Northwestern University

STUDIES IN *Phenomenology &*

Existential Philosophy

Phenomenology and the Problem of History

David Carr

Phenomenology and the Problem of History

A Study of Husserl's Transcendental Philosophy

NORTHWESTERN UNIVERSITY PRESS

1974   EVANSTON

David Carr is Associate Professor of Philosophy
at Yale University

First paperback printing 1980

TO MY PARENTS

Besinnung ist der Mut, die Wahrheit der eigenen Voraussetzungen und der Raum der eigenen Ziele zum Fragwürdigsten zu machen.

Martin Heidegger, *Holzwege*

Contents

List of Abbreviations

The following abbreviations, all of which refer to works by Husserl, are used in the notes and, in some cases, in the text as well:

CM	*Cartesian Meditations,* trans. Dorion Cairns. The Hague: Martinus Nijhoff, 1960.
Crisis	*The Crisis of European Sciences and Transcendental Phenomenology,* trans. David Carr. Evanston, Ill.: Northwestern University Press, 1970.
EU	*Erfahrung und Urteil,* ed. Ludwig Landgrebe. Hamburg: Claassen, 1964.
FTL	*Formal and Transcendental Logic,* trans. Dorion Cairns. The Hague: Martinus Nijhoff, 1969.
Husserliana	*Husserliana: Edmund Husserl, Gesammelte Werke,* gen. ed., H. L. Van Breda. The Hague: Martinus Nijhoff, 1950——.

Volumes cited:

I: *Cartesianische Meditationen und Pariser Vorträge,* ed. S. Strasser, 1950.

II: *Die Idee der Phänomenologie,* ed. W. Biemel, 1950.

III: *Ideen zu einer reinen Phänomenologie und phänomenologischen Philosophie.* Erstes Buch, ed. W. Biemel, 1950.

IV: *Ibid.* Zweites Buch, ed. M. Biemel, 1952.

V: *Ibid.* Drittes Buch, ed. M. Biemel, 1952.

VI: *Die Krisis der europäischen Wissenschaften und die transzendentale Phänomenologie,* ed. W. Biemel, 1954.

VII: *Erste Philosophie.* Erster Teil, ed. R. Boehm, 1956.

VIII: *Ibid.* Zweiter Teil, ed. R. Boehm, 1959.

IX: *Phänomenologische Psychologie,* ed. W. Biemel, 1962.

X: *Zur Phänomenologie des inneren Zeitbewusstseins,* ed. R. Boehm, 1966.

XI: *Analysen zur passiven Synthesis,* ed. M. Fleischer, 1966.

Ideas   *Ideas: General Introduction to Pure Phenomenology,* trans. W. R. Boyce Gibson. New York: Macmillan, 1931.

IP   *The Idea of Phenomenology,* trans. W. P. Alston and G. Nakhnikian. The Hague: Martinus Nijhoff, 1966.

LI   *Logical Investigations,* trans. J. N. Findlay. New York: Humanities Press, 1970. 2 vols.

LU   *Logische Untersuchungen.* Halle a.S.: Max Niemeyer, 1900–1901. 2 vols.

PITC   *Phenomenology of Internal Time Consciousness,* trans. J. S. Churchill. Bloomington: Indiana University Press, 1964.

PRS   "Philosophy as Rigorous Science," in *Phenomenology and the Crisis of Philosophy,* trans. Q. Lauer. New York: Harper Torchbook, 1965.

Acknowledgments

I WOULD LIKE TO EXPRESS my gratitude first to several colleagues at Yale University, whose encouragement, suggestions, and criticisms have been helpful to me in preparing this book. These are Professors Edward Casey, Robert Fogelin, Karsten Harries, and Merold Westphal. Professor David Hoy of Princeton also offered helpful criticisms, and Professor Herbert Spiegelberg of Washington University provided me with some useful documents from the last period of Husserl's life. While I do not wish to implicate any of these persons in the shortcomings of my project, I am sure it has been much improved thanks to their efforts.

Chapter 4 contains a somewhat reworked version of a paper which appeared in *Philosophy and Phenomenological Research* in September, 1973, under the title "The Fifth Meditation and Husserl's Cartesianism." I am grateful to Professor Marvin Farber, the editor of that journal, for permission to use this material. Thanks are also due to Professor H. L. Van Breda, director of the Husserl Archives at Louvain, for permission to consult, refer to, and quote some documents from the Archives.

Finally, I am deeply indebted to my wife, Leslie Carr. Without her encouragement and moral support this book would never have been written.

Preface

THIS BOOK EXPLORES, through a study of Husserl, the relationship between transcendental philosophy and what might be called history-oriented philosophy. The choice of such a broad theme, as well as its relation to Husserl, needs some advance justification and clarification in general terms.

A glance at some of the ironies of the contemporary scene in philosophy suggests a need for such an exploration. Heirs to the British tradition, which had little use for anything called "transcendental philosophy" during its several heydays on the Continent, now often embrace the term or some of the leading ideas associated with it. In 1960 Erik Stenius interpreted Wittgenstein in the *Tractatus* as essentially a transcendental philosopher of the Kantian sort, i.e., one whose aim "is to indicate the *a priori* form of experience which is 'shown' by all meaningful language";[1] a similar interpretation was extended by Specht,[2] and more recently by Toulmin,[3] to the *Investigations* as well. While the approval of the patriarch was thus being assured, contemporary lights were more or less openly pursuing a philosophical program in the transcendental manner. Strawson, for example, introduces his project in *Individuals* with a paraphrase of Kant's very definition of transcendental philosophy—"to de-

1. Erik Stenius, *Wittgenstein's Tractatus* (Oxford: Blackwell's, 1960), p. 220.
2. Ernst Konrad Specht, *The Foundations of Wittgenstein's Late Philosophy*, trans. D. E. Walford (New York: Barnes & Noble, 1969), pp. 176 ff. The book appeared in German in 1963.
3. Stephen Toulmin, "Ludwig Wittgenstein," *Encounter*, XXXII, no. 1 (Jan., 1969), 62.

scribe the actual structure of our thought about the world" [4]—
then goes on to honor Kant with a whole book.[5] Hampshire[6] argues, in effect, to the conditions of the possibility of language
in a way which obviously owes a great deal to the founder of
the transcendental tradition.[7]

Meanwhile, Continental philosophy has for some time been
characterized by a movement not toward but away from transcendental philosophy. Present-day currents have their common
source in a critique and rejection of the two forms of transcendental philosophy which dominated the philosophical scene in
the first decades of this century: Neo-Kantianism and Husserlian
phenomenology. Heidegger, Jaspers, and Scheler attacked their
teachers and predecessors in Germany. They were followed by
the younger existentialists across the Rhine, where a simultaneous left-wing Hegel revival lent ammunition to the anti-tran-
scendental attack. A similar Hegel-and-Marx revival in Germany's
Frankfurt school (Adorno, Horkheimer, Marcuse) was quickly
isolated and exiled during the Nazi years, but has recently
achieved a position of considerable importance in its native
country. The Frankfurt school has made it clear that it is no
friend of Heidegger's or of the French existentialists' but shares
with them its historic point of departure in the criticism of
transcendental philosophy.

Thus, with transcendental philosophy, or some variation of
it, apparently coming into vogue into the Anglo-Saxon world,
it might be wise to ask why some leading European philosophers
have long since thought it *dépassé*. It would be an oversimplifica-
tion, of course, to suppose that all the reasons are the same, just
as it is overly simple to range Husserl and Rickert, not to mention Wittgenstein and Strawson, together under the banner
"transcendental philosophy." Heidegger and the Frankfurt school
are poles apart, while Merleau-Ponty and later Sartre, with their
ambiguous Marxism, perhaps belong somewhere in the middle.

4. P. F. Strawson, *Individuals* (London: Methuen, 1959), p. 9.
5. *The Bounds of Sense* (London: Methuen, 1966).
6. Stuart Hampshire, *Thought and Action* (New York: Viking
Press, 1960).
7. S. Körner summarizes what he calls "the recent remarkable
revival of Kantian ideas and modes of thought in analytic philosophy," in "Transcendental Trends in Recent Philosophy," *The Journal
of Philosophy*, LXIII, no. 19 (1966), 551–61.

Still, in the matter of their common rejection of the transcendental tradition, these disparate figures also agree on a fundamental reason for that rejection. Expressed in widely differing terms, and with different emphasis, it comes down to this: transcendental philosophy in all its traditional forms is rejected primarily because of its inability to come to terms with history or historicity.

This is what was meant at the beginning by the term "history-oriented philosophy": the philosopher's attempt to come to terms with history or historicity, to take history seriously as a philosophical problem. Naturally, transcendental philosophy is able to treat in its own way the "conditions of the possibility of historical knowledge," but this, according to its critics, is an attempt to draw the fangs of history, to render it harmless, and precisely *not* to take it seriously. The result of "coming to terms" with history need not be a philosophy of history in its most familiar and illustrious (or notorious) format, that of Hegel. Not even the Neo-Hegelians of our time provide us with such a large-scale theodicy of world events as is found in Hegel's lectures. The philosophy of history which we find arrayed against recent transcendental philosophy is of a different sort and of perhaps more modest ambitions, but it takes history just as seriously, if not more seriously in the end, than Hegel himself. From this point of view, transcendental philosophy, with its search for the "actual structure of our thought about the world," the concepts or rules which render experience and knowledge possible and condition the way in which the world is given to us, makes its mistaken assumption not in believing that there are such structures, but in supposing that at bottom they are unchanging, ahistorical. Furthermore, it supposes that the knower or experiencer who is subject to such concepts or rules is, to that extent, himself unchanging. This is the transcendental subject which is, it can be argued, indispensable to transcendental philosophy. In spite of all polemics against "psychologism," against the identification of this "pure" subject with man in any anthropological or empirical sense, transcendental philosophy is, after all, talking about man; indeed, it is talking about what has always been thought to be the essence of man, his reason. And in spite of all concessions to the importance of man's changing nature as revealed by psychology, sociology, and history, the message of transcendental philosophy is clear:

whatever else may change and develop, reason does not; dependent as he may otherwise be on his times and circumstances, in his essence man is not historical.

To the opponents of transcendental philosophy, such a revived Platonism ignores the major philosophical insight of modern times. Those who have been taught, by the great thinkers of the last one hundred and fifty years, to appreciate the force of history in man's thought, to grasp the essential historicity of man's consciousness, find such a philosophy naïve. To be sure, it is correct to make the first "transcendental" move from a straightforward consideration of the world to a consideration of the structure of our thought about the world, recognizing, in the words of Kant's "Copernican turn," that "objects must conform to our knowledge" rather than vice versa. But the deepest understanding of history shows that it is precisely these structures that are subject to change, and while the world as given depends on them, they in turn depend on history.[8] Without such insight, any philosophy that attempts to display its supposedly invariant a priori concepts may be doing nothing more than hypostatizing structures that are part of a concrete historical situation. Such a display may be a useful articulation of a historical phenomenon. But a historically sophisticated philosophy will show that it is nothing more than this and account for it in terms of the historical process. In fact, this is the only legitimate task for philosophy once it has made the "historical turn." The curious result of such a historical reorientation is that in a sense the proper subject matter of philosophy is its own history.

To all this the transcendental philosopher can make forceful replies. He can claim that the emphasis on historicity, once it is taken seriously, leads to a particular sort of relativism or skepticism which, like all skepticism, will ultimately contradict itself. He can attempt to show that the argument for the historically limited and thus changeable character of his a priori concepts must presuppose those very concepts as unchanging, since they involve concepts of all possible change. Such rebuttals, however, concede the major point of the objection, which is

8. "Wenngleich Widerspiel des transzendentalen Moments, ist das Traditionale quasi-transzendental, nicht die punktuelle Subjektivität, sondern das eigentlich Konstitutive, der laut Kant verborgene Mechanismus in der Tiefe der Seele." T. W. Adorno, *Negative Dialektik* (Frankfurt: Suhrkamp, 1966), p. 61.

that transcendental philosophy is unable to admit the importance of history or historicity into its account. Is there no way that transcendental philosophy can yield to the compelling demand that it take history seriously without seeing itself destroyed? It seems that the philosophical importance of history must be denied—a difficult task in our day—or the transcendental inquiry must be given up. Such, in broad outlines, is the conflict between transcendental philosophy and what I have called history-oriented philosophy.

Husserl presents us with a unique case study in this conflict. From the moment he began to reflect systematically, sometime around 1907, on the significance of the phenomenological method that had made its "breakthrough" in the *Logische Untersuchungen* of 1900–1901, Husserl placed the new method in the tradition of transcendental philosophy, and to the end of his life the official name of Husserl's philosophy was always to be "transcendental phenomenology." Husserl's 1907 lectures on "The Idea of Phenomenology" resulted at least in part from an intensive study of Kant,[9] and they stress the importance of phenomenology as a means toward a "critique of knowledge," or "critique of reason." Later, though Kant is criticized for almost every aspect of his philosophy, Husserl continues to stress the critical nature of phenomenology and refers to it as "transcendental idealism."[10] In his latest writings, Husserl still presents phenomenology as the fulfillment of the tradition of transcendental philosophy presaged by Descartes and given its decisive impulse by Kant.[11]

Yet in Husserl's last, uncompleted work, *The Crisis of European Sciences*, something apparently new occurs. The *Crisis* has always been seen as significant in Husserl's development because it elaborates for the first time the concept of the *Lebenswelt*. But it contains another dimension which is even more novel in Husserl's work and which is ultimately more significant. Almost exclusive to this book and to the manuscripts from the period in which it was written (1934–37) is an overriding concern not only with the history of philosophy, but also with history and historicity as philosophical problems. In a letter to Roman Ingarden, Husserl speaks of "troubling" problems in the

9. Husserliana II, p. viii.
10. E.g., *CM*, pp. 83 ff.
11. *Crisis*, p. 97.

philosophy of history (*geschichtsphilosophische Probleme*) which he faces in the writing of the *Crisis*.[12] Again and again Husserl insists on the importance of *Geschichtlichkeit* and of the necessity for a new approach to history. Most significantly, he explicitly attacks traditional epistemology for thinking it could ignore history, insisting that the theory of knowledge is a "peculiarly historical task" (*eigentümlich historische Aufgabe*).[13] The *Crisis* as a whole is described by its author as "a telelogical-historical reflection."[14]

Husserl himself, of course, does not seem to regard his new-found concern with history as a break with the transcendental tradition. The "telelogical-historical" reflections serve precisely, he says, as an introduction to transcendental phenomenology. For Husserl, the *Crisis* is a new attempt to explain and ground essentially the same phenomenological philosophy he had been working on since 1907. He admits, to be sure, that it incorporates new insights and approaches, and he regards it as superior to earlier attempts.[15] Furthermore, it would be too simple to claim that the author is "merely" choosing a new mode of presentation while what is presented remains unaffected. Husserl's own clarity on the foundations of phenomenology is still clearly at issue here, and not just his reception by the public. He remarks that he has now finally reached the true beginning of philosophy.[16] Nevertheless, Husserl gives no evidence of regarding his earlier phenomenology as being crucially, not to mention fatally, affected by the new approach. Those who claim that in the *Crisis* Husserl makes a conscious and explicit break with the idealistic or transcendental aspects of his phenomenology have surely not read the *Crisis* carefully and are probably basing their opinion on certain remarks by Merleau-Ponty.

Thus Husserl seems not to be deeply troubled by a possible conflict between a transcendental program and the preoccupation with historical concerns. Does this mean that he does not really "take history seriously," in the sense required by the critics of transcendental philosophy? Some, whose Husserl-picture is formed by the *Ideas*, and who regard such criticism as un-

12. Edmund Husserl, *Briefe an Roman Ingarden* (The Hague: Martinus Nijhoff, 1968), p. 89.
13. *Crisis*, p. 370.
14. *Ibid.*, p. 3.
15. *Ibid.*, p. 155.
16. Husserliana I, p. xxix.

justified in any case, choose to view the historical reflections of the *Crisis* as incidental and to see nothing new at all in the work. But they are just as guilty of ignoring the text as those who see the work as a kind of deathbed renunciation of the author's earlier philosophy. Should we then regard Husserl as having attempted to reconcile what we described above as incompatible alternatives, and judge him on his success or lack of it? These questions are not easily answered because of the state of the book in which all this is found, *The Crisis of European Sciences*. The work is incomplete in more senses than one. Not only does it break off, but the extant text was clearly in such a process of revision at the time of Husserl's death that we cannot regard all its paradoxes as necessarily resolved, even in its author's mind. The *Crisis* is not a finished book that can be subjected to straightforward exposition and criticism but a manuscript in process that must first be interpreted.[17] Adding to the complexity are the many working manuscripts of the period, whose relation to the text of the *Crisis* is not always clear.

What *is* clear, and what makes Husserl an instructive case study in this matter, is that the tension between the demands of transcendental philosophy and those of history is here exemplified in one philosopher. More than this: this tension is not merely found within the writings of one person, as he goes from an earlier "period" in his thought to a later and contradictory one; rather, the tension is dramatically displayed practically within the confines of a single work. It is internal to the very content and development of a manuscript whose inchoate character bears witness to an intense struggle to confront and clarify the issues involved.[18]

17. *Crisis*, pp. xvi–xxi.
18. Secondary literature on the *Crisis* has for the most part been dominated by commentary on the concept of the life-world. Where the concern with history is noticed, the tension between the historical and the transcendental orientations is not. Most commentators offer an exposition of what Husserl says about history without feeling the need to show its relation to his earlier thought. They also fail to recognize that the unfinished character of the *Crisis* calls forth a broader interpretation. (Two recent examples of these tendencies are Hubert Hohl, *Lebenswelt und Geschichte* [Freiburg and Munich: Alber, 1962]; and Paul Janssen, *Geschichte und Lebenswelt* [The Hague: Martinus Nijhoff, 1970].) If the present interpretation is bolder, it is also naturally riskier and more open to criticism.

The following study proceeds from the assumption that an examination centering on Husserl's last work can bring these issues to clarity and immediacy in a way that might not be possible in an abstract confrontation of arguments or even a comparison of opposing philosophers.

Some, to be sure, have argued that Husserl's concern with historicity is to be explained by his confrontation with his former protégé Heidegger. After all, *Being and Time,* with its section on *Geschichtlichkeit* and its homage to Dilthey, was published in 1927, and it is known that Husserl studied it carefully before beginning the *Crisis.* Such a view is not implausible, even though Husserl was strongly critical of Heidegger's book. But it can also be argued, and will be argued below, that adequate reasons for Husserl's turn to history are to be found in his own thought as it developed beyond the period of the *Ideas.* Though the full effects of Husserl's concern for history upon his presentation of phenomenology are not visible prior to the *Crisis,* the train of thought which finally led to them can be traced, even in Husserl's earlier works.

It is helpful, in this connection, to consider a peculiarity of Husserl's philosophical efforts. Husserl scholars and former students have often pointed to two clearly distinguishable aspects of his work. On the one hand there are the rich and detailed phenomenological analyses of more or less isolated topics, of the sort which so impressed readers of the *Logical Investigations* but which were later almost completely confined to lectures, seminars, and working manuscripts, many of which are now available in the publications of the *Nachlass.* Here we find Husserl devoting himself with great intensity to some area of phenomenological *Forschung,* such as perception or logical thinking, time-consciousness or intersubjectivity, with no thought for anything but the insightful penetration of the *Sache selbst.* Here we find the phenomenological method at work. On the other hand there are Husserl's various attempts, comprising most of his published works, to present and ground the phenomenological method in a coherent way, to provide an over-all map of its domains, to justify its claim to fulfill the traditional tasks of philosophy. Here the concrete investigations are drawn in, but they are largely merely referred to, or roughly sketched in an often maddeningly tantalizing way, rather than actually carried out. This is the programmatic Husserl, with the missionary's zeal for saving philosophy and even mankind from its errors, with the mosaic consciousness of having opened up the promised land that is to be explored in endless detail by future generations of researchers. Considering these two aspects of the philosopher's work, many have made it clear that they vastly prefer the concrete Husserl to the missionary Husserl, that they consider him less than successful in his attempts at systematizing the results and assessing the significance of his many investigations. This is why the phenomenological method, much to Husserl's chagrin, was to be appropriated for so many philosophical purposes that were in open disagreement with those of its founder.

These considerations suggest an interesting way of looking at the relation between Husserl's ventures into the realm of history and historicity and his attempt to incorporate them into the transcendental program. It can be argued that in his thoroughly honest and distinterested way, Husserl, in reflecting on consciousness, was finally forced by the *Sache selbst* to take history seriously, and that his death found him only at the beginning of the effort to combine the results with phenomenology in its transcendental interpretation. But did he, or could he, succeed in this effort? It could be maintained—without having to view the *Crisis* as a deathbed conversion—that the attempt is doomed to failure whether Husserl recognized it or not, that he sows here the seeds of the destruction of his own and any other form of transcendental philosophy. Yet, in the *Crisis* Husserl seems sure that the combination will work.

Whether Husserl succeeded, or could have succeeded in his effort, is the question which ultimately interests us in the following study. But first we must understand the train of thought which led him to the problem of history in the first place. We shall begin with a consideration of phenomenology *as* transcendental philosophy, tracing the development of Husserl's approach to the point where he saw it as falling within and fulfilling the demands of the transcendental tradition. Here we shall outline primarily the "classical" position of the *Ideas* (without drawing exclusively on that source) as it grew out of the method practiced in the *Logical Investigations* (Chapter 1). Then we shall turn directly to the *Crisis* and attempt, in a preliminary way, to make clear the novelty of its approach. Here we shall have to establish that the *Crisis* does indeed represent a departure from the "classical" procedure, and that its historical dimension is what makes it different (Chapter 2). Then we shall have to ask: what considerations, growing out of the practice of phenomenology itself, could have led Husserl to so revise his conception of its procedure? These considerations are not explicitly presented in the *Crisis* itself, but we shall see that two themes, pursued by Husserl in different places, come together in such a way as to reveal a specifically *phenomenological* problem of history. These themes are "genetic" phenomenology (Chapter 3) and the theory of intersubjectivity (Chapter 4). Returning to the *Crisis*, we shall then show how these themes come together to form a new part of the phenomenological method which we call "historical reduction," understood as a critique of the philosophical tradition (Chapter 5). But this new aspect of Husserl's method forces him to criticize not only his predecessors but also his own earlier philosophy in one of its most important dimensions, namely, its understanding of the *world*. The notion of the life-world, which emerges from Husserl's historical critique, constitutes an important corrective to a fundamental ambiguity which attended the phenomenological concept of the world prior to the *Crisis* (Chapter 6).

Having articulated Husserl's implicit criticism of his own earlier work, we shall try to state in a systematic way the relation between the historical reduction and the new concept of world as that relation is revealed in the structure of the *Crisis* (Chapter 7). Examining that text in more detail, however, we find that the term *life-world* seems to be applied by Husserl to at least two distinguishable and even incompatible concepts, that of the perceptual world and that of the cultural world (Chapter 8). In search of a resolution to this ambiguity, we turn to another text of the same period, the Introduction to *Experience and Judgment*. But in that text the ambiguity is resolved only by subsuming the perceptual world under the cultural; and phenomenology finds itself faced with a seemingly hopeless impasse, that of historical relativism or historicism (Chapter 9). At this point it becomes finally clear how the acceptance of the historicity of subjectivity threatens the very possibility of transcendental philosophy. But the paradox is that the concept of historicity has been arrived at precisely through the *practice* of transcendental philosophy (Chapter 10). A reflection on this paradox, and on the problem of historical relativism generally, suggests a way in which the *project* of transcendental philosophy must be both radically altered, and at the same time maintained, if phenomenology—and philosophy generally—is to "come to terms" with history (Chapter 11).

Phenomenology and the Problem of History

1 / Phenomenology
as Transcendental Philosophy

THE FOREGOING PREFACE necessarily describes only briefly the project of this study and the broad framework which is meant to justify its undertaking. Even those interested enough to read on may have been puzzled or annoyed by the sort of over-simplifications which are hard to avoid in such a preliminary sketch.

One point seems especially vulnerable to the charge of over-simplification: the term "transcendental philosophy," it might be objected, was used much too loosely. The concept may be a historically meaningful one, but what is questionable is the iden-tification of Husserl with the "transcendental tradition." Husserl may well have seen his phenomenology as belonging to what he considered that tradition to be, continually using the borrowed term "transcendental," but this, needless to say, does not make it so. It is difficult to reconcile Husserl's often grandiose claims for his phenomenology with the quasi-skeptical purposes for which Kant designed his transcendental philosophy, not to mention the even more limited and modest aims associated with the Neo-Kantians and more recent Anglo-Saxon revivals of the notion. There are, of course, similarities in detail, but these are not enough to justify using Husserl, or one aspect of Husserl's work, as exemplary in a broad confrontation between "transcendental philosophy" and "history-oriented philosophy." Does Husserl's phenomenology, prior to the emergence of historical concerns in the *Crisis*, really belong to anything that can legitimately be called the "transcendental tradition"?

This question concerns the presuppositions and over-all sense of our inquiry into Husserl's philosophy of history, and the present chapter is devoted to answering it. We shall attempt to show that Husserl can indeed be seen as a representative, and an important one, of the transcendental tradition. Husserl's phenomenology will be presented "as" transcendental philosophy, i.e., stressing its affinities with what historically goes by that name. Our aim is not to compare Husserl with every philosopher who has ever adopted the term "transcendental," but rather to offer an account of his philosophy in light of certain recognizable conceptions, first articulated by Kant, which can be said to constitute the enduring core of the transcendental tradition.[1] Our picture of phenomenology here will concentrate on the mature period, prior to that of the *Crisis*, in which Husserl used the term "transcendental" to describe his philosophy.

The examination of Husserl's phenomenology from the perspective of the transcendental motif does not merely present us with an aspect or possible view which links it to a historically familiar notion. Rather, it reveals the very essence of phenomenology in its mature form. A concentration, furthermore, on Husserl's conception of the transcendental makes it possible to avoid certain common misconceptions about his thought, particularly those concerning the problem of idealism.

Husserl says that he borrows the term "transcendental philosophy" from Kant,[2] but he often provides his readers with an account of its derivation which apparently differs from that offered by the originator of the term and suggests that the whole similarity might rest on a mere coincidence or a misunderstanding. Kant first speaks, in the *Critique of Pure Reason*, of transcendental knowledge as dealing "not so much with objects as with the mode of our knowledge of objects, insofar as this mode of knowledge is to be possible *a priori*. . . ."[3] Transcendental philosophy is the systematized knowledge of the elements that make up or make possible our way of knowing objects a priori, and the term "transcendental" is also used by Kant to describe

1. Iso Kern has a different purpose in *Husserl und Kant* (The Hague: Martinus Nijhoff, 1964). His aim is to present Husserl's view and interpretation of Kant and Neo-Kantianism (p. viii)—Kern's book has been very helpful to us, however.

2. Husserliana VII, p. 230.

3. *Immanuel Kant's Critique of Pure Reason*, trans. Norman Kemp Smith (London: Macmillan, 1963), B 25 (references are to original pagination).

those elements themselves. This sense of the adjective is used by Kant in a passage which more clearly indicates how he arrived at the term: "the word 'transcendental' . . . does not signify something passing beyond all experience [*Erfahrung*], but something that indeed precedes it [i.e., is] *a priori,* but whose purpose is nothing more than to make experiential knowledge possible." [4] That which goes "beyond all experience" Kant terms "transcendent" (i.e., transcending experience), and while he wishes to distinguish this from the transcendental he apparently sees the latter as being like the former in the important respect that it is not to be derived from experience. It likewise "transcends" experience, then, but in the special sense which Kant stipulates, i.e., as constituting the conditions of the possibility of experiential knowledge itself.

Husserl's explanation of the term "transcendental" takes a different form. In the *Cartesian Mediations* he writes: "neither the world nor any worldly Object is a piece of my ego, to be found in my conscious life as a really inherent part of it, as a complex of data of sensation or a complex of acts. This *'transcendence'* is part of the intrinsic sense of anything worldly," [5] i.e., its *noninclusion,* in the sense described, in the ego or consciousness. The ego itself is called "transcendental" because of its essential character of standing in relation to what transcends it, and "accordingly the philosophical problems arising from this correlation are called transcendental-philosophical." [6] In the *Ideas,* similarly, the term "transcendental" is applied to consciousness because of its "wonderful" capacity to relate to something "that stands over against consciousness itself, something that is other in principle, something not part of it [*Irreelles*], something transcendent. . . ." [7]

Thus the derivation of the term appears to be wholly different. For Husserl the "transcendental" is so named because of its cognitive relation to the transcendent; for Kant it is so named

4. Immanuel Kant, *Prolegomena zu einer jeden künftigen Metaphysik,* ed. K. Vorländer (Hamburg: Felix Meiner, 1957), p. 144 n.
5. *CM,* p. 26.
6. *Ibid.* Kern points out (*Husserl und Kant,* p. 243) that the term was first used by Husserl to designate certain *problems,* rather than consciousness or the ego.
7. Husserliana III, p. 245 (*Ideas,* p. 285). Note: In the case of *Ideas* I, I have for the most part found it necessary to give my own translation. Hence my reference to both the original and the translation.

only by analogy to the transcendent (to which it has no legitimate cognitive relation) by reference to the nontranscendent, i.e., experience (to which it is cognitively related). Of course the term "transcendent" is also used in two very different senses. Kant uses the term *"Erfahrung"* here in a loose sense to refer to the domain of all *possible* sense-experience and experiential knowledge; that is, he is referring to the whole *world* of experience about which scientific knowledge is possible. This is what is surpassed by both the "transcendent" and the "transcendental," whereas for Husserl the world of experience is itself precisely the transcendent because it is not "included in" consciousness. This fact, to be sure, does not remove the difference between Kant's and Husserl's derivation of the term "transcendental"; it even sharpens it. But at the same time it points to the curious fact that, although Kant and Husserl seem to have chosen the same word for very different reasons, they have ended by meaning the same thing by it. This can be seen if we first trace the emergence of the transcendental motif in Husserl's philosophy.

The preoccupation with "transcendental-philosophical problems" and with the notion of transcendental philosophy is what marks the beginning of Husserl's many systematic attempts to establish phenomenology as the fundamental philosophical method, and it is the transcendental motif above all that distinguishes the phenomenology of the *Ideas* and later works from the phenomenology of the *Logical Investigations*. This does not mean, however, that the earlier work can be ignored in a presentation of phenomenology as transcendental philosophy. Husserl himself believed that the essentials of the phenomenological method had made their "breakthrough" in the earlier work and had simply not been reflectively grasped and adequately understood by their author. His retrospective remarks often leave the impression that the phenomenological method had been properly but almost blindly or instinctively *practiced* in the *Logical Investigations*, while the few attempts to characterize the method were wholly inadequate. While it is true that the transcendental character is not ascribed to phenomenology in the early work, it is important not to ignore everything that Husserl says about phenomenology there. Husserl rejects some of his earlier characterizations of phenomenology (e.g., as descriptive psychology),[8]

8. Cf. *LI*, pp. 262–63. Though Findlay's translation is of the second edition, he has included some passages from the first. Cf. *LU*, II, 18.

but others remain at the heart of all later developments, often in veiled form. The transcendental or "Copernican" turn in Husserl's career, and the broadening of phenomenology into a transcendental philosophy, can be seen as a development required in order to fulfill the *aims* of phenomenology as articulated by Husserl in the *Logical Investigations*.

THE PHENOMENOLOGY OF THE *Logical Investigations*

WHAT ARE THESE AIMS? The first volume, *Prolegomena to Pure Logic*, had attacked psychologism by demonstrating the distinction between the subject matter of logic and that of psychology. That is, it showed that logic served its normative function in relation to scientific theory only as a discipline that treats ideal relations among meanings as ideal entities, not as an empirical discipline concerning psychic occurrences in which meanings and their relations are exemplified, i.e., experiences in which something is in fact meant, or in which logical inferences are in fact made. Husserl's notion of a "pure" logic is partially fulfilled as a theory of theory itself in the formal sense, a theory of possible forms each corresponding to a *"possible field of knowledge* [i.e., a *Mannigfaltigkeit*] *over which a theory of this form will preside."* [9] Such a *Mannigfaltigkeitstheorie* would contribute to our understanding of what Husserl calls "the ideal conditions of the possibility of sciences or of theory in general," [10] but it is properly part of formal mathematics and is best left to the mathematicians. There remains a type of reflection "which only the philosopher can provide," which Husserl calls *"erkenntnis-kritisch."* [11]

> The philosopher is not content with the fact that we find our way about in the world, that we have laws as formulae which enable us to predict the future course of things, or to reconstruct its past course: he wants to clarify the essence of a thing, an event . . . [of laws of nature] etc. . . . . And if science constructs theories in the systematic dispatch of its problems, the philosopher enquires into the essence of theory and what makes theory as such possible, etc.[12]

9. *LI*, p. 241.
10. *Ibid.*, p. 232.
11. *Ibid.*, p. 245.
12. *Ibid.* (My insertions and deletions reconstruct the version of this passage given in the first edition. Cf. *LU*, I, 254. I have also

In the latter case, which is relevant for purely logical interests, it is a matter of "scientifically clarifying" the "primitive concepts" which enter into theoretical knowledge as such, e.g., concept, proposition,[13] and "correlate" concepts such as, in this case, object, state of affairs.[14] The philosopher's task is to provide these fundamental concepts with "the 'clearness and distinctness' needed for understanding, and for an epistemological critique, of pure logic." [15]

Husserl's use of Kantian terminology here (i.e., "conditions of the possibility," "critique"), is obvious and intentional,[16] but otherwise his remarks bear little evidence of a distinctively Kantian approach. The question is: what constitutes for Husserl the "clarification" of concepts, which is his stated aim; where is "clarity" to be found? Referring to the "primitive concepts" mentioned above, Husserl says:

> All these concepts must now be pinned down, their "origin" [Ursprung] must in each case be investigated. Not that psychological questions as to the origin of the conceptual presentations or presentational dispositions here in question, have the slightest interest for our discipline. This is not what we are enquiring into: we are concerned with a [logical] origin, or—if we prefer to rule out unsuitable talk of origins, only bred in confusion—we are concerned with insight into the essence of the concepts involved. . . .[17]

Here the author says that we might "prefer" to discard the term "origin" (Ursprung) and even that it is "unsuitable" (unpassend), but Husserl himself is far from discarding it or the notion behind it. In presenting "pure phenomenology" in the second volume as precisely the "clarifying" discipline he has in mind, Husserl writes that phenomenology "lays bare the 'sources' [Quellen] from which the basic concepts and ideal laws of pure

---

substituted the phrase "laws as formulae" for Findlay's "legal formulae," which seems to me misleading.)

13. LI, p. 236.
14. Ibid., p. 237.
15. Ibid., pp. 249–50.
16. Ibid., p. 232: "The historical echoes in the form of our question [into the 'conditions of the possibility' of theory] are of course intentional."
17. Ibid., pp. 237–38 ("logical" inserted in place of "phenomenological" in accord with LU, I, 245).

logic 'flow,' and back to which they must once more be traced, so as to give them all the 'clearness and distinctness' needed for an understanding, and for an epistemological critique, of pure logic." [18] The quotation marks around the words "sources" and "flow" warn the reader again that the terms are not to be taken in an ordinary, psychological sense. Yet in the same paragraph it is stated that phenomenology has the same "domain" or subject matter that psychology treats in a genetic-explanatory way, namely, that of *Erlebnisse*—"experiences"—in this case those of representing, judging, knowing. Introducing the Fifth Investigation, Husserl refers to having dealt with "the sense of the ideality of meanings [*Bedeutungen*] with which pure logic is concerned" in the Second Investigation and continues:

> New questions now arise regarding the kind of experiences in which the supreme genus Meaning has its originative source [*Ursprung*]. . . . We wish to enquire into the originative source of the concept of Meaning and its essential specifications, so as to achieve a deeper-going, more widely ranging answer to our question than our investigations have so far given us.[19]

The philosophical "clarification" of such fundamental notions as meaning, proposition, object, state of affairs, then, consists in tracing their "origins" in *Erlebnisse*—experiences—and yet such tracing is not psychological; the question of origin is not that of how certain "conceptual presentations" arise. What, then, does "origin" mean, and in what sense is phenomenology a tracing of origins? Nothing could be more important for an understanding of Husserl's phenomenology than the answers to these questions, for it is the search for origins in a peculiarly phenomenological, nonpsychological sense which informs Husserl's endeavors from beginning to end.[20] And it is precisely this search which drives

18. *LI*, pp. 249–50.
19. *Ibid.*, p. 533.
20. Eugen Fink, in a famous article approved by Husserl ("Die phänomenologische Philosophie Edmund Husserls in der gegenwärtingen Kritik," in his *Studien zur Phänomenologie 1930–1939* [The Hague: Martinus Nijhoff, 1966], pp. 79–156; English translation in *The Phenomenology of Husserl*, ed. R. O. Elveton [Chicago: Quadrangle, 1970]), stresses the search for "origins" in Husserl's philosophy, but seems to identify this search with Husserl's later work. By pointing to the importance of this notion in the *Logical Investigations*, I hope to show that it is a constant concern throughout Husserl's career, and one which helps to explain his development

him from the phenomenology of the *Logical Investigations* to the "transcendental turn" some years later.

The sense in which phenomenology is a tracing of "origins" can be found in Husserl's "clarification" of logic. He is interested in delineating "the true objects [*die eigentlichen Objekte*] of logical research—and following thereon, the essential species and differentiae of such objects." [21] Because logic is concerned at the highest level with the notion of theory, and because all theoretical inquiry "terminates in . . . statement [*Aussagen*]," [22] it is wise to begin with a treatment of language. If logic has to do with language, however, it is not concerned directly with linguistic expressions as real events but with the *meanings* of these expressions. In first attempting to clarify the distinction between *Ausdruck* and *Bedeutung* (to which the First Investigation is devoted), Husserl is concerned with what constitutes the meaningful use and the understanding of language and distinguishes it from "mere" words or sounds. The answer is that a conscious act "confers" meaning on an expression by referring to something through it, making it (in this sense) an expression *of* something. [23] Such an act is an *Erlebnis*, or at least an aspect of an *Erlebnis*, i.e., something we live in or live through.

Thus certain "objects" of logical inquiry—the meanings of expressions—are related by Husserl to experience; but in what sense are their "origins" traced to experience? The Prolegomena

---

through various stages of his thought. It is surprising that Fink, seeking in a later article to identify "operative" as opposed to "thematic" concepts in Husserl's phenomenology ("Operative Begriffe in Husserls Phänomenologie," *Zeitschrift für philosophische Forschung*, XI, [1957], 321–37), does not mention the concept of *Ursprung*. Even more than the concepts Fink mentions (e.g., *Phänomen, Leistung, Konstitution*), it is one that Husserl presupposes but never explains. The concept and the term figure prominently not only in *LI* but in other early texts as well, e.g., *Die Idee der Phänomenologie* (1907), Husserliana II, p. 56, and the lectures on time-consciousness (1905), Husserliana X, p. 9. One author who does note the early importance of the concept of *Ursprung*, and to whom my whole exposition, especially of *LI*, is greatly indebted, is Robert Sokolowski, *The Formation of Husserl's Concept of Constitution* (The Hague: Martinus Nijhoff, 1964), esp. pp. 38–39, who correctly links this concept with that of *Konstitution*. For some reservations on Sokolowski's treatment, see n. 37 below.

21. *LI*, p. 249.
22. *Ibid.*, p. 250.
23. *Ibid.*, p. 280.

had attacked any attempt to *reduce* such "objects" *to* experiences, in this case to reduce meanings in the logical sense to acts in which something is meant. Is Husserl substituting for a reduction of meanings an account of their creation? Do meanings in the logical sense begin to exist through an act of creation in consciousness? This is also clearly not what Husserl means, for he wishes to insist on the ideal identity of meanings in relation to *all* the acts "through which they become real in human mental life." [24]

But is not the first such act an exception? If we consider an artifact, it is something objective in relation to multiple acts of perceiving it, but it owes its existence to an act of creation, before which no one could perceive it. Is a meaning in the logical sense not something analogous? Not according to Husserl.

> Wherever a new concept is formed, we see how a meaning is realized [*realisiert*, i.e., made real in mental life, as above] that was previously unrealized. . . . There are . . . countless meanings which, in the common, relational [i.e., relative to actual expressions] sense are merely possible ones, since they are never expressed, and since they can, owing to the limits of man's cognitive powers, never be expressed.[25]

Such passages reveal clearly that Husserl is far from asserting the dependence of ideal entities on consciousness. In fact, the phenomenological treatment of *Erlebnisse* in Volume II of the *Logical Investigations* is meant in large part to reinforce the demonstrations of the Prolegomena that logical entities are not only irreducible to consciousness but are also *independent* of it in any sense relative to creation. Not only do such entities not arise and pass away each time they are "realized"; there is no sense at all in which they arise or pass away.

But in that case what sense would there be in speaking of origins? This sense emerges if one pays attention to the way Husserl expresses himself. He turns first to a discussion of language because

> the objects which pure logic seeks to examine are, in the first instance, *given* . . . in grammatical clothing. Or, more precisely, they *come before us* [*sind gegeben*] embedded in concrete mental states [*Erlebnissen*] which further function as the *meaning-*

24. *Ibid.*, p. 333.
25. *Ibid.;* brackets mine.

intention or the *meaning-fulfilment* of certain verbal expressions. . . .[26]

The meaningful use or the comprehension of language does not
create meanings, but it does "realize" them in "human mental
life." It is precisely this "realization" which interests Husserl, the
moment in which something not itself belonging to consciousness, or of the nature of consciousness, is nevertheless *given* to
consciousness. This interests Husserl first of all because it provides the needed reinforcement of the thesis of the anti-psy-
chologist *Prolegomena.* Strict attention to *how* such things as
meanings are given in experience makes it impossible to confuse
them *with* experience: they are given precisely *as* distinct from
experience. When I assert that *P, P* is *given* as something identical that can be asserted again, can be asserted by others, and
could have been asserted before, whether anyone in fact did so
or not.

But Husserl's interest in "realization" or "givenness" goes
much deeper, for the clarification of the purely logical exhibits
a form which belongs to a much broader problem, that of knowledge generally. In being irreducible to and independent of consciousness, logical objects have an "objectivity" which is not
theirs alone. Husserl's treatment of *Erlebnisse* has the function
of elucidating generally "the relationship . . . between the subjectivity of knowing and the objectivity of the content known," [27]
a relationship which corresponds to what Husserl calls the "basic
questions of epistemology":

> How are we to understand the fact that the intrinsic being [*das
> "an sich"*] of objectivity becomes "presented," "apprehended" in
> knowledge, and so ends up by becoming subjective? What does it
> mean to say that the object has "intrinsic being" [*sei "an sich"*],
> and is "given" in knowledge?[28]

Thus the focus of the *Logical Investigations* expands to encompass the epistemological as well as the strictly logical, and much
of Husserl's treatment of *Erlebnisse* is not limited to those whose
object is the logical in the strict sense. For Husserl's problem has
become that of the givenness of the objective in concrete experience generally, whether the objectivity in question is ideal

26. *Ibid.,* p. 250; brackets, and emphasis on "given" and "come
before us," mine.
27. *Ibid.,* p. 42.
28. *Ibid.,* p. 254.

in the sense of logical or mathematical states of affairs, or belongs to the physical world. Because his book is devoted to clarifying specifically logical problems, Husserl does not deal at length with the givenness of physical objects or states of affairs for its own sake, but he uses countless examples from this domain in order to demonstrate the generality of the problem of objectivity and givenness. To Husserl, it is obvious that the physical object can no more be reduced to the consciousness we have *of* it than the ideal object. Nor is it dependent for its existence on our consciousness of it. These points do not require, perhaps, such a vigorous defense as those relating to ideal entities, since the modern tradition (except for Berkeley) has been less inclined to psychologize physical objects.[29] But in either case the needed clarification is achieved by paying attention to precisely *how* such objects are given.

If Husserl looks to *Erlebnisse* for "origins," then, it is clearly not in order to account for the *being* of objects, whether ideal or real. What Husserl does seek in the domain of *Erlebnisse* is the "origin" of precisely that *givenness* of objects of which we have spoken. Not the *being* of objects, but their *being for me* is what has to be accounted for.

This crucial point is, of course, open to a further psychological interpretation that must be avoided if the sense of Husserl's inquiry is to be fully clarified. The search for the origin of an object's givenness might be construed as relating, in Lockean fashion, to the *first time* an independently existing object makes contact with (makes an "impression" on) a likewise independently existing "mind," leaving a trace ("idea") there which becomes a possession of the mind. Husserl's problem of givenness would not be solved by such an account but would simply be raised at a different level: he would ask how the *same idea* can be given in different experiences of it, noting that what *is* given in such cases is not the original object but only the idea of that object. Husserl is interested, in other words, in what makes up the givenness of something *each time* it is given—whether it is a physical object or the idea of that object or even the idea of that idea—and what accounts for the fact that it is *this* that is given (again or for the first time) rather than something else.

29. Berkeley, in fact, by raising the problem of identity, saw that if the ideal had to be psychologized, the physical did too—for the same reasons.

To put the problem in another way: what are the conditions under which something objective can be given as such? Or: what is essential to the givenness of something objective, what must be present?

The answer, which is prefigured in the First Investigation and taken up in the Fifth and Sixth, is the intentional or act-character of consciousness, an act of meaning that refers to the object in such and such a way. Such an act is what we live through, or, more precisely, an aspect of what we concretely live through (the concrete or full *Erlebnis*) when something objective is given; and it is precisely this aspect that cannot be missing.[30] To say that something—anything whatsoever—is given is to say that it corresponds to or fulfills an intention. The intention can also be empty or unfulfilled,[31] in which case all that is really given is the meaning of the intention itself. But objectivity cannot be given without the intention, which is to say that something objective is given only insofar as it is meant as being such and such through an act that "means" it, bestows such a meaning upon it.

This clarification of Husserl's understanding of the search for "origins" already reveals, even in the phenomenology of the *Logical Investigations,* a recognizable and important aspect of the transcendental "motif": first, it is quite obvious that, in keeping with Kant's formula, Husserl is dealing in a sense "not so much with objects as with the mode of our knowledge of objects. . . ." Furthermore, the "objectivity" of objects of various sorts—their nonreducibility to and independence of consciousness—is first acknowledged and even vigorously argued for (just as Kant argued these points against Hume); yet that very objectivity of objects is traced to the subject, or more precisely to conscious acts or intentions. Such acts, furthermore, as Husserl's investigation of them deepens, take on the character of a *synthesis* of various elements into a unity which corresponds to the unity of the object. This is especially evident in the case of complex objects (*Sachverhalte,* states of affairs) meant in complex or "categorial" acts. Such complex acts presuppose and comprise or contain such "simple" acts as the straightforward sense-perception of objects.[32] But even an act of perception is

30. *LI,* p. 337. See also *LI,* p. 567.
31. I.e., an intention in the narrower sense. Cf. *ibid.,* Inv. V, § 13.
32. Cf. *ibid.,* p. 787.

recognized as being complex in character, a synthesis of various elements. (Husserl at this point speaks of sensational contents, *Empfindungsinhalte*).³³

What must not be lost, however, is the objective, even realistic moment in the "tracing" of objectivity to such acts. This moment is even more strongly stated in Husserl's philosophy than in Kant's, but in either case it is a necessary moment if transcendental philosophy is to be kept separate from subjective idealism. To repeat: an act of consciousness which intends an object does not create that object; even as synthesis or "putting together" it does not construct the object. Rather, such an act renders something present; if it is an origin, as we have said, it is the origin of the object's *givenness*, not of its *being*. In the *Logical Investigations*, Husserl's language on this point is clear. In speaking of categorial acts in the Sixth Investigation, he describes them as "acts which . . . *set up new objects [neue Objektivitäten konstituieren]*" ³⁴—new, that is, in relation to objects "constituted" by the simple acts that make them up. Here the all-important word "constitution" makes an early appearance. What it means, however, is that these are "acts in which something *appears as actual [wirklich] and self-given [selbst gegeben]*." ³⁵ Categorial objects are no more invented or fabricated than perceived objects, but are *given* in the categorial act. As Husserl says in another text of the same period, "the recurring expression that in an act 'objects are constituted' always designates the act's character of *rendering the object present [den Gegenstand vorstellig zu machen]*: not 'constituting' in the actual sense." A few years later he notes that "is constituted" is equivalent to "announces itself" (*sich bekundet*).³⁶ As for perceived objects themselves, the perceptive "taking" (*Auffassung*), bringing together various "sense-contents," is not responsible for the existence of the object; what it is responsible for, and *all* it is responsible for, is "*das Dasein des Gegenstandes für mich*"—"the *'being of the object for me.'*" ³⁷

33. *Ibid.*, p. 566.
34. *Ibid.*, p. 787.
35. *Ibid.*
36. These texts of 1903 and 1907 are quoted by René Toulemont in *L'Essence de la societé selon Husserl* (Paris: Presses Universitaires de France, 1962), p. 43, nn. 2 and 3.
37. *LI*, p. 566. My objection to Sokolowski's treatment (*The Formation of Husserl's Concept of Constitution*) is that he often

This "realistic" moment in Husserl's phenomenology must not, however, be construed to mean that he begins with the real separation of subject and object and is faced with the problem of how they relate to one another. The intentionality of the *Erlebnis* is not a real relation.[38] Here again Husserl exhibits a strong similarity to Kant: the objectivity of the object is not postulated metaphysically in advance, but is part of the sense of the object as intended. True, Kant posits the existence of a world in itself, but this is not what accounts for the objectivity of the objects of experience. Rather, it is the character of experience itself that accounts for it. Thus the process of accounting for objectivity is a move from the object back to the experience.

The Radicalization of Reflection

IN CARRYING OUT this reference back from the objectivity of an object to the act which means it, Husserl is still far from executing the full "Copernican turn" in the Kantian sense. In fact, the transcendental aspect of the *Logical Investigations* seems not to have been recognized as such by Husserl when the

---

seems to overlook this distinction between the object's being for me (its givenness) and its being *tout court* (e.g., p. 60: "It can be said that intentionality establishes its own objects of reference. By subjective activity, it constitutes an object"). This difficulty can be traced to one of Sokolowski's first formulations of his problem, what he calls "the paradox of something objective which *exists* only by virtue of subjective mental activity" (p. 16; emphasis mine). This is Sokolowski's paraphrase of what Walter Biemel sees as the origin of the concept of constitution, the fact "dass es Gebilde gibt, die im Denken erzeugt werden müssen, *um zu existieren*" ("Die entscheidenden Phasen der Entfaltung von Husserls Philosophie," in *Zeitschrift für philosophische Forschung*, XIII [1959], 195; emphasis mine). The conception leads to many interpretations of the later Husserl which, in my opinion, are falsely cast. For example, Sokolowski asks (p. 137): "Can [Husserl] mean that subjectivity is not only a *sine qua non*, a necessary condition for the world as real, but also its sufficient cause?" According to my interpretation, subjectivity is in no sense a condition for the world as real, and certainly not a cause.

38. If we adhere to a strict terminology, we should not speak of a "relation" at all, since the expression usually implies the existence of the related terms. Brentano saw this problem, and referred to intentionality as "relation-like" (*ein Relativliches;* cf. his *Psychologie vom empirischen Standpunkt* [Leipzig: Duncker & Humblot, 1911], Appendix I), but Husserl regards the use of the term "relation" unavoidable. (Cf. *LI*, p. 557.)

work was written, in spite of occasional terminological borrowings from Kant. Only in the ensuing years, culminating in 1913 with the publication of *Ideas I,* did Husserl seize upon this aspect of his earlier work and place it within the broadened context of a full-fledged transcendental philosophy.

During these years Husserl was engaged in clarifying the peculiarity of the phenomenological method and exploring its possibilities as a fundamental philosophical discipline. One of his primary concerns was to distinguish phenomenology from *psychology*—even purely descriptive psychology—by securing what he later called the eidetic character of the method. Husserl had already insisted in the *Logical Investigations* that he was not engaged in "genetic" or explanatory psychology; but since he was dealing with the psychic, in the form of certain *Erlebnisse,* he had allowed phenomenology to be characterized as descriptive psychology.[39] It soon became clear to Husserl that the explanatory-descriptive distinction did not provide an adequate basis for characterizing what he had actually been about in the *Logical Investigations* if the objects of description were simply matters of fact in Hume's sense, in this case facts about the psyche. For example, when Husserl argued for the separateness of the ideal object from the act in which it is meant, his claim was not based on an empirical description: he had not enumerated the elements of such acts and simply discovered that the object in fact was not among them. If what Husserl says is true, it is not just factually true—it is true in essence or true of the essence of the *Erlebnisse* in question and of their relation to their objects. The essence of the psychic, not facts about the psychic, is what is "described" in phenomenology, and indeed any factual description—not to mention explanation of facts—presupposes a more or less clear grasp of the essence of the phenomena treated. Husserl's efforts in the *Logical Investigations* to clarify the fundamental distinctions among types of experiences, elements within experiences (various senses of "content," for example), etc., constitute not a description of facts which then had to be explained by genetic psychology (on the analogy of descriptive versus explanatory natural science), as Husserl first thought, but a clarification of the essences, or their corresponding concepts, which determine what count as psychic facts at all. Having recognized this, Husserl devotes a great deal of

39. *LI,* pp. 262–63. Cf. n. 8 above.

argument to showing the legitimacy of sciences of essence as distinct from sciences of fact.[40] This is coupled with an attack on existing psychology for falsifying the psychic by applying to it categories derived from physics. In other words, psychology is accused of failing to attend to the essence of its subject matter, a task properly performed by "phenomenology" in the newly grasped and formulated sense of *Wesenswissenschaft.*

Phenomenology thus formulated, however, still has little import apart from its relation to psychology, even if it is distinct from psychology. For there are many sciences of essence, or possible sciences of essence, according to Husserl, including, for example, all a priori (mathematical) theories of space and motion. On the above reading phenomenology would be distinguished from other sciences of essence only by the domain or region of reality it treats, i.e., the domain of mental or conscious phenomena, and might as well be called a priori or eidetic psychology. Husserl did see phenomenological investigations serving this function and asserted that phenomenology stood in the same relation to psychology as geometry to physics.[41] It had the same scope or domain as psychology but dealt with it in a different way.

The more radical reevaluation of phenomenology, paradoxically, grew out of the fact that, as practiced in the *Logical Investigations,* it was in one sense *narrower* in scope than psychology. It treated the psychic, the domain of *Erlebnisse,* only insofar as this helped clarify first the *logical,* then more broadly, as we have seen, the givenness of the *objective* in general. Placing itself in the service of logic and epistemology, it sought to bring out those aspects and characteristics of the psychic which are relevant to these disciplines, without ever claiming that it was dealing exhaustively—even as an eidetic science—with the psychic. Though the intentional or act-character is an essential element,[42] it is not all there is to consciousness, and Husserl had dealt with the nonintentional only to the extent that it had been necessary to clarify the intentional and keep it distinct.[43] Thus the phenomenology of the *Logical Investigations* derived its focus

40. Cf. *Ideas,* pt. I, chap. I.
41. Husserliana III, p. 5 (*Ideas,* p. 42). Also, *LI,* p. 262.
42. *LI,* Inv. V, § 9.
43. Cf. the discussion of feelings, *LI,* Inv. V, § 15.

from its interest in the objective; it had concentrated on the object-directedness of consciousness constituted in the peculiar quasi relation called intentional.

This objective orientation was developed in two ways which ultimately came together in the "transcendental turn." The first derived from the desire to explore and classify the various types of acts in which consciousness is related to objectivity. Different types of intentions and different manners of fulfillment were found to correspond to different types of objects. Apart from the distinction in general between factual and essential claims and their appropriate forms of fulfillment, and apart from the purely formal conditions of truth for "anything at all" reflected in formal logic, distinction could also be made among regions of reality (for example, the physical, the psychic, the spiritual or cultural) and their distinct forms of givenness. Each of these forms of givenness, in keeping with the general notion of *Ursprung* we have been tracing, corresponds to a type of conscious act which is "responsible" for the givenness, which renders the object present in the manner appropriate to it.

The vast multiplicity which results from this classification is not without its unity. As various types of objects are related to each other, so the acts in which they are given stand in certain orders of priority, dependence, etc. The ultimate unity of all objects, however, is indicated in the concept of *world:* whether the intentional acts of consciousness relate to facts or essences, it is some aspect of the world, or something about the world, that they render present. In lectures, shifting his focus from the "logical" acts of judging, inferring, etc., to those of perceiving, Husserl discovered in its clearest form the manner in which this unity presents itself, not only to the philosopher who reflects upon it but also to any perceiver. In perception it is not only the perceived object that is given: its perceptual background is given with it, a background which in turn presents itself as a mere segment of what can be perceived at all. Without distinguishable boundaries, the background recedes from the distinct to the indistinct or indeterminate. "What is directly perceived, the more or less clearly co-present and determined (or at least to some extent determined) is . . . surrounded by a horizon of undetermined reality [*Wirklichkeit*]" [44] of which we are also conscious. This

44. Husserliana III, p. 58 (*Ideas,* p. 102).

infinite perceptual horizon, partially indeterminate though it may be, is just as surely given as the particular object; indeed, the object could not be given without it.

Now this analysis is confined to sense-perception, and not everything *about* the world is perceived in the strict or narrow sense. Still, everything about the world has some relation to the spatiotemporal structure of the perceived and to this extent partakes of its manner of givenness. The things we see, deal with, enjoy, and value, the persons we encounter, the social institutions we are involved with, are thus *given* together *with* the world of which they are meaningful components.

The concept of *givenness* is thus considerably enriched, and phenomenology, whose function had been to find the "origin" of givenness in certain acts, must take this into account. Obviously, however, one cannot approach the "givenness of the world" as one would approach the givenness of a physical or other sort of object. The world is not an object alongside the others whose objectivity is to be accounted for by reference to an *Erlebnis*. It is the background or horizon of any possible object, and its givenness consists precisely in *being* a background or horizon for something within it.[45] Furthermore, the problem is not that of accounting for its givenness "each time" it is given, since it is always given insofar as anything at all is given. What renders it present to consciousness, then, what is "responsible" for its givenness is not an *"act peculiar to it,* such as an articulated predicative judgment *about* existence";[46] thus the notion of act or intention, understood in the sense of the *Logical Investigations,* seems not to answer the questions of "origin" in this case.

Still, just as the world is given with the object meant, so consciousness implicitly "means" the world at the same time it means the object; every act relating to something about the world is accompanied by this "meaning" of the world, the background against which the particular something stands out. But while such acts necessarily come and go, this meaning of the world persists. Consciousness means the world, yet not in the sense of an *act* of meaning. How then is such meaning to be characterized? Here Husserl seizes on such terms as "frame of mind"

45. Cf. Gerd Brand, *Welt, Ich und Zeit* (The Hague: Martinus Nijhoff, 1955), pp. 13–15.
46. Husserliana III, p. 63 (*Ideas,* p. 107).

(*Geisteshaltung*), "attitude" (*Einstellung*), "belief" (*Glaube*).[47] While such words do not indicate acts as such, Husserl would say that they indicate something more than mere dispositions, since the general attitude is somehow present in or behind each individual act; or, conversely, the act is what it is only as an embodiment or realization of the attitude. Now there are many possible attitudes or frames of mind—for example, one can have a purely aesthetic, a purely practical, theoretical, etc., attitude toward things, where the attitude marks out a sphere or aspect of the world, and gives each particular act its place within that sphere. But here Husserl is speaking of the fundamental attitude which underlies all such "abstractive" attitudes, the attitude whose correlate is the world as such; and this he terms the "natural attitude." Because it does have a correlate, an attitude in Husserl's sense is intentional, like an act; indeed, Husserl believes that this attitude can even be expressed in a "general thesis": the world exists, is there (*da* or *vorhanden*), etc.[48] This brings the notion of attitude closer to that of *belief*, which can be expressed but is not identical with any particular act of expressing it. But this belief is a special one, for its object is the world as such, the domain in which we place, as it were, the objects of our beliefs in the ordinary sense. Hence Husserl's later use of *Weltglaube* as a term more or less equivalent to "natural attitude."

Parallel to this reflection on the world and the natural attitude, Husserl also reflected in another way on the objectively oriented phenomenology of the *Logical Investigations*. This reflection centered on the paradoxical notion of the intentional object. Husserl had taken up Brentano's concept of intentionality—"the relation to a content, the direction to an object" [49]—in order to express the essential character of consciousness which is relevant to his epistemological and logical interests, the character of relatedness involved in the peculiar concept of "act." [50] Attempt-

47. The first term is common in *Die Idee der Phänomenologie* (1907) (Husserliana II), the second in the *Ideas*, and the third (in the form *Weltglaube*) in the *Cartesian Meditations*.

48. Husserliana III, p. 63 (*Ideas*, p. 107). But cf. *CM*, p. 17: "the being of the world . . . is so very obvious that no one would think of asserting it expressly in a proposition." We shall have more to say about this problem on pp. 173–78 below.

49. *LI*, p. 554.

50. For Husserl "intentional experience" and "act" are equivalent terms. Cf. *ibid.*, Inv. V. § 13.

ing to clarify this notion, he insisted that the objective term of this relation is not, as suggested by the term "content," a "mental" object bearing some resemblance or other relation to a "real" object outside consciousness. The intentional relation is not a relation between two elements *within* consciousness; what is meant in the experience is the object itself, whether the object in question is a tree, a mathematical state of affairs, or even the god Jupiter. "This intentional experience may be dismembered as one chooses in descriptive analysis, but the god Jupiter will naturally not be found in it" any more than one could discover a tree or a mathematical relation there.[51] The mathematical relation has ideal status, not psychic existence; the tree is physical, not mental; and the god Jupiter does not exist physically, mentally, or any other way.

At the same time, however, the description of the experience would not be adequate unless mention is made of that *of* which it is the experience or *to* which it refers; this reference or intention, after all, is part of what makes it what it is. "In the very essence of an experience lies determined not only *that*, but also *whereof* it is a consciousness." [52] But this fact has peculiar consequences for phenomenological inquiry. The description of the object meant does not belong, strictly speaking, to the description of the act, since the object is not part of the act being described. Yet phenomenology is in some sense required to describe it. The paradox of phenomenology, as this term was understood in the *Logical Investigations,* is that it was conceived as a description of the psychic, yet finds itself forced to refer *beyond* consciousness in order to make its description complete.[53] Does this mean that phenomenology must pass beyond each conscious act and describe the object of that act as well?

Husserl's ultimate answer to this question arises from a distinction made in the *Logical Investigations* themselves. Addressing himself there to the problem of the intentional object, Husserl points to the possibility of distinguishing between "*the object as it is intended,* and the *object* (period) *which* is intended." [54] Each intentional act grasps an object in a certain way, takes it *as* something, while the object may have "in itself" other possible determinations not taken into account at all. To use Husserl's

51. *Ibid.*, pp. 558–59, 593–94.
52. Husserliana III, p. 80 (*Ideas*, p. 120).
53. *LI*, p. 576, n. 1.
54. *Ibid.*, p. 578.

example, the person I represent as Germany's emperor (in 1900) could also be represented as the son of Emperor Friedrich III, the grandson of Queen Victoria, etc. This distinction does not refer, it should be noted, to *two objects;* the object meant and the object *as* meant are the same,[55] and there is no question here of a third entity set up *between* the subject and the object "in itself." Nor does the distinction introduce any difference in the ontological status of the object: the object *as* meant is no more dependent upon the act which means it than the object meant. A certain person, by being represented as Germany's emperor rather than Queen Victoria's grandson, does not thereby become dependent on my act of representing him; nor does his status of being Germany's emperor depend on it.

What the distinction does introduce, however, is two different ways of *considering* the object, one of which certainly is dependent upon a certain act of representing the object. Considering the object as meant refers back to some particular act of meaning it. Furthermore, a consideration of the object *as* meant introduces a certain "neutrality" to the consideration, since the object "in itself" may not turn out to be exactly as it was meant. A straightforward position on the object is thus withheld, an "epochē" is effected regarding it. Such consideration then takes on a "hypothetical" character; the object becomes a supposed or putative object—the object as it *would* be if it *were* "in itself" what the intention claims for it.[56] Such a "hypothetical" object can be described in great detail. But the description takes on a peculiar character which distinguishes it from any other sort of description. Two important features must be noted: First, the description derives all its material, so to speak, *from* the intentional act which serves as its point of reference; if it remains true to its character of a consideration of the object as meant it cannot free itself from this dependence. But second, it is still a description

55. *Ibid.,* p. 595.
56. In *FTL* (p. 206) Husserl speaks of "neutralized" experience as "as-if experience." Cf. J. N. Findlay, *Meinong's Theory of Objects and Values* (Oxford: Clarendon Press, 1963), p. 344: ". . . some languages often employ subjunctives to express references and connections that only obtain in someone's thought, where cruder languages employ misleading indicatives. It would have been well if, instead of saying that we were thinking of a golden mountain or of what *is* golden and mountainous, we were to say that we were thinking of what *were* a golden mountain, or what *were* golden and mountainous."

not of that act itself but precisely of the object of that act as meant in the act.

How can it be maintained, however, as we did above, that this object as meant is not dependent on the act that means it? Is it not the case, that, without the act that means it, there would *be* no object as meant? To answer this it is necessary to reaffirm the hypothetical character of the type of consideration under discussion. The description of the object as meant, by taking on its "neutral" character, is describing not something *that* is as it is, but something as it *would be* if it *were* as it is meant to be. If something were as it is meant to be in a certain act—Germany's emperor, for example—then it *would* not *be* dependent. To describe it as it *would be*, then, is to describe it as *independent*.

This much is suggested, then, by the distinction between the object meant and the object as meant. As Husserl recognized, this distinction, with its resulting "neutrality-modification" in regard to the object under consideration, is something quite natural, something ordinarily involved in many everyday situations. Above all, it is involved in any sort of critical *reflection*, in which the object as meant is "compared" with the object meant to see whether it "corresponds" or whether the original meaning should be cancelled or corrected. "Natural reflection," as Husserl calls this procedure,[57] need not always be critical—in an autobiography or personal history, for example, it can be purely descriptive—but it seems always to involve considering *both* the object meant and the object *as* meant at least in order to achieve a sort of contrast. It involves supposing, in other words, that the object *is* such and such, *has* such and such determinations, to which the object as meant can be compared. The whole distinction, in fact, seems to make no sense without this supposition. It can easily be seen, however, that in this sense the "natural" consideration of the object as meant thus depends upon an *act of meaning* the object per se, and that this object, in a further reflective move, can in turn be considered the object *as* meant. Critical thinking can be subjected to further criticism. In autobiography, objects and events as seen in one's youth are presented by reference to those objects as they really are now, yet the latter can in turn be considered, in a latter installment of the autobiography, merely "as meant" in the composition of the original autobiography.

57. Husserliana VII, p. 259; *CM*, pp. 33 ff.

At this point, reflecting on natural reflection with its distinction between the object meant and the object *as* meant, Husserl introduces a twofold radicalization of reflection as the basis of a philosophical method. Such radical reflection proposes first to consider every possible object meant exclusively in the sense of object *as* meant. Through this *radical epochē,* "we effect a reduction . . . to the meant, purely as meant . . . [and] accordingly, not to objects simpliciter but to the *objective sense.*" [58] Thus it does not engage in the "straightforward" or unreflected intention of the object, which accompanies reflection in its natural form, in order to hold up a standard or point of comparison with the object as meant. Such radical reflection neutralizes or "brackets" the object, as in the case of natural reflection, but not *for the purpose* of comparing or contrasting it with the "real thing." *Both* the "real thing" and the "supposed thing" of natural reflection become, in Husserl's radical reflection, two versions of the object as meant, which is then not further criticized by reference to anything.

Husserl saw this operation of "neutralization" or "bracketing" at work in Descartes' systematic doubt, and compared his procedure to the latter in both the *Ideas* and the *Cartesian Meditations.* But he also insisted that he was not, like Descartes, even attempting to *doubt* the existence of the object, but was merely "extracting" the moment of bracketing that is involved in the process of doubting,[59] just as it is involved in natural reflection. Descartes' attempt to doubt, of course, is connected with his ultimate purpose of *removing* doubt, where possible, by restoring belief in the object. In this sense, the real object still functions as the standard against which the meant object is measured.

But if such radical reflection is not undertaken for the purpose of critiques or contrast, as in the case of natural reflection, what does it achieve? What it does, according to Husserl, is to bring out in its clearest form precisely that givenness of the objective whose elucidation he had sought from the start; and furthermore, because the consideration of the object as meant carries with it a reference back to the act of meaning, it elucidates such givenness precisely by reference to the nature of the conscious act which belongs essentially to the *Erlebnis* in which it is given. Since it considers in this way not only the supposed

58. *CM,* p. 56.
59. Husserliana III, p. 66 (*Ideas,* p. 109).

thing but also the "real" thing of natural reflection by reference
to the act in which *it* is meant, it is in a position to describe in
general the *standards* by which natural reflection measures the
real, the criteria according to which the illusory is rejected and
"objectively true being" [60] is established. Questions of natural reflection, of which scientific questions are one type, are always
concerned with how the "experienced . . . world is to be determined in truth in respect to individual realities, their properties, relations and laws; and especially how [it is to be de-
termined] in 'objective' truth, which makes our knowledge independent of the relativity of 'merely subjective' manners of
appearance." [61] The principles according to which it does this are
indeed *invoked* in natural reflection but are not thematic. Only
radical reflection, which is in a large part a reflection on natural
reflection (though not only on this), is in a position to do this.
Attending as it does to different kinds of givenness, describing
in its oblique way different kinds of objects as meant, it at the
same time brings out and describes the different kinds of acts
that relate to them. Objects-meant as belonging to different regions of reality are meant in different ways; different procedures
are involved in each type of meaning for determining "objectively
true being."

Phenomenological reflection is thus distinguished by its re-
fusal to pose the "in-itself" as a standard by which the "for-me" is
measured. But there is yet another sense in which it is radical.
One can reflect, in the manner described, upon particular objects, or in general upon a particular sort of object—i.e., one can
consider it *merely* as meant—without at the same time performing the same act of reflection upon its background. I could, for
example, reflect upon persons in this way, without reference to
persons "in-themselves," yet at the same time not include in my
reflection the physical world. This would be to forget, however,
that persons have bodies and, *as* meant, the spatiotemporal world
in which they live and move is given with them. This brings us
back to Husserl's reflections on the world and the natural attitude. Insofar as phenomenology passes beyond the conscious act
to describe the object of that act as meant, it is forced to include
in its considerations the horizon "meant with" the object—ultimately the world itself, whose givenness is implied in the given-

60. Husserliana VII, p. 272.
61. *Ibid.*, p. 246.

ness of the object. Proceeding as it does from the object to its horizons, its consideration of the *world* is undertaken from the same standpoint as the consideration of the object: that is, it is a consideration of the *world as meant*. This is, of course, exactly the kind of consideration we carried out before in order to illustrate Husserl's move from the individual act to the "natural attitude" underlying it. Only such a consideration, involving as it does a reference to the act (or in this case attitude) of meaning, is capable of revealing that act for what it is. But this consideration, as in the case of the individual object, must be explicitly grasped and radicalized: phenomenology, insofar as its descriptions encompass the whole *world,* must confine itself to a consideration of the world exclusively *as meant* without invoking, as standard of comparison, the world "in itself."

TRANSCENDENTAL PHENOMENOLOGY

THIS REPRESENTS the ultimate radicalization of phenomenological reflection, which Husserl calls the "phenomenological reduction." The reduction is simply the phenomenological epochē, extended to encompass the whole world and carried out consistently as a philosophical method. Once it is achieved, the development is complete whereby the descriptive psychology of the *Logical Investigations* is transformed into a transcendental philosophy. In intentional acts of consciousness, Husserl found the "origin" of the givenness of the objective, the process by which the *an sich* enters into experience and thus becomes "in a certain sense subjective." Forced to the recognition that what it must describe is not only the act but the object as well, Husserl's phenomenology overflows the boundaries of anything that can legitimately be called psychology, whether eidetic or empirical. The consideration of objects in turn expands to become a consideration of the whole world; yet Husserl makes this consideration entirely dependent upon reference to consciousness by considering the world strictly as meant; and here the reference to consciousness discovers not an act, strictly speaking, but an attitude, the "natural" attitude.

In a certain sense the basic scheme or pattern of the *Logical Investigations* is maintained even after the development just described is completed. Where he had previously found in the act the "origin" of an object's givenness, Husserl now finds in the natural attitude the "origin" of the world's givenness. As in the earlier work, Husserl's procedure involves a rejection of any form of subjective idealism. The world is no more reducible to the act in which it is meant than are the real or ideal objects discussed in the *Logical Investigations.* "The world," as he says in the *Cartesian Meditations,* is "not a piece of my Ego, to be found in my conscious life as a really inherent part of it, as a complex of data of sensation or a complex of acts." [62] This "nonincluded-ness," it will be recalled, is what Husserl terms "transcendence." Nor is there any question of the world's having a real dependence on consciousness for its being. The natural attitude, in other words, does not create the world. As before, these philosophical insights are gained by paying attention precisely to the sense of the act—or in this case the attitude—in which the world is meant. "Only an uncovering of the horizon of experience ultimately clarifies the 'actuality' and the 'transcendency' of the world. . . ." [63] As the subject matter of phenomenology's descriptions, the natural attitude exhibits the *nature* of the world-as-given by being at the same time the source of that givenness.

In spite of such similarities to the *Logical Investigations,* however, Husserl's revised and expanded phenomenology is placed in an entirely new dimension. This derives primarily from the fact that it is the world, rather than this or that object, whose givenness is now being traced to consciousness, the domain of *Erlebnisse.* The world, we have noted, is not just another object; it can be looked at as the "universe" of the philosophers, the realm of all possible objects. In the *Ideas* Husserl speaks of it as *"omnitudo realitatis,"* [64] or "the totality of objects of possible experience [*Erfahrung*] and experiential knowledge." [65] To be sure, Husserl's approach to a treatment of the world is not that of the cosmologists, old and new, but in keeping with our earlier remarks he is speaking of the *same thing* they are. And it is the world as a whole, rather than anything *in* the world, that is now being placed "over against" consciousness, since it "transcends" consciousness.

But the obvious consequence of this approach is that, in considering consciousness, phenomenology seems to place it outside the world. Just as the world is not part of it, it is not a part

62. *CM,* p. 26.
63. *Ibid.,* p. 62.
64. Husserliana III, p. 6 (*Ideas,* p. 44).
65. *Ibid.,* p. 11. (*Ideas,* p. 52). We shall have occasion on pp. 144–50 below to question this early formulation.

of the world. How is this possible? Insofar as consciousness can be subjected to any kind of consideration at all, it would seem to become an "object" (of consideration) and thus to belong to the world, the "totality of objects of possible experience." Also, quite apart from this "formal" argument, is it not obvious that consciousness, whether my own or someone else's, is something that is encountered in the world along with other things, something that stands in certain kinds of relations to its surroundings within the world horizon?

Husserl admits that in natural reflection consciousness is indeed encountered in the world as a "property" or mode of existence of certain entities that have bodies, that it is thus the object of its own kind of experience in which it is given in the context of the spatiotemporal world. At the same time the theory and practice of radical reflection or phenomenological reduction shows that it is possible to *consider* consciousness—the same consciousness—under a different aspect, namely, exclusively in terms of its intentional or act-relation to the world as a whole. And this consideration, while it sees consciousness in *relation* to the world, is forced by its recognition of the very nature of that relation to separate consciousness from the world, to place it, in a sense, "outside." Husserl admits, indeed wishes to insist, that the phenomenological consideration of consciousness is based on a kind of *experience* (*Erfahrung*).[66] He chooses this term because he wishes to insist that radical reflection, like natural experience, involves a direct grasp of individual occurrences, in this case acts of consciousness. At the same time this "experience" is such that its object is no longer an object in the sense of belonging to the world. If reflection is truly radical, this is how its object is *given*.

We can now see why Husserl's radical reflection is called transcendental reflection, why the reduction is transcendental reduction, and in what sense phenomenology is transcendental philosophy. First, in Husserl's sense of the term "transcendental," the world as a whole is *transcendent* in relation to consciousness; it is something meant in consciousness which is "other in principle . . . not part of" consciousness. Phenomenology is concerned first with the world *as* transcendent, i.e., with its givenness *as* transcendent to consciousness; and it is concerned second with consciousness itself, but exclusively as *transcendental*

66. Husserliana VIII, p. 163.

consciousness, i.e., insofar as it transcends itself in meaning the world. Phenomenological considerations, then, whether of the world or of consciousness, stand under the sign of the problem of transcendence. Phenomenology looks at everything, so to speak, from the perspective of this problem.

But Husserl's phenomenology fulfills in large measure the Kantian notion of transcendental philosophy as well. We have already noted that there is a sense in which phenomenology deals, in Kant's phrase, "not so much with objects as with the mode of our knowledge of objects . . ."—that is, it is reflective. But for both Husserl and Kant it is the radical character of this reflection that counts, and Husserl's and Kant's modes of reflection are radical in the same way. Kant proceeds from the objectivity not of particular objects but of the whole world of experience and possible experience. His conception of "nature" (or sometimes, loosely, *Erfahrung*) corresponds to Husserl's conception of world as "the totality of objects of possible experience and experiential knowledge." [67] Like Kant's pure understanding, consciousness for Husserl is not part of the world, but "transcends" it in a certain sense by standing over against it; yet, like the "transcendental" in Kant, its "purpose is nothing more than to make experiential knowledge possible." For both Husserl and Kant this means first that "the transcendental," even though it "transcends" the world, consists purely in its intentional character, its character of standing in relation to the world. At least as far as transcendental philosophy is concerned, it has no meaningful or legitimate mode of existence apart from this relation.

The character of the relation is such, however, that the two terms are not on an equal basis. The transcendental is related to the world in the sense that it provides the ground or origin of the world-as-given. What this means is that the character of the world-as-meant, the way in which it presents itself, finds no justification in the world itself; the world as meant finds its only justification in the act that means it, which in turn has no further justification. The objectivity of objects, their givenness as objective or transcendent (in Husserl's sense), is established or legitimized, for both Husserl and Kant, by virtue of the transcendental meaning-of-the-world discovered in radical reflection.

67. Kant calls nature *"der Inbegriff aller Erscheinungen"* (*Critique of Pure Reason*, B 163); Husserl's expression is *"der Gesamtinbegriff von Gegenständen möglicher Erfahrung"* (Husserliana III, p. 11).

The recognition of this relation is compared by Kant with the Copernican revolution in science: "hitherto it has been assumed that all our knowledge must conform to objects," whereas Kant shows that "objects must conform to our knowledge" [68] in virtue of "laws [prescribed] *a priori*" by the understanding "to nature, the sum of all appearances." [69] Once Husserl's concept of "objects" expands to take in the world as a totality, he has made the full transcendental turn and is in a position to embrace Kant's conception of the Copernican revolution.[70]

Both Husserl and Kant dissociate themselves from any form of subjective idealism, and they do this in similar ways. It is not the world *schlechthin* that "must conform" to our way of knowing in the Copernican revolution, but rather the world as meant. Transcendental philosophy *itself* makes no pronouncements, positive or negative, about the world-in-itself, even though it relies on the distinction *between* the world-in-itself and the world as meant. To be sure, the two philosophers have radically different ways of making this distinction. For Husserl the object as such corresponds to a straightforward or nonreflective intention, a consideration of the object which does not refer to its givenness to consciousness; whereas Kant's thing-in-itself is conceived as the correlate of a postulated mode of intelligence radically different from our own. Husserl finds such a conception unintelligible,[71] and ultimately rejects the *Kantian* conception of the transcendent, the conception which led Kant, by analogy, to use the term "transcendental." But Kant proceeds from a concept of the objectivity of *nature* which corresponds to *Husserl's* conception of the transcendent; and this objectivity, in turn, is not considered "straightforwardly" (i.e., simply taken for granted) by Kant as if it were the world-in-itself, but is considered strictly *as meant* in natural scientific thinking. This is, in effect, Kant's "phenomenological reduction," which reveals the *character* of the meaning of which nature is the correlate and upon which its status or validity as objective depends.

68. *Critique of Pure Reason,* B XVI.
69. *Ibid.,* B 163.
70. Husserliana VII, p. 240.
71. In a penetrating analysis, Iso Kern, *Husserl und Kant,* pp. 119–34, criticizes Husserl's actual references to the Kantian thing-in-itself as inappropriate, but finds Husserl's genuine rejection of the thing-in-itself in his rejection of the Kantian *intellectus archetypus.*

There are, of course, many other crucial differences between Husserl and Kant that must not be overlooked. Husserl sees in Kant, for one thing, a confusion of nature with the world. For Husserl, it is not only the objectivity of nature, as it is represented in the theory of the physicist, that must be accounted for by reference to the transcendental. There is much in the world that is not reducible to spatiotemporal nature (e.g., persons and cultural entities), and there is even much of spatiotemporal nature itself (so-called secondary qualities, for example) that cannot be grasped by the physicist's mathematical approach, but which is nevertheless given as objective (transcendent) and thus has to be accounted for transcendentally. For Husserl, Kant either identifies the world with (scientific) nature, in which case he simplifies it beyond recognition; or he simply takes for granted other forms of objectivity, failing in the end to provide a transcendental account for everything that is in need of such an account.

Another important difference between Kant and Husserl concerns the emphasis placed on the concept of *act* as opposed to that of *rule*. It could be argued that the two transcendental philosophies are only formally similar in grounding the objectivity of the world in something called "the transcendental," whereas what is actually understood by this term is in each case totally different. That which ultimately renders possible the objectivity of the world-as-meant is, for Kant, a set of pure concepts, principles, or rules, not acts of consciousness. This was the Neo-Kantian interpretation of Kant which attacked Husserl for distorting transcendental philosophy into a confused kind of psychology. The controversy between the Neo-Kantians and the phenomenologists in the twenties and thirties centered around this issue,[72] and Husserl did indeed attack Kant, at one point, for being "too ontological" by stressing the "form" of the world and failing adequately to ground that form in subjectivity.[73]

Actually, this opposition of Husserl and Kant was vastly exaggerated; the real difference is one of emphasis. Kant's "rules,"

72. Fink, in "Die phänomenolgische Philosophie Edmund Husserls in der gegenwärtigen Kritik," sums up this controversy and refers to two books: Rudolf Zocher, *Husserls Phänomenologie und Schuppes Logik* (Munich: Ernst Reinhardt, 1932); and Friedrich Kreis, *Phänomenologie und Kritizismus* (Tübingen: J. C. B. Mohr, 1930).

73. Husserliana VII, p. 281.

after all, are rules for doing something—judging or "synthesiz-ing"—and Kant does not fail to use the term "consciousness" for the agent of synthesis. And it is quite obvious that, insofar as consciousness is being considered purely in this light—purely insofar as it is subject to the transcendental rules—conscious-ness is itself transcendental, i.e., it is not part of or subject to the determinations of that which is determined by its activity (the world). Husserl, for his part, by emphasizing consciousness as act, does not conceive of an arbitrary or capricious agent whose whim determines how the world is. In relation to spatio-temporal things, for example, "we are not fully free," [74] even in what we can imagine, let alone what we can perceive. Rather, we are bound to the *essence* of "thinghood" or to what constitutes the ontological region of "things" in the world, and this region *"pre-scribes rules for the course of possible intuitions*—and that means [in this case] possible perceptions." [75] Such rules are pre-cisely those standards we spoke of earlier, criteria that are in-voked in order to distinguish "objectively true being" from illu-sion. Such rules are the "principles which, as ideal conditions of the possibility of scientific objectivity, function as norms govern-ing the whole enterprise of empirical science." [76]

Phenomenology and Idealism

IN ANY CASE, it should be clear from our presentation that phenomenology cannot be accused of a "psychological" ap-proach to transcendental philosophy. This is true because the "common" subject matter of phenomenology and psychology, consciousness, is subjected in phenomenology to an essential rather than a factual consideration, and because consciousness is considered as subject to rules or nonempirical norms rather than empirical laws. But even more important than this is the fact that consciousness is approached not as a part of the world but rather as standing "outside" the world in virtue of its intentional relation to it. This is why Husserl insists again and again[77] that

74. Husserliana III, p. 366 (*Ideas,* p. 413).
75. *Ibid.*
76. *IP*, p. 46. Cf. *FTL*, p. 16: phenomenology "intends to bring to light the system of transcendental principles that gives to sciences the possible sense of genuine sciences."
77. E.g., Husserliana III, p. 4 (*Ideas,* p. 42); *PRS,* p. 115.

the source of phenomenological descriptions is not "inner experience" or "inner perception" in the usual sense. Such inner perception makes sense only by opposition to "outer perception" and is based on distinguishing two types of objects, the psychic and the physical respectively, *within* the world. Inner perception then concentrates on one region of the world to the exclusion of the other. We have seen that phenomenology, because of its intentional view of consciousness, is and must be as much a description of the world as of consciousness. A discipline whose subject matter is not primarily the psychic can hardly be called psychology. At the same time phenomenology, in virtue of its radical reflection or phenomenological reduction, is a special way of looking at the world, namely, *as meant,* that is, by reference to the intentional activity of consciousness. By comparison to "straightforward" sciences of the world, phenomenology is distinguished not by its subject matter, since it, too, is a science of the world, but by its *attitude,* the sign, so to speak, under which all its reflections on the world stand.[78] "Phenomenological reduction is precisely nothing other than a change in attitude through which, consistently and universally, the experienced world [*Erfahrungswelt*] is regarded as world of possible experience, that is, the experiencing life is considered for which the experienced is . . . experiential sense with a certain intentional horizon"[79]—the ultimate horizon being, of course, the world. As Ricoeur puts it, "the reduction is a conversion which causes the 'for-me' to emerge" from every straightforwardly given object.[80]

Just as phenomenology is a special way of looking at the world, so too it is a special way of looking at consciousness. In a sense it is the *discovery* of transcendental consciousness, the emergence of the possibility of something that can be "considered" and yet lies outside the world. But it should be clear that while consciousness, from this point of view, does not belong to the world, it is nevertheless not worldless. On the contrary, as transcendental, it has no other mode of being than that which relates it to the world[81]—i.e., its intentional character, which is precisely a nonbelonging relation to the world. As Husserl says,

78. Husserl describes the *epochē* as a "change of sign" (*Vorzeichenänderung*), Husserliana III, p. 74 (*Ideas,* p. 212).
79. Husserliana VIII, p. 436.
80. Paul Ricoeur, *Husserl: An Analysis of His Phenomenology* (Evanston, Ill.: Northwestern University Press, 1967), p. 176.
81. Husserliana III, p. 195 (*Ideas,* p. 233).

it "is what it is solely in relation to intentional objectivities." [82] This is why no consideration of consciousness is possible, under this attitude, which is not at the same time a consideration of the world, and why Husserl's conception of subjectivity is no more ontological or metaphysical than psychological. As long as consciousness is considered psychologically, it is considered a member of a distinct region of being. In the *Ideas,* when Husserl introduces the phenomenological reduction by moving from natural to radical reflection, he speaks of the domain of consciousness as an *Urregion.*[83] But this can only mean that, from the phenomenological point of view, consciousness, by "encompassing" the world, becomes the region of all regions, and reference to it as *a* region can only be confusing. Phenomenology is not an ontology of consciousness; it does not consider consciousness alone, it does not distinguish consciousness from other forms of being and then relate it to them in the ontological manner. Husserl admits, of course, that a phenomenological or intentional *psychology* is possible.[84] Here consciousness would be treated as intentional but could not be considered *only* in its intentional relation to the world; it would have to be related ontologically as well. For example, human consciousness is considered not only as aware of its body, but also as dependent on its body in the psychophysical sense. Such a consideration would be required by an *attitude* which places consciousness within the world.

Again, the attitude, not only toward consciousness but toward the world, reveals itself as the crucial factor. According to Husserl's conception, every "natural" attitude, or every variation of *the* natural attitude, is ontological. That is, it considers its objects as comprising a distinct region of reality, and takes certain things for granted about that region. Also possible *within* the natural attitude is an explicit ontology, i.e., a discipline which *articulates* what is "taken for granted" about a particular region.

82. *CM*, p. 65.
83. Husserliana III, p. 174 (*Ideas*, p. 212). An author who correctly sees the consequences for phenomenology of this misleading notion is Lothar Eley in *Die Krise des Apriori* (The Hague: Martinus Nijhoff, 1962), p. 15 and *passim*. Jacques Derrida mentions the same problem in Husserl, *L'Origine de la géométrie*, translated with an introduction by Derrida (Paris: Presses Universitaires de France, 1962), p. 151 n.
84. Though its ultimate possibility is questioned in the *Crisis,* p. 257.

Phenomenology's transcendental attitude, however, is distinguished by the fact that it is nonontological.[85] This is true not because it considers the whole world, rather than some region: a formal and material ontology of the whole world (of all its regions) is also possible, and such, according to Husserl, is the character of most traditional philosophy. Rather, phenomenology is nonontological because of the way it considers the world—purely as meant by consciousness—and because of the way it considers consciousness—purely as meaning the world, and thus as not belonging to the world.

That is why Husserl so often stresses the mental efforts required not only to achieve the phenomenological reduction but also to sustain it, to avoid "falling back" into some variation of the natural attitude. The image of falling, of a gravitational pull on consciousness, corresponds to Husserl's use of the term "natural" in the expression "natural attitude." It is of the nature of consciousness to ontologize, to consider its object "straightforwardly," simply as being. Even in natural, critical reflection, the natural attitude is not left behind. In phenomenological reflection, with its radicalization of reflection's neutrality-modification, consciousness must constantly fight against its tendency to ontologize both itself and the world, remaining, as it were, in a state of continual suspense. In this sense, it is the most "unnatural"[86] or "artificial"[87] of attitudes, constituting, as Husserl said, nothing less than a "revolution of the natural way of thinking."[88]

Supposing, however, that such an attitude is attained and sustained and the world is successfully considered exclusively as meant: what has become, one might ask, of the world *which*

85. We are using the term "ontology" here in *Husserl's* sense, which claims to be no different from the traditional sense. "Ontology" in this sense should not be confused with Heidegger's "fundamental ontology" (*Being and Time,* trans. John Macquarrie and Edward Robinson [New York: Harper & Row, 1962], pp. 32 ff.), which stands in roughly the same relation to ontology as Husserl's phenomenology. In fact, of course, Heidegger calls his own method "phenomenological," though its relation to Husserl's is notoriously problematic. See the famous exchange between Husserl and Heidegger on the *Encyclopedia Britannica* article in Husserliana IX, p. 601.

86. Husserliana VIII, p. 121.

87. Husserliana IV, p. 180.

88. Husserliana VII, p. 240.

is meant, the "world-in-itself"? Phenomenology, we have seen, involves refusing to consider the world in this sense, whether in order to contrast it with the world-as-meant or to use it as a critical standard. Does this mean that it denies the existence in itself of the world or assigns to it no other existence than that which it has in the mind or in consciousness?

Husserl has indeed been accused of making such a move, and many of his statements, especially in his later years, support the accusation. Many other statements, however, support the view that Husserl holds on to the literal sense of what was just asserted: phenomenology simply *refuses to consider* the world as in itself; it simply places the whole question "in brackets." To consent to such a consideration of the world would be, after all, to "ontologize," whether by assigning the world a status independent of consciousness or (as Husserl is accused of doing) by denying it any existence except in consciousness. In the *Cartesian Mediations,* which for some commentators documents Husserl's move to pure idealism, Husserl still affirms the character of phenomenology as reflection which consistently maintains its "epochē with respect to the being or non-being of the world." [89] As Husserl states in the *Ideas* and repeats many times, the phenomenological attitude involves neither a negation of nor even a doubt concerning the world's existence.[90] Nor does it involve "securing" the existence of the world *against* skeptical doubts, as in Cartesianism, or "securing" the objectivity of science, which many see as the task of Kantian transcendental philosophy.[91]

This does not mean that the "decision" as to the being or non-being of the world is not a matter of interest to phenomenology. In a sense the "decision" has been made and is irrevocable—in the *natural attitude:* the world exists, and is neither reducible to nor dependent for its being on consciousness; and all the sciences of the natural attitude are dependent on this "decision." In order to be a description of the world-as-meant, phenomenology must describe the world in this way, precisely *as* it is meant. As we have seen, it derives all the content of its descriptions from the act or attitude of consciousness to which it refers back; and as the fundamental attitude, underlying all other attitudes and all acts, the natural attitude is anything but neutral.

89. *CM,* p. 34.
90. Husserliana III, p. 67 (*Ideas,* pp. 110–11). See also Husserliana V, p. 153; Husserliana VI, p. 410.
91. Husserliana VII, p. 246.

With this, another paradoxical feature of the phenomenological attitude is revealed: while consciousness must constantly strive to keep itself free of the natural attitude, it is at the same time in a sense bound to it, because it is not only an object of description itself but also the source of phenomenology's description of the world. The phenomenologist must continue to live in the natural attitude in order to be vitally aware of what it is he is describing. Phenomenological reflection, in which consciousness turns on its own acts and attitudes, seeks to describe articulately what it has previously only lived through; but it must have the original living-through as the constant source of its description if it is to avoid becoming empty talk or philosophical invention.[92] The intricacy of not losing touch with the natural attitude while at the same time not falling into it completely makes up one of the difficult aspects of phenomenology which never ceased to occupy Husserl.

In any case we can see that, in this sense, neither the natural attitude nor the being-in-itself of the world are lost in phenomenology; the natural attitude is lived through and then described *as* it is lived through; the world-in-itself is meant in that attitude and is then described *as* meant. What is not done, or what should not be done, is to confuse the natural and the phenomenological attitudes or to place them on the same plane, as if they presented an alternative between "realism" and "idealism." Quite apart from the question of whether the natural attitude, or its "thesis," corresponds to anything like philosophical realism, the phenomenological attitude is not, as we have seen, a *different* ontological thesis which seeks to overcome the natural attitude in *this* sense by putting itself in its place. Husserl is not one of those philosophers, who, in Strawson's words,[93] seeks to reform our thought about the world. Rather, he is content, like Kant and Aristotle, to describe that thought. "Phenomenological explication does nothing but *explicate the sense this world has for us all, prior to any philosophizing . . . —a sense which philosophy can uncover but never alter. . . .*"[94] If phenomenology were to replace the natural attitude, to declare it invalid, it would by that same step become empty, for it would have nothing to describe. Phenomenology is a way of looking at the world which seeks to be non-

92. *Crisis*, p. 176. Cf. *CM*, p. 35; Husserliana VIII, p. 96.
93. *Individuals* (London: Methuen, 1959), p. 9.
94. *CM*, p. 151.

ontological. It is a different way of looking at the world, which must remain aware of, but not overcome, its difference from the primary way of looking at the world, the natural attitude. It can only pass beyond the natural attitude by remaining partly within it.

All the same, is phenomenology not "idealistic"? Certainly not in the sense that the world is reduced to consciousness or made a product of it, comparable to a product of imagination. Still, in considering the world merely as meant, is it not reducing the world to a mere meaning, something dependent upon an act of meaning for its existence? This would be so, and phenomenology would have to be considered an idealism, if it *claimed* that the world *is* such and nothing else; but instead of doing this, phenomenology makes use of a possibility which is always open and precisely *considers* the world purely as meant without transforming its consideration into a philosophical (or ontological) claim. Referring to this procedure, Ricoeur has found a particularly appropriate expression: "it entails a methodological rather than a doctrinal idealism." [95]

The characterization of phenomenology as "methodological idealism" is in keeping with our own presentation of phenomenology as first and foremost a *"way* of looking at things." We have seen that it is not concerned with a special region of reality, the psychic, but takes the whole world as its subject matter. In this sense it shares its subject matter with all sciences, including metaphysics (or ontology), if the latter is considered the science of all being. Instead of being distinguished by its subject matter, then, phenomenology is distinguished by its way of approach or attitude. Husserl expressed this in his first systematic exposition of phenomenology, the five lectures of 1907, when he said that phenomenology is "above all . . . a method and attitude of mind [*Geisteshaltung*]." [96]

PHILOSOPHY AS RIGOROUS SCIENCE

BUT THE QUESTION presents itself: even if such a frame of mind is possible, why adopt it? There must be some point in

95. Ricoeur, *Husserl*, p. 36. Ricoeur also thinks (pp. 36–37, 89, 176) that Husserl goes beyond this position to a "doctrinal" (metaphysical or ontological) idealism.

96. *IP*, p. 19.

assuming this new and most "unnatural" of attitudes. Why go through the rigors of radicalizing reflection, of performing the "phenomenological reduction" and making the effort to sustain it, at all?

We have seen that the thoroughly consistent or radical consideration of the object purely "as meant" refers back to, and thus forces, an explicit consideration of the conscious acts and underlying attitudes in which the object's "being meant" consists. When we spoke above of the emergence of the concept of world in Husserl's philosophy, primarily in his phenomenology of perception, we recounted just such a consideration. Reflection on the perceptual object as meant reveals its givenness against the background of its horizon—ultimately the world itself—and at the same time consciousness' "meaning" of that horizon. We saw that the act—any act—has its own sort of "horizon," which is not itself an act but an attitude, ultimately the "natural attitude" or *Glaube* in the world itself. The consideration of perceptual objects, then, *as meant* in perception, leads to the consideration of the world; the world itself is considered as meant, and this consideration leads in turn to the recognition and characterization of the natural attitude. Now what is important is that this process of reflection reveals something that had not been seen before—the "horizontal" character of perception and its ultimate rootedness in the natural attitude—and that *could* not be seen except by virtue of the method of radical reflection. "The phenomenologist . . . does not inquire with merely a naïve devotedness to the intentional object purely as such. . . . If that were all he did, the intentionality, which makes up the intuitive or non-intuitive consciousness itself . . . would remain 'anonymous'." [97] Natural reflection remains within the natural attitude, which is to say that its consideration of objects as meant does not expand to take in the ultimate horizon of the world. Living *in* the natural attitude, it is unable to *see* the natural attitude. Furthermore, because it is busy *invoking* those norms and standards of the natural attitude by which the real is determined in various regions, it is unable to see those standards for what they are, to describe their relation to the natural attitude itself and to the acts they normatively determine. Without the radicalization of the phenomenological reduction, in other words, a description of consciousness would be incomplete at best; it would not ac-

97. *CM,* p. 47.

complish the discovery of transcendental consciousness in its full range and complexity.

In one sense this is justification enough for the adoption of the phenomenological attitude: it permits something to be seen that was not seen before and could not be seen without it. Or, to be more precise, it *is* such seeing: Husserl criticized himself for his early "Cartesian" presentations of the reduction in which he seemed to "bracket" or "neutralize" the world first and then had to explain what to do next, namely, to investigate consciousness under the new attitude.[98] Actually, the change of attitude by which the world is converted into the meant, and the conscious meaning of the world emerges, is one movement; the *quasi*-negative moment of neutralization, the *quasi*-renunciation of the natural attitude, *is* the positive moment by which the previously hidden characteristics of transcendental consciousness are revealed.

For Husserl, simply seeing needs no justification beyond itself. Its motivation is nothing other than simple wonder ($\theta\alpha\nu\mu\acute{\alpha}\zeta\epsilon\iota\nu$) to which Husserl, following Plato and Aristotle, traces the beginning of philosophy.[99] In this sense, the phenomenological attitude is a purely theoretical rather than a practical attitude, one which, to be sure, involves its own kind of practice and method but whose ultimate purpose is simply to see or to know.

Thus phenomenology is a new "way of looking at things" which reveals something previously unrecognized. But does it have only its novelty to recommend it? Once it is discovered, does it simply take its place among the possible attitudes we can adopt and discard, becoming one more theoretical enterprise alongside the others?[100] For Husserl, on the contrary, the phenomenological attitude has a dignity and superiority over all other theoretical attitudes, which permits philosophy, for the first time, to assume its long-claimed position in regard to the sciences. Phenomenology is one theoretical attitude among others, but it is the only one in a position to fulfill all the requirements inherent in the notion of theory. How is this so?

The answer lies in the nature of what it is that phenomenology reveals. We have spoken of acts and attitudes, norms and

98. *Crisis*, p. 155.
99. *Ibid.*, p. 285.
100. *Ibid.*, p. 136.

standards, involved in the process by which consciousness means the world, the "origin" of the world's givenness. Underlying them all is the natural attitude itself, the *Weltglaube* or world-life whose correlate is the world as horizon. Here we referred to the "decision as to the being or non-being of the world" as one which is "already made" in the natural attitude, one in which the phenomenologist does not take part, but in which he is interested as a theme. Considered phenomenologically, what is of interest about this "decision" is that it is, of course, not really a decision at all in any ordinary sense. There is no point at which such a decision is made, no call for any such decision. In this sense the term "belief" is better, but again the *Weltglaube* bears few of the earmarks of any ordinary belief: it is not subscribed to on the basis *of* experience or even accepted on hearsay from others; there is no evidence, probable or otherwise, for it, no imaginable circumstance in which experience would provide grounds for making this belief more firm than it already is. On the other hand, there are no circumstances in which this belief could be called into question, no grounds against it, no doubts suggested by contrary evidence. Thus Husserl calls *Weltglaube* a "universal 'prejudice' [*Vorurteil*]." [101]

And this is indeed one of the most remarkable things that comes to light when natural attitude is revealed in phenomenological reflection: there is such an attitude or belief, and it can, according to Husserl, be expressed as an affirmation; yet it appears to be totally arbitrary, totally outside the sphere of justification or denial.

But it is not only the natural attitude or *Weltglaube*, in this general sense, that has this character. In the natural attitude, the world is not simply given as such, but is given as the ultimate horizon of a multiplicity of objects and states of affairs which fall into various types and whose ultimate forms Husserl calls "regions" of reality—nature, the psychic, the spiritual or cultural. Correlatively, consciousness of the world as horizon is only the background for the concrete life of consciousness consisting of acts relating to objects falling into these types. Now the particular truths and evidences of experience and science, which constitute one's "actual" world, the concrete and determined content of the world, are not themselves arbitrary, of course; they are justified to greater or lesser degrees (and can also turn out to

101. *CM,* p. 35.

be unjustified and thus "cancelled") by reference to what counts as the justification which is appropriate to them. "What counts as justification" is nothing other than those norms and standards referred to above which allow us to determine "objectively true being." But these norms and standards are no less arbitrary than the natural attitude itself. In fact, they are nothing but the forms according to which the natural attitude is concretely actualized in conscious life, the guidelines according to which its general intention toward world-content is fulfilled. The ultimate rules of justification are not themselves subject to justification, and it is inappropriate to demand it for them. They too constitute a set of "prejudices," presuppositions, or what Husserl calls *Selbstverständlichkeiten:* they are simply taken for granted.

Now "the whole aim of transcendental philosophy is to go back to these fundamental *Selbstverständlichkeiten*," [102] i.e., "the taken-for-granted [*selbstverständliche*] pregivenness of the world in living experience and the further *Selbstverständlichkeiten* that are built upon it." [103] Whereas actual world-life consists in simply taking these norms and standards for granted and applying them, even when reflecting in the natural way (i.e., "critically"), the transcendental attitude has the character of *reflecting upon* such norms and the manner in which they are applied. It *consists*, really, in becoming aware of them for what they are, that is, as "prejudices." The phenomenological reduction is nothing other than the process or method of such coming-to-awareness. In the process, such prejudices lose their character as prejudices, because they are no longer accepted blindly and unquestioningly. To be sure, they are not challenged, as we have seen, with a view to replacing them with other beliefs or norms. Nor is there an attempt to buttress them, to remove their prejudicial character by providing them with a justification. As we have noted, Husserl states that phenomenology explicates *"the sense this world has for us all . . . a sense which philosophy can uncover but can never alter."* [104] The firmness of our beliefs is neither lessened nor strengthened, but there is a sense in which the phenomenologist, in reflecting upon them, does not really subscribe to them, at least not in the manner of the natural attitude he has left behind. Rather, he grasps them, recognizes them for

102. Husserliana VII, p. 247.
103. *Ibid.*, p. 246.
104. *CM*, p. 151.

what they are, and understands their position in relation to one another and their over-all role in the concrete life of consciousness. In Husserl's words, he transforms a *Selbstverständlichkeit* into a *Verständlichkeit;* he transforms something taken for granted into something understood.[105]

In this way phenomenology reveals not only its difference from all other forms of inquiry, but also its superiority over them. Every project of knowledge distinguishes between the merely supposed, conjectured, or vaguely meant and the grounded or justified, and aims at arriving at the latter. This is true of all the sciences, but they succeed in arriving at justified assertions in their respective spheres only by taking for granted the process of justification itself and the standards of justification that apply to those spheres. Now philosophy has always sought to be "the universal and in the radical sense 'rigorous' science," i.e., "the science of ultimate justification or, what comes to the same thing, of ultimate responsibility for itself, in which, then, no predicative or pre-predicative *Selbstverständlichkeit* functions as *unquestioned* ground of knowledge." [106] How can this philosophical project be realized? "It takes place in a decisive and fruitful way only through systematically working out the method for inquiring back into the last conceivable presuppositions of knowledge." [107] And this is precisely the method, says Husserl, of phenomenological reduction. Because its very subject matter is those "last conceivable presuppositions of knowledge," insofar as it recognizes them in their entirety for what they are, phenomenology is in a position to be a "presuppositionless" science in the sense that it *itself* has no prejudices: what it recognizes, to the extent that it recognizes it, it does not take for granted. Thus phenomenology is in a position to realize the perennial goal of "philosophy as rigorous science."

Such, in broad outlines, is the conception of phenomenology as transcendental philosophy presented by Husserl in his various "introductions" prior to 1936. Then, under the title *The Crisis of European Sciences and Transcendental Phenomenology,* Husserl published the beginning of a new introduction, to whose peculiar features we shall now turn.

105. *Crisis*, p. 180.
106. Husserliana V, p. 139; emphasis mine.
107. *Ibid.*

Philosophy and History
in the *Crisis*

HUSSERL'S NEW INTRODUCTION to phenomenology begins in an unexpected way. Its title and opening theme seem to
derive from what the author admits is a kind of popular cliché.
Talk of a "crisis of science" is "heard so often these days," he
says.[1] Is there any truth in it? Husserl admits the prima facie
implausibility of the idea if one takes it to mean that the sciences
are on the point of some sort of internal breakdown. On the contrary, revolutionary upheavals in physics and mathematics have
led to important theoretical renewals, and have only strengthened
the universal admiration accorded these disciplines as models of
scientific rigor and accomplishment. The humanistic disciplines,
too—included, of course, in the broad German concept of *Wis-
senschaft*—are undoubtedly making great progress.

Husserl wishes to defend the notion of the crisis, however, in
another sense. There exists a "general lament about the crisis of
our culture" in which science is seen as being implicated.[2] Science
not only makes great theoretical progress but also contributes to
material comfort and prosperity; yet it insists on excluding in
principle precisely the questions whose answers we most des-
perately need: "questions about the meaning or meaninglessness
of the whole of this human existence."[3] Even the sciences of man
insist that the scientist take no valuative position in his inquiry.
Hence a hostile attitude toward science among the "younger generation": "In our vital need—so we are told—this science has

1. *Crisis*, p. 3.
2. *Ibid.*, p. 5.
3. *Ibid.*, p. 6.

[45]

nothing to say to us." [4] In spite of its great theoretical and practical successes, there is a crisis of science. It consists in "the loss of its meaning for life." [5]

It was not always this way, Husserl reminds us. Modern theoretical disciplines trace their origins to a time—the Renaissance —when it was generally believed that it was precisely science which was destined to give meaning to life. To be sure, it was science in a most elevated sense, as an overarching system of truth of which the special sciences are merely coordinated branches, which was assigned this role. In other words it was philosophy which was the ground and unity of science and the fullest realization of man's essential trait, his reason. His infinitely increasing theoretical and practical "mastery and possession of nature" [6] would free him from its bonds and would go hand in hand with his growing ability to shape his own life, to derive its rule from reason alone. Such mastery of self and world was not proclaimed as something that had already been accomplished, of course, but was announced as a distant goal. Yet, through the Renaissance, rationalism, and the Enlightenment, nothing seemed to stand between man and its realization but time.

How great the contrast between that time and ours! The belief in the possibility of philosophy as the ultimate unification and ground of all special sciences has been shaken by repeated failure. The efforts of the past and present offer "philosophies, never philosophy." [7] And as for the otherwise rigorous and successful but isolated and fragmented disciplines that remain, they are neither willing nor able to address themselves to those very concerns which, for the Renaissance, ultimately justified their existence. With the failure of philosophy, the sciences as a body are "decapitated," as Husserl says; [8] or, to adopt an analogy of Descartes', they are branches that flourish but have no trunk and no roots. And the very civilization that began by placing its trust in science in Descartes' sense, modern Europe, is similarly rootless.

Husserl's introductory picture of the crisis of European sciences is expressed with a pathos that readers familiar with his

4. *Ibid.*
5. *Ibid.*, p. 5.
6. Cf. Descartes, *Discourse on Method*, in *The Philosophical Works of Descartes*, trans. Elizabeth S. Haldane and G. R. T. Ross (Cambridge: At the University Press, 1967), pt. VI.
7. *Crisis*, p. 17.
8. *Ibid.*, p. 7.

earlier works doubtless find surprising. What is the way out? Many, Husserl notes, have already drawn the conclusion that the scientific or philosophical ideal was mistaken from the beginning, that the error lay in looking to knowledge for salvation. The failure of our sciences, which are the legacy of rationalism, proves that reason is an idol that must be renounced as the source of meaning for life. Husserl finds a contradiction in such "irrationalism." "Does it not have to convince us, if we are to listen to it, with rational considerations and reasons?" [9] Such an appeal to noncontradiction may not, in turn, convince the irrationalist, but in any case there is another alternative. Perhaps the modern concept of reason, and that of science in both the broad and the narrow senses, was falsely cast; perhaps the present irrelevance of science for life derives not from reason itself or the ideal of knowledge, but from a misguided conception of what rational knowledge should be like and how it is to be achieved.

Rather than simply defending once again—or else skeptically rejecting—this rationalistic ideal, one should renew the search for a genuine and attainable philosophical science. Husserl admits that, after the repeated failure of philosophy, considerable faith is required if the ancient idea of rational knowledge and its relation to life is still to serve as a goal. The choice, however, is between the pursuit of a goal that has eluded man for milleniums and the surrender to the absurdity of irrationalism.

Once the choice is suggested, and the alternative of irrationalism rejected, Husserl's reflections imply an obvious question: what *is* the proper conception of science or philosophy, of rational knowledge, and how can it be realized? Only a science clearly aware of its proper task and secure in its method can do justice to the demand that knowledge be not only relevant, but also of decisive significance for life.

The New Departure of the *Crisis*

How do we go about answering this question? Husserl's approach now takes an interesting turn. Announcing "The project of the investigations of this work," he says:

What is clearly necessary (what else could be of help here?) is that we *reflect back,* in a thorough *historical* and *critical* fashion,

9. *Ibid.,* p. 16.

in order to provide, *before all decisions,* for a radical self-understanding: we must inquire back into what was originally and always sought in philosophy, what was continually sought by all the philosophers and philosophies that have communicated with one another historically.[10]

He thus prepares the way for the ensuing Part II, some eighty pages long, on "Clarification of the Origin of the Modern Opposition between Physicalistic Objectivism and Transcendental Subjectivism," [11] in which he discusses the rise of modern mathematical science beginning with Galileo and its influence on philosophy from Descartes to Kant. The two subdivisions of the larger Part III, dealing respectively with the life-world and psychology, also begin with historical discussions.

To most readers, such a train of thought is probably understandable and legitimate, almost expected at this juncture. Husserl has begun by joining in a certain critique of the times: we find ourselves in crisis, he says, and we need a way out. Historical considerations suggest themselves immediately. They can show us how we got into the crisis in the first place and can sharpen our awareness of its nature. The historical approach is, however, unusual for Husserl. The question which arises from Husserl's exposition of the crisis of science is, as we have seen: what is the proper conception of science and how can it be realized? Three times before in his career, in writings designed for publication as introductions to phenomenology, Husserl had begun by stressing the need to discern the genuine idea of rational knowledge or science. "Philosophy as Rigorous Science" is the title and theme of a lengthy essay of 1910, while in *Formal and Transcendental Logic* (1929), Husserl places reflections on the true nature of science in general, and on that of philosophical science in particular, near the beginning of his book. The same is true of the *Cartesian Meditations,* first published in French in 1931. What is more, the "crisis" theme is not lacking in these works. In the 1910 article, philosophy, or science, is seen as having failed at its task, and the question seems open as to "whether philosophy is to continue envisioning the goal of being a rigorous science, whether it can or must want to be so." [12] Husserl sees the ideal of philosophy threatened by two dominant currents of the time, naturalism and

10. *Ibid.,* pp. 17–18.
11. *Ibid.,* p. 20.
12. *PRS,* p. 75.

historicism, which constitute respectively an adulteration and a weakening of the will to rigorous science,[13] and he subjects each to a thorough critique. In *Formal and Transcendental Logic* and the *Cartesian Meditations* Husserl speaks of the belief in autonomous philosophy and science which the modern age has placed in a position corresponding to that previously held by religious faith. "But meanwhile this belief too has begun to languish"; we find ourselves confronted with a "splintering" of philosophy, a growing accumulation of philosophical literature with no hope for unity. This is the "unhappy present" which Husserl compares with the philosophical confusion lamented by Descartes in the first pages of the *Discourse*.[14]

In none of these works, however, does Husserl feel the need to embark on historical investigations. There are historical references, to be sure: "From its earliest beginnings"—so begins the 1910 essay—"philosophy has claimed to be rigorous science"; and Husserl mentions several historical figures in whose work this claim can be seen. In the *Cartesian Meditations*, of course, Descartes is the subject of some discussion at the beginning, and *Formal and Transcendental Logic* begins with a brief discussion of the whole tradition. But there is nothing here to compare with the lengthy "historical and critical" reflections of the *Crisis*, which deal in some detail with Galileo and Descartes, Hume and Kant, which mention almost every other major philosopher of the modern period, and which treat this period as a development of occurrences rather than dealing with philosophers as isolated figures. The earlier works we have discussed, after announcing the "crisis" and pointing to the need for a clarification of the genuine concept of science, seem to proceed under the assumption that we need only reflect on what science truly is, or should be (the essence of science), in order to see the errors of its enemies and false prophets and start it on the road to realization. Not that this is an easy task, to be sure, but in any case it seems not to require the aid of history. The other works published during Husserl's lifetime, from the *Philosophie der Arithmetik* (1895) to the *Encyclopedia Britannica* article on "phenomenology" (1928),[15] are similarly lacking in such involved historical expositions.

What is the significance of Husserl's novel approach? A

13. *Ibid.*, p. 77.
14. CM, pp. 4–5, Cf. *FTL*, p. 5.
15. 14th ed., Vol. XVII. Cf. the original German version in Husserliana IX, pp. 237–301.

hurried and inattentive reading of the *Crisis* might yield the following view: true, such an extended preoccupation with the history of philosophy may be unusual for Husserl, but he is, after all, leading up to the same transcendental phenomenology he had been propagating since 1913. Nothing is more natural than for a philosopher to discuss the views of prominent historical predecessors, either to seek their support or to criticize them before presenting the "true" solution to the problems they were unable to solve. Husserl's earlier works contain many criticisms of past philosophers, and the only thing that distinguishes the *Crisis* is that its historical treatment is more comprehensive. Perhaps the method of "historical introduction" was simply chosen as a new and more impressive way of presenting phenomenology to the public.

Some factors suggest that Husserl might indeed have been concerned about the public reception of his work. Seldom has a philosopher been more oblivious to public (or academic) tastes in his single-minded dedication to following his own lights; but Husserl was human enough to be affected by the external "success" of his work. He was increasingly embittered by the tendency of his former students to go their own philosophical ways; he felt that he had been misunderstood by his critics; now his work was being eclipsed by the increasingly popular *"Existenzphilosophie."* While Husserl was convinced of the errors of his opponents, it must have occurred to him that the difficulty and abstractness of his earlier works might have been at fault. The academic community was encouraged to turn its back on him, of course, by the fact that as a Jew Husserl was now officially an undesirable in his own country. Thus it was necessary for him to publish abroad, perhaps for an unprepared public.

Furthermore, while the "crisis" theme is not new to his work, as we have seen, Husserl here for the first time chooses to employ it in the very title of his essay. This in itself might reflect a desire to give a striking and impressive appearance to his book. Also, the crisis seems to have worsened, for Husserl, and it is also more deeply and broadly conceived. Again contemporary philosophy is accused of failing to fulfill its ideal function; but part of its function is to secure meaning for life and to serve as a guide for the community as a whole. In this sense philosophers are, or should be, says Husserl, "functionaries of mankind," [16] and the

16. *Crisis*, p. 17.

failure of philosophy or science is at the same time a crisis of culture. Such was one philosopher's approach to a time of great po-
litical and social turmoil, a time in which everyone agreed that
Europe had reached some kind of turning point. For Husserl, in
one sense, the failure was more that of the community than of
philosophy. He felt that he had at least made a few steps toward
establishing philosophy in the role for which it was destined; but
"philosophy is not a private matter," he says,[17] perhaps somewhat
regretfully. Taking seriously the role of a functionary of mankind, with the reluctance of one returning to Plato's cave, Husserl
may be determined to do all he can to help make himself understood.

A new mode of presentation is called for, then, and the
heightened sense of living in a time of crisis brings with it the
desire to find out how the crisis developed. A historical introduction can draw the reader along for a time on a plane with which
he is familiar, before plunging him into the rigors of the phenomenological reduction. Besides, *Existenzphilosophie* had brought
with it a revival of the historically oriented philosophy of the nineteenth century. Husserl's novel approach could be seen as a con-
cession to the temper of the times.[18]

If such were truly the character of the historical framework
of the *Crisis* and Husserl's primary reason for adopting it, one
might remark on its novelty but not be inclined to ascribe to it
any great significance for the *content* of phenomenology. According to this view, Husserl has simply changed the frame, not the
picture. Those familiar with the *Nachlass* can even challenge the
idea that such a historical introduction is new to Husserl. He may
not have used it in his books, but in at least one important lecture
course, given in 1923–24 under the title *Erste Philosophie*,
Husserl devoted twenty-seven lectures, before the "systematic
part" of the course began, to a "historical introduction" or "history
of ideas," as he calls it.[19] Not only do the historical sections of
the *Crisis* repeat many of the themes of the *Erste Philosophie;*
they are considerably shorter and less comprehensive than the

17. Husserliana VI, p. 439 (a passage not included in the *Crisis*).
18. Cf. Suzanne Bachelard, *A Study of Husserl's Formal and
Transcendental Logic,* trans. Lester E. Embree (Evanston, Ill.:
Northwestern University Press, 1968), p. 142 n.
19. Husserliana VIII, p. 3. The designations "historical introduction" and "Systematic part" stem from Landgrebe but were approved by Husserl.

lectures of a decade before, which are not confined to the modern period but deal with Greek philosophy as well,

THE ROLE OF HISTORICAL REFLECTION

THE HISTORICAL INVESTIGATIONS of the *Crisis,* however, exhibit features which distinguish them sharply from anything Husserl has done before. These features make it impossible to dismiss them as external embellishment chosen for effect or timely relevance, and they prove, as we shall see, to be of decisive significance for phenomenology itself.

A first appreciation of this can be achieved by examining the terms in which Husserl introduces his "history of ideas" of 1923 and comparing it with what he says about the "historical and critical reflections" of the *Crisis* in 1936. In the *Erste Philosophie* Husserl begins with general remarks about his choice of a title, drawing on the literal sense of Aristotle's term to sketch the idea of a science that is first "in itself," a discipline that constitutes the "beginning" of science in the most fundamental sense. Such a genuine beginning is not to be found, unfortunately, among the heritage of Western philosophy. "On the other hand," says Husserl, "I am convinced that with the breakthrough of the new transcendental phenomenology a first breakthrough of a true and genuine First Philosophy has occurred; but only, so to speak, in a first and still imperfect approximation." His purpose in the lectures is "to raise this approximation to the highest possible level" by developing phenomenology as the fulfillment of the idea of First Philosophy.[20]

"I preface this first with an introduction," Husserl says (*Ich schicke zunächst eine Einleitung voraus*), "which is meant to procure for us the indispensable inner preconditions for our undertaking." [21] The success of phenomenology as First Philosophy would mean "nothing less than a reform of philosophy as a whole" and, in consequence of this, of all sciences as well. But the will to such a reform must proceed from the awareness of the need for reform: "The spiritual situation in general fills the soul with such deep dissatisfaction that it is simply impossible to continue living under its forms and norms." [22] Husserl wishes to com-

20. Husserliana VII, p. 6.
21. *Ibid.,* p. 7.
22. *Ibid.*

municate his own dissatisfaction and then establish in his lis-
teners the "inner preconditions"—i.e., the will to reform—by
exhibiting the failure of philosophy and the sources of that failure
(*die inneren Motivationsquellen solcher Lage*). Such reflections,
Husserl says, must take a historical form.

In short, Husserl has begun with another variation on the
"crisis" theme! But in this case the crisis is not fully recognized
as such, at least not by all. Before proceeding to its resolution, we
must have full awareness of the nature of the crisis by reflecting
historically on how it arose. A historical *Rückblick*, Husserl con-
cludes, "*soll uns also zur seelischen Vorbereitung dienen*"—i.e.,
it is designed to prepare us psychologically or to put us in the
right frame of mind. It is for this that the historical introduction
is "indispensable"—and we can conclude that if the proper frame
of mind were already present, one could proceed straightway to
phenomenology.

In the *Crisis*, however, Husserl's very point of departure is
the widespread presence in the public mind of the sort of "deep
dissatisfaction" he sought to awaken in his students in 1923. But
historical reflections are now called for with even more urgency
than before and for much more compelling reasons. "What else
could be of help here," Husserl asks rhetorically in the passage
quoted above, "in order to provide . . . for a radical self-
understanding?" We gain a conception of the "task which is
truly our own" as philosophers, he says later, "only through a
critical understanding of the total unity of history—*our* history." [23] The critical-historical reflections in which Husserl is engaged are described as "the philosopher's genuine self-reflection
on what he is *truly seeking*" (*auf das, worauf er eigentlich
hinaus will*).[24] Historical reflections are thus linked to the
philosopher's endeavor in a more positive and intimate way than
before. Whereas in the *Erste Philosophie* they are needed to
awaken dissatisfaction with the failure of philosophy and hence
the will to reform it, here they are required in order to make the
philosopher aware of exactly what he has to do: of his genuine
task, of what he is truly seeking as a philosopher. Such awareness is not only positive in character but is actually presupposed
by the negative awareness of past failure: one must know the
task of philosophy in order to see that it has failed in the past.

23. *Crisis,* p. 71.
24. *Ibid.*

The later conception also seems to involve a kind of indispensability the earlier one does not have: we *must* be aware of the task of philosophy in order to philosophize properly; acquaintance with the mistakes of past attempts may help us in avoiding them, but if we philosophize properly we should avoid them in any case. Here historical reflections are not merely helpful, it seems, but necessary. What is more, only such reflections, says Husserl, can procure *radikales Selbtverständnis*, a radical understanding of ourselves—one of the primary aims, it should be noted, previously claimed for phenomenology itself.

But why do these aims require precisely *historical* investigations? Husserl first calls for them because the exposition of the contrast between the present feeling of crisis and the optimism of the Renaissance has "reminded us that we as philosophers are heirs of the past in respect to the goals which the word 'philosophy' indicates, in terms of concepts, problems, and methods." [25] And later: historical reflections are needed to reveal the "task which is truly our own" because "we . . . not only have a spiritual heritage, but have become what we are thoroughly and exclusively in a historical-spiritual manner." [26] "A historical . . . reflection of the sort under discussion is thus actually the deepest kind of self-reflection aimed at a self-understanding in terms of what we are truly seeking as the historical beings [*historisches Wesen*] we are." [27]

Such a justification for historical procedure clearly goes far beyond what Husserl has said earlier, and ascribes to the expositions of the *Crisis* a significance those of the *Erste Philosophie* do not have. If such a procedure is necessary because we are not only "historical beings" but also are what we are "thoroughly and exclusively" in a historical manner, then historical reflection would belong to any attempt by such historical beings to embark upon the philosophical task. Who are "we" who are so "thoroughly" historical? Offering no limitations, historical or classificational, to his application of this term, Husserl would seem to be departing from what he regards as something like an essential human trait. Something in the nature of those who do philosophy makes it necessary that they do it this way— or such is the impression given by Husserl's remarks. Such a conception differs in substance, as can be seen, from one which

25. *Ibid.*, p. 17.
26. *Ibid.*, p. 71.
27. *Ibid.*, p. 72.

proposes a historical *Rückblick,* aimed at those who may not be aware of the failures of philosophy, in order to put them in the "frame of mind" to want to reform it.

We are not arguing, of course, that the notion of a "frame of mind" as such is of no importance for phenomenology. Nothing is more intimately involved in the actual *business* of phenomenology, as we saw in the previous chapter, than the establishment of the appropriate *Geisteshaltung* or *Einstellung.* But the frame of mind sought by the historical investigations of the *Erste Philosophie* seems to be outside of and prior to the actual *phenomenological* change of attitude—something which finally begins only in the "systematic part" of the lectures, as might be expected from earlier writings, with the "theory of phenomenological reduction." Historical reflection simply does not belong to the "systematic" pursuit of phenomenology itself. We should note, too, that in the *Erste Philosophie* the historical procedure is dictated by the need for *"seelische Vorbereitung"*—a term we have translated, not quite literally but accurately enough, as "psychological preparation." This is not a term that Husserl would use for any thing that belonged essentially to the establishment of the phenomenological attitude. The "deep dissatisfaction" and the "will to reform" Husserl seeks to engender through his historical introduction in 1923 might be described as public or private moods which come and go, and at times it might be necessary to awaken them. The historical reflections of the *Crisis* are justified in other terms. If their point is still that of establishing a frame of mind, this frame of mind is now differently conceived, and the need to establish it is now seen by Husserl as a permanent or essential and not merely a possible or occasional need. Historical reflection would, on this interpretation, belong essentially, and not incidentally, to the business of putting philosophy on the right road.

We do not wish to minimize the important similarities between the historical aspects of the *Crisis* and the historical introduction to the *Erste Philosophie.* Later we shall attempt to show that Husserl's preoccupation with history in his last work can be traced to developments in earlier writings, not the least important of which are the lectures of 1923–24. Not only do the actual discussions of philosophers in the two texts exhibit common features; there are also isolated general remarks on historical procedure in the *Erste Philosophie* which remind one of the *Crisis:* "The point of these consideration is nothing less than to lay bare the unity of motivation, persisting throughout millenia, which has lived in all philosophy as the driving force of its development, insofar as it sought to become the true philosophy . . . ," he says at one point in the lectures.[28] And a few pages later: ". . . we are in the process of showing, from many different sides in connection with the historical-critical material, that the sense of philosophy itself, and of the method required by that sense, drives toward an intuitionism. . . ." [29] These remarks occur rather late in the historical introduction, and finally, at the beginning of the "systematic part," looking back upon the historical introduction, Husserl credits it with having shown not only the need for philosophical reform but also the direction in which such a reform lies—that of "a science of transcendental subjectivity." [30] He even goes so far as to say that an anticipating conception, a *Vorbegriff*, of such a science "in the most general terms," has emerged.[31] It must be remembered that the *Erste Philosophie*, like the *Crisis*, was not a finished book but a "manuscript in progress," and Husserl's interpretation of his own procedure seems to have changed gradually throughout the lectures, with an increasing appreciation of what the historical introduction could accomplish. But the passages we have just quoted are almost fleetingly introduced into the text, and their points are not further pursued. In any case, while they attribute a perhaps more elevated purpose to the historical investigations than the introductory passages quoted earlier, even they do not convey the conviction, so strong in the *Crisis*, of a *necessary* connection between historical reflection and the foundation of philosophy.

What Husserl says about historical procedure in the *Crisis* rules out the possibility, then, that such procedure was chosen in order to meet the needs of a particular public, to prepare it "psychologically" for what he had to say. Of course, the question of interpretation is slightly complicated. If Husserl was in fact bent on a popular effect, he might have exaggerated rhetorically the importance of his historical expositions. There is no doubt that the passages we have quoted imply the *necessity* of a historical introduction to philosophy, but should they be taken completely seriously? Husserl insisted that they should. In a lengthy

28. Husserliana VII, pp. 141–42.
29. *Ibid.*, p. 147.
30. Husserliana VIII, p. 4.
31. *Ibid.*

preface designed for the published version of Part III, in which
Husserl looks back upon the previous section that had already
appeared, he insists again on the importance of the investigations there and explicitly denies that the historical method of
introduction was "chosen incidently for the sake of an impressive
presentation." [32]

But even more indicative of the importance ascribed by Husserl to the historical approach is his recurring preoccupation
with the method, aims, and presuppositions of his own procedure. In the preface just mentioned, the passage quoted introduces a four-page retrospective interpretation of the foregoing
Part II of the *Crisis*, obviously designed to avert misconceptions
of its historical treatment. Husserl apparently felt that such an
exposition was necessary, in spite of the fact that he had already
interrupted the historical sequence of Part II itself at two points
for separately titled sections dealing exclusively with method,
once at the end of his long section on Galileo (§ 9l: "Characterization of the method of our exposition")[33] and once later (§ 15:
"Reflection on the method of our historical manner of investigation").[34] Similar attempts to characterize his historical procedure
turn up in manuscripts apparently considered for inclusion in
the *Crisis* but not found in the last remaining version of the text.
One must conclude that Husserl was unhappy with the reflections on method that had appeared in Part II, either because
he thought they were poorly expressed or because he was himself
not entirely clear on the matter. The latter interpretation, it must
be said, is borne out by the texts themselves. The usual point of
departure is a negative one: "The type of investigation that we
must carry out, and which has already determined the style of
our preparatory suggestions," says Husserl in the middle of Part
II, "is not that of a historical investigation in the usual sense." [35]
Or, as it is worded in the text that has acquired the title "The
Origin of Geometry" and which was obviously meant for inclusion in the *Crisis* in connection with Galileo: " . . . our investigations are historical in an unusual sense, namely, in virtue
of a thematic direction which opens up depth-problems quite unknown to ordinary history, problems which, [however], in their

32. Husserliana VI, p. 441.
33. *Crisis*, p. 57.
34. *Ibid.*, p. 70.
35. *Ibid.*

own way, are undoubtedly historical problems." [36] While Husserl is thus clear in his claim that his historical approach differs fundamentally from history in any ordinary sense, he is less clear in explaining exactly what constitutes the difference and wherein, precisely, his new approach to history consists. Different treatments of the subject stress different aspects of the problem, and it is difficult to find in them a clear statement of what Husserl is about. One important and recurring theme is that the historical introduction to philosophy leads to—or implies, or even presupposes—a theory of history as such. As it is expressed in "The Origin of Geometry": "Our considerations will necessarily lead to the deepest problems of meaning, problems of science and of the history of science in general, and indeed in the end to problems of a universal history in general." [37] We shall have occasion later to examine the many strands that are often confusingly interwoven in these reflections on the historical method of the *Crisis,* and to defend our suggestion that Husserl had not achieved clarity on this matter even for himself. For now it suffices to have pointed out that Husserl was convinced enough of the importance of his historical procedure to be deeply concerned with clarifying its method.

There is nothing to compare with this, by contrast, in the *Erste Philosophie.* The term "history of ideas," [38] used by Husserl to describe the historical introduction to the lectures, suggests that he sees his exposition as falling within a well-established and easily identifiable realm of discourse that needs no further clarification. To be sure, the account of philosophy's development has been accompanied by a "constant radical critique," [39] through which the need for a science of subjectivity has emerged. But the notion of a "critical history" seems to present no methodological problems for Husserl. Or, if it does, these problems are not methodological problems involved directly in the formulation of first philosophy itself, and are not pressing enough to keep him from proceeding to its systematic development. We pointed out earlier, of course, that Husserl fleetingly justifies his historical introduction in terms similar to those of the *Crisis*—"to lay bare the unity of motivation . . . which has lived in all philosophy," to show the necessity of a science of sub-

36. *Ibid.,* p. 354.
37. *Ibid.,* p. 353.
38. Husserliana VIII, p. 3.
39. *Ibid.,* p. 4.

jectivity, etc. These aims, along with others, turn up in Husserl's attempts to clarify the historical procedure in his later work. But in the *Crisis*, as we have seen, Husserl becomes aware that these aims are incompatible with history in any ordinary sense and are so important that the matter requires immediate and serious methodological clarification.

What can we conclude from the great importance Husserl obviously attributes to his historical procedure? The *seelische Vorbereitung* sought in the *Erste Philosophie* was the awakening of the will to reform through dissatisfaction with the past and present situation in philosophy. We have tried to show by reference to Husserl's remarks that the historical introduction of the *Crisis* is considered to be more intimately and essentially bound up with the construction of philosophy itself than such a conception would justify. We noted, among other things, Husserl's remark that historical reflection provides for the necessary *radikales Selbstverständnis*—radical self-understanding—and pointed out in passing that this is one of the achievements otherwise claimed for phenomenology itself. Has historical reflection somehow merged with phenomenological reflection?

Here we might be accused of an ambiguity in translation. The word almost always used by Husserl to describe his historical exposition is *Besinnung*—or some combination like *Rückbesinnung* or *Selbstbesinnung*—a word properly translated by "reflection," provided this is understood in a broad and nontechnical sense. It signifies a contemplative and deliberate consideration of something, "thinking it over" carefully and unhurriedly, taking everything into account. True, its object in the main is oneself, or some particular plan or mode of one's action; and, indeed, Husserl's most common variant of the term is *Selbstbesinnung*. But should it be confused with *Reflexion*, in Husserl's technical sense, which refers to consciousness directed at itself, and which in its transcendental form is the cornerstone of phenomenological method?

Many of the late manuscripts not included in the *Crisis* text deal with the notion of *Besinnung* and of historical *Besinnung* in particular. At one point Husserl writes: "The historical reflection [*Besinnung*] we have in mind here concerns our existence as philosophers and, correlatively, the existence of philosophy, which, for its part, *is* through our philosophical existence." [40]

40. *Crisis,* p. 392.

Here the word *Existenz* is used three times, in a sense loosely borrowed from Jaspers and Heidegger, a usage that also often occurs in the *Crisis* (at another point he speak of *"existenziale Selbstbesinnung"* [41]). In a note Husserl explains that "the reflection in question is a particular case of that self-reflection in which man as a person seeks to reflect [*sich besinnen*] upon the ultimate sense of his existence [*Dasein*]. We must distinguish between a broader and a narrower concept of self-reflection [*Selbstbesinnung*]: pure ego-reflection [*Ichreflexion*] and reflection [*Reflexion*] upon the whole life of the ego as ego; and reflection [*Besinnung*] in the pregnant sense of inquiring back [*Rückfrage*] into the sense or teleological essence of the ego." [42]

These passages indicate both a close relation and a distinction in Husserl's mind between *Besinnung* and *Reflexion*. They make possible the view that the historical aspects of the *Crisis* belong in the category of "existential" reflections carried out by "the human being as a person" (*der Mensch als Person*), who in this case happens to be a philosopher. Such reflections are, then, after all, "psychological" in character, designed to put him in the right frame of mind to begin *reine Ichreflexion*, which, as is known, ultimately *deprives* him of his status as *Mensch* or *Person* and constitutes the actual procedure of philosophy. Such an interpretation would again attribute to the *Crisis* a thought structure similar to that of the *Erste Philosophie*.

The passages leave many questions open, however. While Husserl suggests that *Selbstbesinnung* is a possible activity proper to persons as such, and not just to philosophers, he does not deny that philosophical *Reflexion* might be essentially linked with a *Besinnung* of the personal and historical sort. We shall have occasion later to explore the relationship between these senses of *Besinnung* and *Reflexion* and to discover considerable convergence between them. For present purposes, a more immediately accessible argument against the view expressed in the foregoing paragraph is presented by a glance at the over-all structure of the *Crisis*, again comparing it with that of the *Erste Philosophie*. The 1923–24 lectures were neatly divided, as we have seen, into the "historical introduction" and the "systematic part." In the *Crisis* this distinction fades almost

41. Husserliana VI, p. 486 (not in translation).
42. *Crisis*, p. 392 n.

to the point of disappearing. Part II is perhaps more purely historical than what follows, both in its title ("Clarification of The Origin of The Modern Opposition between Physicalistic Objectivism and Transcendental Subjectivism") and in its content. But well into Part III A, with its more "systematic-" sounding title ("The Way into Phenomenological Transcendental Philosophy by Inquiring back from the Pre-given Life-World"), Husserl is still discussing Kant ("philosophizing with Kant," as he puts it[43]); and the concept of the life-world that is crucial in this *Auseinandersetzung* actually emerges gradually in Part II out of the discussion of Galileo. If Husserl later finally "leave[s] the reference to Kant behind" [44] in order to devote his expositions directly to the concept of the life-world, it is only to return at the beginning of Part III B ("The Way into Phenomenological Transcendental Philosophy from Psychology") to a long exposition of the historical development since Kant, with special reference to psychology. The ensuing attempt to work out a phenomenological psychology, and to show its relation to transcendental phenomenology, evolves concurrently with a critique of modern psychology with its Cartesian and Lockean background.

In short, the distinction between systematic and historical investigations, if it is still valid for Husserl at all, hardly figures in the make-up of the *Crisis*. The first part of the *Erste Philosophie*, of course, is both historical and critical and is thus more than a mere narrative; but its subject matter is clearly the historical figures, while the second part devotes itself exclusively to the *Sache selbst*. In the *Crisis*, narrative, criticism, and "pure" phenomenological theory and analysis are found side by side at almost every stage in the work. To be sure, an interweaving of "straightforward philosophy" with references to and criticism of past and present philosophers does not in itself obliterate the distinction between the "historical" and the "systematic"; but if we consider our earlier conclusions about the essential or necessary character of historical investigation for the construction of philosophy, this distinction becomes blurred in any case. If the historical is truly a necessary part of the process of "doing" philosophy, then it is just as systematic as the

43. *Ibid.*, p. 111.
44. *Ibid.*, p. 120.

nonhistorical. The make-up of the *Crisis,* then, reinforces our earlier conclusions, drawn from Husserl's own remarks on his procedure, about the importance of the historical reflections, and sharpens the contrast between the late work and the *Erste Philosophie* of 1923–24. If we consider, in addition, Husserl's brief preface to the *Crisis,* which accompanied the appearance of its first two sections in *Philosophia* in 1936, we find more reinforcement:

> "The work that I am beginning with the present essay, and shall complete in a series of further articles in *Philosophia,* makes the attempt, by way of a teleological-historical reflection upon the origins of our critical scientific and philosophical situation, to establish the unavoidable necessity of a transcendental phenomenological reorientation of philosophy. Accordingly, it becomes, in its own right, an introduction to transcendental phenomenology." [45]

Here the work as a whole, and not just part of it, is described as "teleological-historical reflection," and this work is further characterized as being "in its own right" (*eigenständig*) an introduction to transcendental phenomenology, not a preface to "systematic" or nonhistorical work for which it merely prepares the way.

HISTORICAL REFLECTION AND PHILOSOPHICAL METHOD

THE FOREGOING CONSIDERATIONS make it impossible to dismiss the historical framework of the *Crisis* as a mere résumé and critique of past attempts to solve philosophical problems before presenting their true solution, the true philosophy itself. Such a résumé, familiar enough since the first book of Aristotle's *Metaphysics,* is not a *material* part of philosophy; it could just as well be left out, though it might be chosen for the sake of an impressive presentation. Husserl's own remarks express the conviction, as we have seen, that he is not engaged in anything as familiar as a mere "history of ideas," and his preoccupation with his own procedure reflects his estimation of its importance for his project as a whole. The almost constant interweaving of the historical and the nonhistorical in the *Crisis* reinforces the implication drawn from Husserl's remarks that historical reflec-

45. *Ibid.,* p. 3 n.

tion belongs essentially to the foundation of the "true philosophy," that the very distinction between the "historical" and the
"systematic" breaks down.

The idea that the way to philosophical truth passes through
the history of philosophy is now new in itself, but for Husserl
it is not only new but almost startling in contrast to his earlier
views. "Zu den Sachen selbst!" was the motto of the early
phenomenological school gathered about Husserl. What it meant
primarily was best expressed by Husserl in "Philosophy as
Rigorous Science": "The impulse of research must proceed not
from philosophies but from things [*von den Sachen*] and from
the problems connected with them." [46] To deal with the history
of philosophy is to deal not with the *Sachen* but only with what
others have *said* about the *Sachen.* Husserl objected not to the
history of philosophy as a discipline, of course, but only to the
tendency to confuse it with philosophy itself, either in the manner of *Weltanschauungsphilosophie* or as an attempt to conjure
a doctrine of one's own by ingeniously mixing and stirring the
doctrines of others. In the *Ideas,* to ward off any such temptation
from the start, Husserl laid down what he called the "philosophical epochē": "Expressly formulated [it] consists in this,
that we completely abstain from judgment respecting the doctrinal content of all preexisting philosophy, and conduct all our
expositions within the framework of this abstention." [47]

Husserl immediately qualifies this dictum by permitting
references to "philosophy as a historical fact," especially for
purposes of criticizing one or another of its representatives, and
then launches into an attack on naturalism and its psychologiza-
tion of ideas. Criticism of other philosophical views is not unusual in Husserl's writing, and in any case it is clear that in the
"philosophical epochē" he is warning against assuming or taking
over some philosophical view, or "even the concept of philosophy" [48] itself, simply because it was espoused by some prominent
thinker or even an impressive number of such thinkers.

Husserl's treatment of philosophical history in the *Crisis* is
by no means merely an attempt to lean for support on the great
figures of the past, and even less an example of scissors-and
paste syncretism. But at the same time it is much more than a

46. *PRS,* p. 146.
47. Husserliana III, pp. 40–41 (*Ideas,* pp. 80–81).
48. *Ibid.,* p. 41 (*Ideas,* p. 80).

mere critique of this or that philosophical view, something thrown in, so to speak, alongside the actual business of philosophy, something perhaps helpful but ultimately dispensable. We still have to examine more closely what Husserl is about, or thinks he is about, in reflections he calls not only "historical" and "critical" but also "teleological." That such reflections should constitute, "in their own right" as Husserl says, an introduction to phenomenology; that the way into "phenomenological transcendental philosophy" should involve a passage through the history of philosophy—this is what is important and new about the *Crisis*. It is hardly the case that Husserl had come round to the belief that philosophy could proceed without direct recourse to the *Sache selbst,* basing itself entirely, as it were, on hearsay. The historical reflections of the *Crisis* are not only at the same time critical but are also interwoven with investigations of a nonhistorical character. Nevertheless, the contrast between Husserl's earlier and later views on the relation between philosophy and its own history presents a puzzle that needs to be further explored.

Of course, our own presentation of the earlier or "classic" Husserlian phenomenology neglected the inevitable transformations, of varying degrees of magnitude and importance, which occurred prior to the *Crisis*. Various accounts have been given of "phases" or "turning points" in Husserl's development,[49] and one of these accounts may be of help in explaining the philosopher's use of historical reflections. Rudolf Boehm[50] has shown the emergence, in manuscripts from the period of the *Erste Philosophie,* of a deepening preoccupation with the problem of the "way into" phenomenology and of the novel conception that the Cartesian "way" of the *Ideas* was not the only possible one. Husserl's publications of the ensuing years then make use of some *alternative* "ways": while the *Cartesian Meditations* (1929) repeat the approach of the *Ideas,* the same period produces an introduction to phenomenology based on psychology (the *Ency-*

49. Cf. Fink's prefatory remark to his edition of Husserl's "Entwurf einer 'Vorrede' zu den 'Logischen Untersuchungen' (1913)," *Tijdschrift voor Philosophie,* I (1939), 106–33; further, Walter Biemel, "Die entscheidenden Phasen der Entfaltung von Husserls Philosophie," *Zeitschrift für philosophische Forschung,* XIII (1959), 187–213; Paul Ricoeur, *Husserl: An Analysis of His Phenomenology* (Evanston, Ill.: Northwestern University Press, 1967), pp. 3–12, 29.

50. Husserliana VIII, editor's introduction, *passim.*

clopedia Britannica article) and one based on logic (*Formal and Transcendental Logic*). And in the *Crisis,* finally, each of the two subdivisions of Part III corresponds to a different "way into phenomenological transcendental philosophy," one "from the pre-given life-world" and the other "from psychology." In reflecting on and taking up the different ways into phenomenology, Husserl is not concerned merely with the didactics of teaching his method but is departing from certain more or less familiar spheres of inquiry which, if pursued far enough, he thinks, lead inevitably to the "transcendental turn."

Husserl never talked about the history of philosophy as a possible "way into" phenomenology. But it is not hard to imagine that, especially after his growing appreciation in the *Erste Philosophie* of how much could be accomplished by a critical history of philosophy, Husserl might finally have adopted such an idea. There is no doubt that of the many facets of Husserl's treatment of history, one certainly reflects a role comparable to the way into phenomenology from psychology, from the life-world, from logic: if one pursues a particular line of inquiry, in this case into the history of philosophy, in a way which does complete justice to the subject matter, one is led in the end to see the necessity of the "transcendental-phenomenological reorientation." Is this the way to approach the anomaly of Husserl's preoccupation with history?

This interpretation proves to be untenable, as can be seen in the structure of the *Crisis* itself. Husserl is quite conscious here of the notion of alternative ways into phenomenology (he speaks at one point of the advantages and disadvantages of different ways),[51] and the two sections of Part III are in their very titles presented as parallels or alternative ways (from the life-world and from psychology). But these two sections are not presented alongside the predominately historical Part II, as if it were yet another parallel, but are introduced by it and at the same time find themselves embedded, so to speak, within the historical framework of the *Crisis* as a whole. Moreover, Husserl never speaks of his historical reflections as if they constituted an alternative way into phenomenology.

What he does say about these reflections, in fact, makes it impossible to consider them merely an *alternative,* as we have seen. If our exposition and interpretation of Husserl's remarks

51. *Crisis,* pp. 154 ff.

is correct, historical reflection is a necessary and not merely a possible component in the business of "establishing" philosophy. Whereas Husserl had moved in 1923 from the belief in a single necessary procedure to that of alternative procedures, in 1936 he seems to have returned to the idea of a necessary procedure, but now a different one. Or, to put it more accurately: to judge by the *Crisis*, whichever of several nonhistorical alternatives, or whichever combination of them, is chosen, each must be prefaced or accompanied (or both) by historical reflections. These are called for, as we recall, because of the very nature of those who do philosophy. While various domains can be investigated which will lead them, in Husserl's view, to the transcendental turn, in each case they remain "historical beings" and *for this reason* must reflect "historically and critically."

This brings us to the central problem posed by this late development in Husserl's philosophy. The historical character "through and through" of those who do philosophy makes it necessary, says Husserl, that they reflect critically on the history of philosophy *in order* to "do" philosophy properly, i.e., in order to truly begin philosophy for the first time. *Why* is this so? Human beings could *be* historical in some sense without having, for that reason, to reflect historically when it comes to philosophy. What is Husserl's concept of the historicity of the potential philosopher? In his concept lies the only explanation for the new demand, in Husserl's last work, that the foundation of philosophy occupy itself with, or at least pass through, the history of philosophy. Where is such a concept to be found in Husserl's work? Since the historical procedure first appears in the *Crisis*, does the concept of historicity also emerge here for the first time?

It is true that the full-fledged concept of historicity—that is, the concept developed to the point where the demand for historical reflection follows from it—can be found only in the *Crisis* and in manuscripts which date from the same period. Even in the *Crisis* it often appears in veiled form, as an operative rather than an implicitly stated concept. In part it can be extracted from the way Husserl actually goes about his historical reflection —something we have spoken little of up to now—in part it is involved in the philosopher's various remarks about his procedure. It is in the manuscripts and related texts, above all, that the most direct and explicit treatments are found.

It is hardly to be expected, however, that a problem with

which Husserl is so preoccupied could have occurred to him overnight, as it were, or even have entered his thinking from an outside source—such as Heidegger's *Being and Time* (with its chapter on *Geschichtlichkeit*), which Husserl seems to have studied carefully, for the first time, in 1932. We intend to show, in fact, that the concept of historicity has its roots in reflections on various subjects going back as far as 1913, and that its emergence in the *Crisis* is the effect of an accumulation and confluence of trains of thought which ultimately force Husserl's new introduction to phenomenology to take on its peculiar form.[52] In the following chapters we shall attempt to trace these roots to earlier writings and, by constant reference to the *Crisis*, show how they bear fruit later on. Not only will this procedure enable us to understand Husserl's approach to history with a degree of clarity which the *Crisis* itself, because of its inchoate character, does not allow; but it will also reveal, I hope, the manner in which the pursuit of transcendental philosophy gives rise, of its own accord, to the problem of historicity. We shall then have to deal with the question of whether, after this occurs, transcendental philosophy can remain intact.

52. Hans-Georg Gadamer (*Wahrheit und Methode*, 2d ed. [Tübingen: Mohr, 1965]), who has much to say about the relation between the later Husserl and Heidegger's *Being and Time,* also notes explicitly (p. 230) that Husserl's late turn to history was not set off by a confrontation with Heidegger (Gadamer also mentions Dilthey in this context), but was a consequence of elements in his own thought.

3 / Genetic Phenomenology

THERE ARE TWO THEMES in Husserl's phenomenology which can be said to have "resulted" in the late "historical turn" described in the previous chapter. While it is impossible to retrace Husserl's actual train of thought, it is at least possible to show that these themes, when developed and combined, suggest and make understandable the historical framework of the *Crisis*. These themes fall under the following headings: (a) genetic phenomenology; (b) the phenomenology of inter-subjectivity.

As we shall see, neither of these themes of the *Crisis* period is really new. In fact, each can be traced to the very beginnings of Husserl's phenomenological writings. It is the case, however, that as Husserl's career progressed he became increasingly preoccupied with these themes, devoting progressively more thought and exposition to them. We shall try to show that the inevitable result of this development was a qualitative change in the nature of phenomenology.

THE TEMPORAL DIMENSION

PHENOMENOLOGY AS TRANSCENDENTAL PHILOSOPHY was described in Chapter 1 as the search for the "origin" of the givenness of the objective—in the broadest sense, the world—a search which led to the characterization of consciousness as transcendental in relation to the world. The originating function of transcendental consciousness was found in its act- or intentional character; acts were further characterized as synthesis, following certain patterns subject to certain rules which could ultimately only be described, not further justified. Acts as syntheses were found to stand out upon a background of belief or attitude whose underlying stratum was described by Husserl as the natural attitude or *Weltglaube*.

Husserl's point of departure was always: *how* is the world given? In his earliest writings on transcendental phenomenology, especially the *Ideas*, this question was first answered in the following way: the world is given first and foremost in that individual things are given, and these individual things fall into various types. The search for origins in consciousness must follow these types as guidelines. Thus, while phenomenology (as we have seen) is not itself "ontologically committed," it takes its point of departure from a pregiven notion of "what there is," or what kinds of things there are, in order to ask how these things are given; the "material and formal ontological regions [are] indexes pointing to transcendental systems of evidence."[1] Consciousness is described in terms of such systems—i.e., the types of syntheses, the types of relation between intention and fulfillment (evidence), which correspond to these types of objects. The resulting subjective-objective typology is the articulation of the *Selbstverständlichkeiten* through which consciousness transcends itself in "meaning" the world. What truly exists, or what in truth belongs to the world, is determined according to these conscious "procedures" corresponding to the various regions. And the world is given precisely as that which is found to "truly exist" in this sense.

In the *Cartesian Meditations* Husserl characterizes such descriptions, which "concern particular types and . . . arrange them in their systematic order,"[2] as *static* phenomenology, and states that it must be supplemented by *genetic* analysis. The need for a transition of this sort can be seen by examining the complexity that must be accorded the act or synthesis in order to do justice to its originating function. Acts, as we have seen, are synthetic in the sense that they unify a multiplicity in rendering something present. Every such act, Husserl points out, "is indeed (in the broadest sense) a meaning of its meant [*Meinung seines Gemeinten*] but . . . this something meant [*dieses*

1. *CM*, p. 62.
2. *Ibid.*, p. 76.

Vermeinte] is more . . . than what is meant at that moment 'explicitly' "[3] We have already encountered the "implicitly" meant [das Mitgemeinte] in the example of the background or surroundings of a perceived object. Similarly meant, of course, are its hidden sides: these too, are not explicitly presented, in all their determinations, in the manner of the side which faces the perceiver. But these "internal horizons," as Husserl calls them, belong just as surely to the object-as-meant, and neither they nor the "external horizon" of the object's surroundings could possibly be lacking from the perception as a whole. The perceived object owes its givenness to a conscious act which means more than what is explicitly given.

Now the horizons of a given object correspond in the act to surplus meaning or "meaning more [Mehrmeinung] at that moment," but they are also, Husserl says, "predelineated potentialities" of consciousness.[4] That is, the implicity meant at one moment is something that can be explicitly meant at another. The relation of actuality and potentiality in a "static" analysis reminds us that experiences are not only related to objects but are also related to one another in a temporal continuum;[5] but it also forces the recognition that consciousness has a peculiar temporal structure which distinguishes it from any ordinary sequence of events. When the potential becomes actual, "replacing" the previous content, what *was* actual is not simply wiped out but has a way of remaining or being retained by the new actual consciousness. The new actual consciousness presents itself *as* the actualization of a possibility that was contained in the previous one. Whether as a goal-oriented activity or simply as receptive passivity, consciousness is always such that what is directly given stands out against the background of what it replaces in the temporal flow. Thus the "living present"[6] which constitutes the direct or self-givenness (*Evidenz*) of something is accompanied by its protention of open and more or less determined possibilities, and by its background of the just-past and

3. *Ibid.*, p. 46.
4. *Ibid.*, p. 45.
5. See Ludwig Landgrebe, *Phänomenologie und Geschichte* (Gütersloh: Gütersloher Verlagshaus G. Mohn, 1968), pp. 14–15. See also Hans-Georg Gadamer, *Wahrheit und Methode*, 2d ed. (Tübingen: Mohr, 1965), p. 236. Both Landgrebe and Gadamer are comparing Husserl and Dilthey in this regard.
6. FTL, p. 319.

retained. The consciousness of anything "now" takes in or "means" these temporal "horizons," just as surely as it does the spatial surroundings and internal horizons of a perceived object —with the important difference that the past and future *do* not exist.

Husserl had originally developed the concepts of "retention" and "protention" in the lectures of 1905, where his point of departure was the question of the "essence of time." In keeping with the pattern of the *Logical Investigations*, this question was reinterpreted as the question of the "origin" of time, i.e., the search for those forms of consciousness "in which the primitive differences of the temporal are constituted intuitively and authentically as the originary [*originären*] sources of all certainties [*Evidenzen*] relative to time." [7] The concepts of retention and protention, as the peculiarly temporal modes of being conscious of the nonactual, were the results of that search.

Husserl's later insistence on the move from static to genetic analysis is occasioned by the recognition that these forms of consciousness are also relevant to the point of departure of *transcendental* phenomenology, i.e., the problem of how the world is given. At least at the level of perception, in the case not only of events but of objects, too, givenness itself must be regarded as a temporal affair. It is the temporal structure of consciousness that makes it possible for a perceived thing, for example, to be meant in a determinate way beyond what is presently and explicitly given about it. That is, not only is the givenness of an object spread out over time, but each temporal phase of its givenness also retains those preceding it and draws them together in its determination of the object. From the temporal point of view, then, the object-as-meant involves an advancing nucleus of actual givenness and what Husserl calls the deposit (*Niederschlag*) or sediment of the no-longer given but retained. In this way the givenness of an object has its "origin" in a synthesis whereby a manifold of temporal phases are taken as the "appearances" of a particular thing. The drawing-together of the actual and the nonactual, which was the synthesis of static analysis, must be interpreted as a temporal drawing-together in order to be adequately described.

Husserl is careful to insist that it is still description, and

7. Husserliana X, p. 9 (*PITC*, p. 29); often I have substituted my own translations for those of Churchill.

essential description at that, that interests him. In the first edition of the *Logical Investigations* he had distinguished phenomenology from psychology as "pure description" rather than a "genetic" account of experiences, and by the latter he had meant an explanation in causal terms.[8] In other words, after a particular experience or type of experience had been described, psychology could investigate experimentally the circumstances associated with it and the variations in the experience itself. It could thus arrive at *laws* concerning the factors required to bring about certain occurrences in the realm of *Erlebnisse*. Such factors could be *external* to the experience itself—events "in the world," physiological events, or even psychological events available to empirical examination by outside observers (or by oneself after the fact). Introducing the notion of *phenomenological* genesis in his later work, Husserl clearly has something else in mind. First, he is interested as always in features inherent in an experience itself which can be revealed by reflection directly upon the experience; and these are genetic features in virtue of their attesting to a temporal development in which a dependence of *sense* is revealed. In other words, *what* is given, and *how* it is given, "presupposes" a *definite* temporal background, and such "presupposing" is found to be a feature of the experience itself, rather than being discovered by deductive or inductive inferences after the fact. Second, Husserl is of course interested in genesis as an essential feature of consciousness, and as before is describing not facts but patterns which facts follow, the "pure possibilities." Within this framework, Husserl regards the transition from the static to the genetic a move from the abstract to the concrete, one which places the problem of the "origin" of objectivity in its true perspective. It adds a "third dimension," the temporal, to what was previously described in "cross section."

For Husserl, the introduction of genetic considerations makes phenomenological analysis more concrete in several ways. In *Formal and Transcendental Logic* he speaks of an object-as-meant as the "product" of an intentional genesis which must be "unfolded" or retraced if the givenness of the object is to be understood.[9] "Genesis" is also used synonymously with "constitution" at this point. Beginning with any object, one could

8. *LU*, II, 4.
9. *FTL*, p. 207.

and should describe its givenness in terms of a genesis peculiar to it; and different types of genesis correspond to different types or regions of objects. The "founded" awareness of a person or aesthetic object, for example, which is complex from the static point of view because it involves personal or aesthetic apperception in addition to mere perceptive consciousness, would have a correspondingly complex genesis. From the formal point of view (i.e., without respect to the varying material regions), complex objects or states of affairs of differing levels of generality, which are reflected in judgments of various forms, would also be subject to genetic analysis.

In each of these cases, following the laws of the temporal form of consciousness, the actual or self-giving (intuitive) *cogitatio* of something new passes by way of retention into nonself-giving or "empty consciousness" (*Leerbewusstsein*);[10] its successor follows it, pushing it "farther back," etc. "Continuous retentional modification proceeds up to an essentially necessary *limit*. That is to say: with this intentional modification there goes hand in hand a *gradual diminution of prominence;* and precisely this has its limit, at which the formerly prominent subsides into the *universal substratum*—the so-called 'unconscious,' which, far from being a phenomenological nothing, is itself a limit-mode of consciousness." [11] In moving beyond the limit of conscious retention, the past *cogitatio*, according to Husserl, becomes an acquisition (*Erwerb*) or possession (*Habe*) which can be reawakened in recollection. In this way the temporal determination of an object's givenness need not be an unbroken, short-range continuum but can be spread over many "occasions" separated by shorter or longer spans of conscious activity directed elsewhere.

Such descriptions proceed from the problem of how an object is given as a unity through a temporal multiplicity of "appearances," and they tend to follow the "classification" procedure of static phenomenology, simply adding a temporal dimension to each type of subject-object correlation revealed through the phenomenological reduction. But Husserl's turn to genetic analysis has even broader implications. In *Formal and Transcendental Logic* Husserl describes genetic analysis as being "directed to the whole concrete nexus [*Zusammenhang*] in which each

10. *Ibid.*, p. 209.
11. *Ibid.*, p. 319; cf. *EU*, p. 336.

particular consciousness stands, along with its intentional object as intentional." [12] By "concrete nexus," Husserl means here a temporal or genetic context which extends beyond reference to a particular object. That is, an object or state of affairs is present to consciousness not only with the temporal background of its own givenness but also against a temporal background of other objects and states of affairs. The consciousness which can be analyzed genetically in relation to one particular object, event, or state of affairs has had experience of others as well; and this experience may well be relevant to the analysis in question. Whatever the present offers, it stands out against such a "substratum of sedimented prominences which, as a horizon, accompanies every living present. . . ." [13] The form of consciousness, which had concerned Husserl when he was interested in the primary intuition of temporal difference, is now considered as replete with content: the temporal background is not just "past" but *something* past.

With this approach, the focus of phenomenology is shifted slightly. If the world's givenness is still traced to the intentional character of consciousness, this character is now seen to have a much more complicated structure. We have seen that Husserl's concept of *Erlebnis* was not that of a capricious act *ex nihilo* but was bound to certain patterns that represent possibilities. But here the act, in Husserl's conception, is bound in a still more determinate way. The "realization in human mental life" or "givenness" of something objective is not merely the actualization of something which was a priori possible, but follows on and is linked with certain retained actualities which form a stock of acquisitions. With this the "originating" function of the act takes on a new character. *Erlebnisse* do not simply form a chain which could be expressed in a conjunction of judgments. Husserl's use of the "background"- or "horizon"-image for the temporal dimension of consciousness makes unavoidable the notion that the actual character of the objective, the "how" of its givenness to consciousness, is determined or "influenced" by this retained and possibly reawakened stock. For, as in the case of the spatial framework from which the image is borrowed, what is given is a *Gestalt* comprising both foreground and background, and the background cannot be changed without changing the

12. *FTL*, p. 316.
13. *Ibid.*, p. 319.

whole. For example, we noted that, because of retention, every new consciousness presents itself as the actualization of a possibility that was contained in its predecessor. But since its predecessor had a more or less definite protention of what was to come, the new consciousness is more than just the actualization of a possibility: it is either the confirmation of the expected, a determination of the previously undetermined, or a disconfirmation and surprise. Also involved in Husserl's conception, of course, is a logical or cognitive framework in which the "background" is made up of accomplished judgments or protojudgments which become "beliefs" or "persisting opinions." [14] In the *Logical Investigations,* in attacking the "feeling" theory of self-evidence, Husserl had developed a sort of operational definition in which the self-evident is seen as a norm for all rational creatures.[15] Later, the self-evident is seen as a norm set within the dynamic flow of individual consciousness: "Every evidence 'sets up' or 'institutes' [*stiftet*] for me an *abiding possession*. I can 'always return' to the itself-beheld actuality . . ." [16] Of course, this is the claim, so to speak, attached to an intuitive consciousness as it is vitally present and then becomes nonactual by way of retention; which is not to say the claim cannot be called into question by a conflicting experience, with the possible result that the original "insight" is unmasked as false and rejected entirely. Until challenged, however, such a "possession" stands ready to be reawakened, and, of course, it need not be *actively* reawakened. The possibility of its passive reawakening points to its continued quasi-presence—which can be viewed as a kind of "influence" on the course of conscious activity. In the form of a premise for explicitly logical inference, or merely as the source of motivation for nonlogical "association," such a possession must be viewed as a determining factor in the "originating" function of consciousness. The past, as Husserl points out, is also paradoxically under the "influence" of the present. Short of the possibility of being cancelled completely, the sense of a retained acquisition may be transformed by being "seen" from the ever new perspectives of the changing present.[17] On each occasion of its being reawakened, it may, though it is in principle

14. Husserliana IV, p. 111.
15. *LI*, p. 769.
16. *CM*, p. 60.
17. *FTL*, p. 321.

"the same," have different significance, thanks to the content of the present.

One peculiarity of "reawakening" is of particular interest to Husserl and is of the utmost importance for our problem. A particular belief, opinion, or conviction enters the stock or background of consciousness in virtue of an original act of self-giving consciousness or insight (intuition) through which something is given. As an acquisition, such a belief can be characterized as the "result" of such activity. But in the process of reawakening, it is often only this "result" that figures in relation to the present. "The 'result' of the earlier originative activity is picked up again and something new is made with it; but picking it up does *not* involve *repeating the activity*." [18] Of course, in the case of a perceptual judgment, for example (as opposed to a mathematical or logical one), the conditions may not permit an actual repetition, but even here a memory can reproduce the perceptual conditions on which the judgment is based. In the case that interests Husserl, however, not even this occurs, and the result is an interesting hybrid in the framework of intention and fulfillment set up by the *Logical Investigations*. Such a belief constitutes neither a "mere" or empty intention nor a fulfilled one, but rather one which functions in consciousness *as if it were fulfilled*, because in principle (by virtue of its having been) it can be fulfilled again or, as Husserl says, "reactivated." It carries a kind of guarantee that it can be "cashed in" at any time.[19]

Such cases of nonactive reawakening interest Husserl partly because of their obvious importance in deductive reasoning and hence in science. "Without them there would be no science." [20] His model is the use made of a theorem previously proved in geometry, for example, to prove something else, without having to go back and prove the original theorem. We shall soon see that this conception of reawakening and its accompanying conception of science play an important role in the emergence of the problem of history.

THE IMPLICATIONS OF GENETIC ANALYSIS

BUT WHAT MUST BE CONSIDERED FIRST is the effect of the whole "genetic" dimension of phenomenology on the concep-

18. *Ibid.*, p. 322.
19. *Ibid.*, §§ 23–24.
20. *Ibid.*, p. 328.

tion of transcendental consciousness as such. The scheme which served as the account of transcendental origins from the static point of view was that of act-object, or *cogito-cogitatum*, as Husserl says in the *Cartesian Meditations*. The act, as we have seen, is given a further context in the consideration of attitude, whose fundamental form, the natural attitude, is correlated to the world, the object's background. With the introduction of the temporal dimension, another problem of origin is raised, for acts are now seen as spread out in a temporal manifold. From the genetic point of view, in serving the transcendental function of "constituting" an object in the world, any particular act must draw itself together with other acts in the continuum, which themselves, in turn, serve the same function. In other words, another problem of unity-in-multiplicity is raised, not that of the unified object versus its multiple appearance this time, but that of the unity of consciousness in relation to its own temporal multiplicity. Husserl traces the origin of this unity (or the origin of the givenness of consciousness to itself as unified) to "an all-embracing 'cogito,' synthetically comprising all particular conscious processes . . ." and whose "cogitatum" is the transcendental life itself.[21]

With the conception of this all-encompassing synthesis, Husserl has arrived, as he recognized even in the time lectures of 1905, at the *ultimate* source or transcendental origin, for the givenness of the world is ultimately dependent upon the unity of consciousness. In those lectures Husserl had referred to this synthesis as the work of "absolute subjectivity," or what was paradoxically described as the "time-constituting flux." [22]

We shall not enter into all the complexities and problems which attach to Husserl's notion of time-consciousness. Of interest to us here is the notion that the temporally ordered constitution of the world goes hand in hand with, indeed is made possible by, the self-constitution of consciousness itself, the production of its own unity-in-multiplicity. In the First Cartesian Meditation, speaking of consciousness as revealed in transcendental reflection, Husserl uses the Cartesian term "ego cogito," but when he finally turns to a discussion of the "ego" in its own right, in the Fourth Meditation, this turns out to be conceived more as a *result* than as a *source* of the universal

21. *CM*, pp. 42–43.
22. Husserliana X, p. 75 (*PITC*, p. 100).

cogito referred to in the framework of time-consciousness.[23] Husserl's "ultimate source," discussed above, is usually characterized as "transcendental subjectivity," the "transcendental life," the "flowing-static present," or "living present," and is not conceived as an agent called "ego" which stands outside of time and whose acts constitute time and its contents. The ego in a substantive sense does become important, however, in the context of the problem of the self-constitution of transcendental subjectivity, where it can be seen in varying degrees of concretion. From the formal perspective the ego can be considered a mere "pole" on which the multiplicity of acts is predicated. But as each act, with its particular content, takes its place among the stock of sedimented and potentially revived acquisitions, consciousness is constituting itself as a "substrate of habitualities," [24] a concrete nucleus of particular beliefs, convictions, and dispositions to act. There develops through such self-constitution a "persisting style," a "personal character." [25]

An important refinement on this concept of self-constitution is added in certain manuscripts of roughly the same period and later. In one of these Husserl writes: "The ego is heir to itself [beerbt sich selbst], and its heritage lies in itself as its persisting 'character.' . . ." This "self-inheritance" and "self-generation" "consist[s] in the fact that every actus immediately becomes a habitus and as such goes into the ego as its maintainance of itself [Sich-selbst behalten]." "But self-maintainance [Selbsterhaltung]," he goes on, "has yet another and more pregnant sense, [that of] prescribing for the ego a particular composition (Aufbau) as that toward which I am always 'aiming' without necessarily having set it explicitly as a goal." [26] In other words, the self is constituted for itself (or given to itself) not only as what it already is—its stock of accumulated experiences or habitus—but also as a prescribed pattern of activity in the form of a style to be maintained, whether one is fully conscious of this as a goal or not.

This notion of the habitually persisting style or orientation of conscious life, also called interest (Interesse) by Husserl, together with the related concept of goal and goal-setting

23. Husserliana IV, p. 112: "Das eine reine Ich ist konstituiert als Einheit mit Beziehung auf diese Stromeinheit."
24. CM, p. 66.
25. Ibid., p. 67.
26. Husserl Archives MS. A V 5, p. 11.

(*Zwecksetzung*), assumes an increasingly important role in the manuscripts of the *Crisis* period. Not only do these concepts of conscious activity add to the general theory of the ego and of self-constitution; they also refer to a specifically *transcendental* function, i.e., a function related to the way the world is given, as can be seen in the following passage:

> Conscious of the world as a horizon, we live for our particular ends, whether as momentary and changing ones or as an enduring goal that guides us. [The latter] can be a goal that we have elected for ourselves as a life-vocation, to be the dominant one in our active life, or it can be one that we have somehow drifted into through our upbringing. In this case a self-enclosed "world"-horizon is constituted. Thus . . . we may permit ourselves to be indifferent to everything else, and we have an eye only for this horizon as our world and for its own actualities or possibilities—those that exist in this "world"—i.e., we have an eye only to what is "reality" here (what is correct, true in relation to this goal) or "unreality" (the incorrect, the mistaken, the false).[27]

As can easily be seen, what this concept of *Zwecksetzung* does is to make more concrete and place in the temporal context the notion of *attitude* we have already discussed—attitude, that is, in the narrower sense of marking off, within the world of the *natural* attitude as a whole, a particular region or zone of interest to the exclusion of others. We have already seen the importance of attitude in relation to the general transcendental problem of the givenness of the world. Now, in the context of genetic phenomenology, attitude can be seen as the longer-range *temporal* structure of consciousness which lies behind (or ahead of) individual acts and gives them their horizons and thus their sense. Naturally, within the natural attitude as a whole, many long- and short-term attitudes and interests are compatible; they can also be set aside or bracketed for a time and taken up again. In any case, such a theory not only supplements the theory of acts and their relations, providing a picture of the structure of the world as given; it also makes more concrete the theory of the ego by revealing it as a self-constituted unity not only of acts but also of interests and goals.

The ego can be considered even more broadly—and more concretely, according to Husserl—if it is taken to include the *objects* of its own personal experience, the particular content of

27. *Crisis*, p. 379.

its world, and even the particular potentialities which are commensurable with this content. Many forms of conscious activity and many forms of objectivity are a priori possible, but not all such forms are compossible, i.e., compatible with all others. Borrowing this notion from Leibniz, Husserl refers to a concrete ego, including "its world," both actual and potential within the limits of the compossible, as a "monad." [28] Any particular conscious act must be considered—concretely—as proceeding from such a monadic consciousness, a consciousness with its own habitualities and its own world.

Genetic analysis, then, adds considerably to what must be included in the phenomenological concept of consciousness. We have seen this conception grow in complexity, beginning with the simple notion of *Akt-Erlebnis* in the *Logical Investigations*. The act was further conceived as synthesis and was then given the background of attitude, with a corresponding expansion of the notion of intentionality. All this was developed in answer to the question of how something objective can be given. Now we see that the concept of intentionality is not capable of answering this question until the temporal dimension is added. The givenness of anything is the "product" of a particular genesis that must be traced. The "constitution" of anything objective is a temporal affair. But such a particular constitution, in turn, cannot be understood except in the context of the genesis of consciousness itself, i.e., in terms of its self-constitution as a substrate of habitualities and of goals, and in the fullest sense as a "monad."

Of interest for our topic is the fact that Husserl uses the terms "history" and "historicity" in this context. Referring to judgments in *Formal and Transcendental Logic* as "products of a 'constitution' or 'genesis,'" he says that an "essential peculiarity of such products is precisely that they are senses that bear within them, as a sense-implicate of their genesis, a sort of historicalness [*Historizität*]" and that for every sense-formation [*Sinngebilde*] one can inquire into its sense-history [*Sinnesgeschichte*].[29] In another context it is stated not only that "every single process of consciousness, as occurring temporally, has its own 'history,' that is: its *temporal genesis*," but that any such particular "history" finds its place within the

28. *CM*, pp. 67–68.
29. *FTL*, p. 208.

temporal unity of a particular conscious *life* as a whole, which has its own "history" in such temporal unity.[30] In the *Cartesian Meditations* Husserl says that "the ego constitutes himself for himself in, so to speak, the unity of a *'history.'*"[31]

Now in these passages the term "history" is clearly not used in its usual sense, and Husserl shows his awareness of this in using quotation marks or expressions like "so to speak," or "a sort of historicalness." To be sure, history involves time, development, "genesis"; but except in expressions like "personal history" or "case history," the term is usually used to refer not to individual experience but to mankind, to particular societies or to particular human activities involving many persons, e.g., the history of philosophy. And of course the "problem of history" that was discussed in connection with the *Crisis* was related to history in this more usual sense. When he states that as philosophers we are "historical beings," "heirs to the past," etc., Husserl clearly means history in the broader sense, and the past he has in mind is not merely that of the individual—it involves philosophy as a human or at least as a European activity.

What is the relation between the two senses of history? Here Husserl seems to be borrowing something from the usual notion of history and applying it to the individual sphere. Yet we have suggested that it is in part Husserl's concept of "history" in the individual sphere that gives rise to the introduction of historical considerations (in something more like the usual sense) into phenomenology. Since the difference between the "unusual" and the "usual" senses of the term seems to correspond to the difference between the individual and the community, it is well to turn our attention next to Husserl's reflections on the problem of intersubjectivity.

30. *Ibid.*, p. 316.
31. *CM*, p. 75.

4 / Intersubjectivity

As DEPICTED SO FAR in our exposition, Husserl's phenomenology takes its point of departure from consciousness conceived as *individual* consciousness. This point of departure was taken for granted in the *Logical Investigations* and was made more explicit in the theory of the *Ich*, which was first treated in *Ideas* I and further developed in the *Cartesian Meditations*. In this last work, published in 1931, Husserl tacitly admits to a rather remarkable fact: in the thirty years since the inception of phenomenology Husserl had published no systematic or extensive treatment of the problems falling under the heading of intersubjectivity, e.g., the problem of our experience of another consciousness and of the concept of a plurality of subjects. True, he had treated such themes in lectures and unpublished writings—they occupy an important position, for example, in the now available second volume of the *Ideas*,[1] and Husserl himself traces his handling of the problem to lectures given in 1910.[2] It is nevertheless worthy of note that this problem, like that of genetic phenomenology, was not publicly assigned a place within phenomenology until Husserl was seventy years old.

Today, with so many unpublished manuscripts available through the work of the Husserl Archives, one is tempted to overlook the significance *for Husserl's own development* of the distinction between the published and the unpublished works.

1. Husserliana IV, §§ 29, 43 ff.
2. *FTL*, p. 243 n; also Husserliana V (*"Nachwort"*), p. 150, n. 2.

We now know that both genetic phenomenology and the problem of intersubjectivity had occupied Husserl for many years prior to their first appearance in print, and we can trace their development.[3] But certain criteria are invoked in the choice of what to publish which are not invoked either in choosing material for lectures, which often have an experimental and improvised character, or, obviously, in purely private *Forschungsmanuskripte*. Even if the two themes mentioned had been dealt with by Husserl before 1913, the fact is that in that year he published his "General Introduction to Pure Phenomenology" (the *Ideas*) and saw fit to ignore both of them, or at least not to accord them the important position they occupy in the "Introduction to Phenomenology" (the *Cartesian Meditations*) of 1931. Obviously, certain conclusions about Husserl's attitude can be drawn from this fact: either he felt that these themes were not important enough to be included in an uninitiated reader's first meeting with phenomenology; or he was not satisfied with his own treatment of them. Perhaps both considerations were involved. The second conclusion is supported by the fact that *Ideas* II, in which both subjects receive some treatment, was meant to be published along with the first volume but was continually held back for revision and was never published at all during Husserl's lifetime. Yet the fact that Husserl published only the first, "introductory" volume, which does not treat these themes, supports the first conclusion. In any case it is clear that his attitude had changed by the time of the *Cartesian Meditations*, where the two problems occupy important positions.

We shall try to show, as we have said, that Husserl's fully developed treatment of the problem of intersubjectivity has important implications related to the emergence of the concept of history in the *Crisis*. Before that can be done, it is necessary to understand just what Husserl considers the "problem of intersubjectivity" to be. His conception of the problem is obscured by the manner and the context in which it is given its best-known and most fully developed exposition, that is, in the Fifth of the *Cartesian Meditations*.

3. Three new volumes of Husserliana (Vols. XIII–XV), which have just appeared at this writing, contain manuscripts devoted to intersubjectivity dating from 1905: *Zur Phänomenologie der Intersubjektivität: Erster Teil, Zweiter Teil, Dritter Teil*, ed. Iso Kern (The Hague: Martinus Nijhoff, 1973).

THE PROBLEM OF THE FIFTH MEDITATION

WHAT DOES HUSSERL SEEK in the Fifth Meditation? According to the title, the "Uncovering of the Sphere of Transcendental Being as Monadological Intersubjectivity." But in the first paragraph it appears that this task must be undertaken because of the objection that phenomenology, as described in the preceding four meditations, could "be branded . . . as transcendental solipsism." [4] By introducing the problem in this way, Husserl has placed a great obstacle in the way of his readers' understanding of what he is about.

Husserl's characterization of phenomenology as (transcendental) idealism[5] seems to make it susceptible to the charge of solipsism, an objection often raised against idealism. One concise definition of this objection states that solipsism "consists in holding that the individual *I* . . . with its subjective modifications, is all of reality, and that other *I*'s of which one has a representation have no more independent existence than persons in dreams;—or [it consists] at least in admitting that it is impossible to demonstrate the contrary." [6] By seeming to present his theory of intersubjectivity as an answer to such an objection, Husserl gives the impression that he is setting out to demonstrate or prove, deductively or inductively, the "independent existence" of other "*I*'s."

The impression that the standard problem of solipsism is at issue is reinforced by the Cartesian "presence" which gives the *Meditations* their name. Husserl has presented the phenomenological reduction as a variant of the Cartesian systematic doubt, as he had already done in the *Ideas;* and he has credited Descartes with seeing "that *ego sum* or *sum cogitans* must be pronounced apodictic, and that accordingly we get a first apodictically existing basis to stand on" [*einen ersten apodiktischen Seinsboden unter die Füsse bekommen*]." [7] But, once established upon this *Seinsboden,* what do we do? Descartes' idea of proceeding from this point is, of course, to be able to assert the existence

4. *CM*, p. 89.
5. *Ibid.*, pp. 83 ff.
6. *Vocabulaire technique et critique de la philosophie*, ed. André Lalande, 8th ed., (Paris: Presses Universitaries de France, 1960), p. 1008.
7. *CM*, p. 22.

of God and the rest of the world, including other egos, with the same degree of certainty, even if by inference rather than immediately, as that attaching to the assertion *ego sum*. And it is precisely against the failure of Descartes and others that the objection of solipsism is ordinarily raised. Now Husserl explicitly dissociates himself, early in the *Meditations*, from Descartes' attempt to prove the existence of "the rest of the world" [*die übrige Welt*] by using the *ego sum* as an "axiom." [8] But by raising the objection of solipsism in the Fifth Meditation and by presenting his theory as an answer to it, Husserl seems to be returning to the Cartesian approach, hoping to ascribe independent existence to other egos, if not to the rest of the external world, with a degree of certainty comparable to that of the *ego sum*.

This becomes plausible if we consider Husserl's reasons for rejecting Descartes' procedure. It is impossible to move by inference from one's own ego to "the rest of the world," because the ego is not a "tag-end of the world," i.e., it is not "part" of the world at all. As Descartes failed to realize, though there are different ways of considering the ego, the ego of which one has apodictic certainty is transcendental: its relation to the world and the things in it is intentional and not that of a part to a causally interrelated whole. Consequently, "inferences according to the principle of causality," of the sort used by Descartes, are ruled out. [9] Thus we cannot prove the existence of other egos considered as part of the world's causal nexus. But what about other egos considered as transcendental? The problem, as Husserl announces it in the Second Meditation, is how "other egos— not as mere worldly phenomena but as other transcendental egos —can become positable as existing and thus become equally legitimate themes of a phenomenological egology." [10] And at the beginning of the Fifth Meditation the problem of solipsism is stated in this way: "But what about other egos, who surely are not a mere intending and intended [*Vorstellung und Vorgestelltes*] *in me*, merely synthetic unities of possible verification *in me*, but, according to their sense, precisely *others*?" [11] Thus other egos seem to demand a treatment which goes beyond the consideration of them merely as intentional objects, for they

8. *Ibid.*, p. 24.
9. *Ibid.*
10. *Ibid.*, p. 30.
11. *Ibid.*, p. 89.

are intentional subjects. Husserl seems to be admitting that he asserts that everything else has the status of merely something intended or represented "in me," and he is now faced with the question of whether other egos have merely the same status. His "denial of solipsism" would then take the form: "no, others as transcendental egos in fact exist outside me," or the like.[12]

This could explain the fact that Husserl says he is addressing himself to the problem of *transcendental* solipsism. But in fact the transcendental character of the problem seems to involve much more, for the objection is described as calling into question "the claim of transcendental phenomenology to be itself transcendental *philosophy* and therefore its claim that, in the form of a constitutional problematic and theory moving within the limits of the transcendentally reduced ego, it can solve the transcendental problems pertaining to the *Objective world*." [13]

Not just a particular type of entity which has a status different from other entities, but the objective world as a whole, then, seems to be at issue. How is this so? Husserl explains the objectivity of the world in this way: "I *experience* the world . . . *not* as (so to speak) my *private* synthetic formation but as other than mine alone [*mir fremde*], as an *intersubjective* world, actually there for everyone, accessible in respect of its Objects to everyone." [14] Husserl has indeed already insisted on the *transcendence* of the world, as we have seen, by saying that "neither the world nor any worldly Object is a piece of my Ego, to be found in my conscious life as a really inherent part of it, as a complex of data of sensation or a complex of acts." [15] Accounting for transcendence is the task which gives transcendental philosophy its name. But while such transcendence is "part of the intrinsic sense of anything worldly," he goes on, ". . . anything worldly necessarily acquires all the sense determining it, along with its existential status, exclusively from

12. Those who interpret Husserl's project in this way usually judge that he has not succeeded. This is Sartre's conclusion in *Being and Nothingness*, trans. Hazel Barnes (New York: Philosophical Library, 1956), p. 235. This interpretation also seems to be the foundation for Quentin Lauer's opinion that Husserl meant to provide an "additional guarantee for the validity of subjective constitution" and failed. See his *Phenomenology: Its Genesis and Prospect* (New York: Harper & Row, 1965), p. 150.

13. *CM*, p. 89.

14. *Ibid.*, p. 91.

15. *Ibid.*, p. 26.

my experiencing, my objectivating, thinking, valuing, or doing. . . ." [16] Our previous discussions have clarified this apparent paradox. Transcendence is conceived as the nonreducibility
of what is meant to the particular act or acts in which it is
meant. But the meant surpasses any particular act or acts by
always being the reference point of other *possible* acts implied
in any *actual* one. Until the Fifth Meditation, all such acts,
actual and possible, are conceived as mine. By introducing the
problem of objectivity, Husserl is simply drawing on a sense of
transcendence involved in the natural attitude which is stronger
than the sense previously developed. The objective is not only
irreducible to any particular acts of mine; it is also not reducible
to *all possible* acts of mine, my whole actual and possible stream
of consciousness, because it is identically the same for others
and their acts as well.

Now if "the claim of transcendental phenomenology to be
itself transcendental *philosophy*" is threatened by the objection
of solipsism, it is because phenomenology seems to be incapable
of dealing with the stronger sense of the *transcendence* of the
world. It can account for the weaker sense of transcendence
(the transcendence of my particular act or acts) because of its
concept of the relation between actuality and potentiality in the
stream of consciousness. But up to now it has no concept of
the alter ego to whose acts the stronger sense of transcendence
refers.

The "objection of solipsism" thus takes on a sense very
different from its traditional one: not the *existence* but the very
concept of the alter ego is needed in order to answer it. But
the character of the concept required must be further specified.
It is not equivalent, for example, to the concept of a multiplicity
of egos: Husserl is not concerned with showing that *different*
egos are possible or conceivable. In a sense the possibility of
different egos has already been taken into account by the very
eidetic approach of phenomenology. By taking the *particular*
objects of transcendental reflection as merely exemplary, Husserl seeks to describe the structure of any consciousness at all.
That not all possibilities can be construed as possibilities of *my*
consciousness is ruled out by the concept of the monad as
a system of compossibilities. Not all possibilities of consciousness are compossible with all others, and certain conceivable

16. *Ibid.*

possibilities would rule out my actual present and past. These would have to be other than they are, a different stream of consciousness involved in a different system of possibilities. The monad as such a system of compossibilities makes no sense except by reference to other possible systems, and this is why Husserl speaks in the *Cartesian Meditations* not only of the *eidos* of consciousness, whose instances could potentially all belong to one stream of experience, but of the *eidos ego,* whose instances are different and incompatible streams of experience.[17]

True, Husserl says that the eidetic approach presupposes "neither the actuality nor the possibility of other egos." [18] But it is necessary to distinguish between *different* egos and *other* egos in the sense of the alter ego referred to in the Fifth Meditation. The eidetic approach conceives of different egos without conceiving of any relation among them, other than their essence and their difference. But the concept of objectivity, introduced in the Fifth Meditation, places ego and alter ego in intentional relation, since the ego refers his world, or the things in it, to others. The ego in the fullest sense, i.e., the monad, may differ from my own. But the problem now is to make sense of the alter ego *for* that ego, whoever he may be. The concept of objectivity, after all, is part of the natural attitude; it is the ego of the natural attitude that refers the objects of his experience to others. The task which arises is to explain *how* the other exists *for him,* not *whether* the other exists as such.

What is sought, then, is a specifically phenomenological concept of the alter ego, that is, one that will fit into the over-all scheme of phenomenological investigation, the scheme indicated by the words *ego-cogito-cogitatum-qua-cogitatum.* And when Husserl places the objection of "solipsism" into the mouth of his imaginary critic, it is the possibility of just such a concept that is being questioned in principle. The critic doubts not Husserl's ability to prove that others exist, which is not in question, but his ability to make "phenomenological sense" of other egos. There is simply no place in the phenomenological scheme, he argues, for the alter ego. In that scheme everything must be either *ego, cogitatio,* or *cogitatum,* and the alter ego presents us with the apparent paradox of a *cogitatum cogitans.*

17. *Ibid.,* p. 71.
18. *Ibid.,* p. 72.

Husserl has his opponent say that other egos "are not a mere intending and intended [*Vorstellung und Vorgestelltes*] in me," as if he, Husserl, were simply asserting that everything else *is* just that. But this is a very naïve statement of the results of the first four meditations; and Husserl seems aware of this in his use of the words *Vorstellung* and *Vorgestelltes*. One could object to Cairns's translation of this passage on the ground that Husserl is suggesting that the "problem of solipsism" arises only if such a naïve view is taken: to say that everything is something intended in (or by) me is equivalent to saying it is "merely my representation" (*Vorstellung*). Thus transcendental idealism would be transformed into subjective idealism. But Husserl does not answer his imaginary opponent by reiterating the distinction between transcendental and subjective idealism, so one suspects that the latter's case does not rest merely on this confusion. A more accurate statement of the phenomenological procedure, as we have seen, is that it considers everything meant purely *as* it is meant (*cogitatum qua cogitatum*) and withholds any other attitude toward it.[19] It thus arrives at a full account of its being-for-me or its sense. But even with this view it could be argued that the alter ego is not susceptible of this kind of treatment: he cannot even be considered purely as meant; or, to the degree that he is, he is no longer an ego. Thus the concept of the ego in general is incompatible with the phenomenological concept of something given, at least if the alter ego is to be considered transcendental and not merely worldly. To the extent that he is given he is not a transcendental ego, and to the extent that he is a transcendental ego he is not given.

The difficulty is explained best in a manuscript bearing the title "Das Ich und sein Gegenüber." Here Husserl refers to that which *gegenübersteht,* i.e., the *Gegenstand* or object, and brings up the problem of considering the other subject as object.

> The non-ego, the object that is not a subject, is what it is only as a *Gegenüber,* only as something constituted with relation to an ego or an open multiplicity of egos. . . . [But] the ego is *gegenüber for itself,* it is for itself, constituted in itself. Any ego can also be *gegenüber* for another or several other egos, [i.e.] a constituted

19. The *cogitatum qua cogitatum* goes back to a distinction in the *Logical Investigations* between "*the object as it is intended,* and the *object* (period) *which* is intended" (*LI,* p. 578).

object for them, grasped, experienced by them, etc. But it is also precisely constituted for itself and *has* its constituted surrounding world consisting of non-egos, mere "objects". . . .[20]

In this passage the problem of the alter ego is not raised as an objection to phenomenology as such, or even as a difficulty. Husserl is simply pointing out that if the other person is to be considered in his being-for-me (the standard phenomenological move), he must also be considered as being-for-himself, unlike any other kind of object. As usual in the phenomenological attitude, his "being-in-himself" is simply not at issue. What is at issue is how he is given. But it is easy to see how this formulation is transformed into the "solipsistic objection" of the Fifth Meditation: how can the other person be considered purely as being-for-me, in accord with the phenomenological reduction, when he is essentially for himself— not merely an object but a self-constituting stream of experience with "his own" world? Others are not *Gegenstände* but *Gegen-Subjekte*, as Husserl says at one point in *Ideas* II;[21] how can something that is not a *Gegenstand* be given at all in the phenomenological sense? Perhaps the *an sich* can be considered purely as *für mich*, but how can the *für sich* be so considered? Up to now, the universal characteristic of any concrete object has been its position within the horizons of the world. An object is spatiotemporally situated in relation to my own body and a spatial horizon and ultimately is causally related to its surroundings. But if the other ego is to be transcendental, his relation to his surroundings is not of this sort. His relation to the rest of the world is not that of a part to a whole or that of a thing to its surroundings. Rather, the world is *for* him, his relation to it is purely intentional; he can no more be considered a part of the world than I can. But how can anything be given except as being in the world?

Thus, if the other cannot be accounted for—phenomenologically—*as* other subject, how can the intersubjective sense of the objective world be given a phenomenological account? The only account of objectivity, then, according to the critic, is "transcendental realism," [22] which simply dogmatically assumes the existence of a multiplicity of egos without providing an

20. Husserliana IV, p. 318.
21. *Ibid.*, p. 194.
22. *CM*, p. 89.

account of their givenness to each other. But to accept this view, of course, is to give up the phenomenological attitude altogether.

What Husserl has done by raising the issue of solipsism is to articulate the problem he faces and even to give a preview of the solution he proceeds to offer. He is convinced that the alter ego is given in experience—the other must be considered an object in some sense—but he must show that the other is given *as* a *Gegen-Subjekt*, i.e., "not as mere worldly phenomenon, but as another transcendental ego." With the statement of the problem the first step of the phenomenological reduction has already been performed—the object has been transformed into the object-as-meant, the "how of its givenness" has been brought into view. But Husserl must account for this givenness of the other subject in the usual way: he must correlate it with the activity of the conscious subject *to whom* he is given. "We must . . . obtain for ourselves insight into the explicit and implicit intentionality wherein the alter ego becomes evinced [*sich bekundet*] and verified in the realm of our transcendental ego; we must discover in what intentionalities, syntheses, motivations, the sense 'other ego' becomes fashioned in me. . . ." [23] But the first step of the analysis already contains the second: by performing the reduction of *what* is meant and considering it purely *as* meant, one is already made aware of the intentional act of meaning it. Thus the direction of Husserl's inquiry is already outlined: he must lay bare the form of experience through which consciousness intends not merely an object within the world, as in the case of a perceived object, but another subject with its own stream of experience and its own objects.

There are further complications. While the other is not merely an object in the world of things given to me, he is nevertheless related to that world, and this in two ways: first he is given to me somehow through his body, which is part of the world as a perceived object; second, this object and the rest of my world must be *for him* as well as for me. Husserl must point to a form of my experience through which another subject is given as an individual when his body is given and through which the world becomes the world for both of us.

What Husserl does is to explicate the experience of others

23. *Ibid.*, p. 90.

first by pointing to certain features it shares with other forms of experience already treated in the *Meditations* and elsewhere. The experience of others is in some ways analogous to perception and in some ways analogous to recollection. By showing how it is analogous and then how it is different, he hopes to have provided an account that can be understood in the context of the phenomenological theory as a whole.

As for the other's body, it can be construed as "transcendent" in the weak sense, i.e., purely in relation to my own actual and possible acts of consciousness. Everything that can be so considered belongs to what Husserl calls the sphere of ownness (*Eigenheitssphäre*).[24] But in the actual experience of another, in which the body is grasped *as* body (*Leib*) and not just as a physical object (*Körper*), it is subjected to what Husserl calls an " 'analogizing' apprehension":[25] it is taken as the organ or expression of a consciousness, by analogy to my own body in relation to my own consciousness. The consciousness *of* which it is the manifestation is intended by virtue of an act Husserl calls "appresentation"—the consciousness of something as co-present (*mitgegenwärtig*) that is not itself directly presented to consciousness.[26]

How is such an act to be understood? Appresentation, Husserl points out, is what occurs in ordinary external perception, where the intention includes the other side of the object as "co-present."[27] This is different from what Husserl calls *Vergegenwärtigung*, rendering present to consciousness something that is not present either spatially or temporally, as in imagination or recollection. What is appresented is always the complement of what is presented, forming a kind of continuum with

24. *Ibid.*, p. 92.
25. *Ibid.*, p. 111. A great deal of discussion has been occasioned by the way in which Husserl accounts for this apprehension. He seems to be asking for the experiential conditions under which one would be motivated to take a particular object as another person. His account has been attacked by A. Schutz in "Das Problem der transzendentalen Intersubjektivität bei Husserl," *Phil. Rundschau*, V (1957), 81–107, and defended by M. Theunissen in *Der Andere: Studien zur Sozialontologie der Gegenwart* (Berlin: de Gruyter, 1965), pp. 64 ff. We leave this whole discussion aside, concentrating on the analysis of such apprehension itself, whatever its preconditions may be.
26. *CM*, p. 109.
27. *Ibid.*

it. Of course, one can also remember the other sides of a perceived object, or one can imagine what they are like, perhaps constructing a determined image on the basis of certain evidence; but one need not do this, whereas the appresentative consciousness, whether more or less determinate, necessarily accompanies presentation in perception. The presented is what it is (the side of a thing) only *together* with the appresented. The appresented belongs to the (internal) horizons of what is presented; it is intended in a horizon-consciousness, not an independent act. Now the other consciousness, according to Husserl, is given in a similar act as copresent *with* the body, as its "other side," so to speak; it is not something imagined in a separate act. Again, the presented (in this case the body as *Leib,* not as mere *Körper*) is what it is only together with the appresented.

Husserl is quick to point out the primary difference between appresentation in perception and in *Fremderfahrung:* the copresent side of the perceived object may be simultaneously present to others and may be present to me at an earlier or later time; while the other consciousness can never be anything but copresent to another and is present only to itself.[28] One might mention other ways in which this relation of the copresent to the present is a special one, not comparable to such a relation in the perceived object. The present (the other's body) is organ or expression of consciousness, thus bearing a relation to the copresent that is comparable to nothing else. Thus the analogy to perception is only partial, but it is helpful in avoiding certain misunderstandings arising from the distinguishability and the supposed discontinuity between "mind" and "body." Just as Husserl attacks the sign-theory of thing-perception, where the sense-datum is a mental sign or indicator of the thing that lies behind it,[29] so he opposes the view that the body is the "sign" of a separate mind, something that announces or gives evidence of its existence. What I *see* in perception is the thing itself, even though only a side is, strictly speaking, presented to me. Likewise, in the experience of someone else, "what I actually see is not a sign and not a mere analogue, a depiction in any natural sense of the word; on the contrary, it is someone else. . . ."[30]

28. *Ibid.*
29. Husserliana III, p. 99. (*Ideas,* p. 136).
30. *CM,* p. 124. See also p. 121.

While this analogy to perception is helpful in explaining the mediating role of the other's body in *Fremderfahrung*, and while it goes some way toward clearing up the apparent paradox of the object which is a subject, it does not itself take account of *what* is ultimately given through the "analogizing apprehension": another stream of consciousness. In order to illuminate this central point, Husserl introduces a comparison to a different phenomenological dimension, that of recollection.[31] Recollection, of course, is a special sort of *Vergegenwärtigung*, an act which "renders present something that is not present"; it is distinguished from an act of phantasy, for example, by locating its object in the past, and, what is more, in *my* past. It is, as Husserl says, in essence the consciousness not only of something past, but also of this something as having been perceived or otherwise consciously experienced by me.[32] Thus with a greater or lesser degree of explicitness, recollection renders present not only the object of the experience (e.g., a musical performance) but also the experience itself. In this sense "the immediate 'I' performs an accomplishment through which it constitutes a variational mode of itself as existing (in the mode of having passed)," a process Husserl describes as "depresentation" (*Ent-Gegenwärtigung*).[33] What is constituted, an experience, is a stream of consciousness, and this stream is distinct from and in a sense different from the stream which constitutes it. It can also involve a different spatial location, as Husserl points out in a manuscript ("then I was in Paris, now I am in Freiburg").[34] In any case, one "original" living present renders another, as past, present to itself, which is similar to what happens in *Fremderfahrung*. To be sure, this is only an analogy, as Husserl makes clear, and not an explanation;[35] but at least it makes somewhat

31. *Ibid.*, pp. 115–16, 126 ff. A clearer exposition of this point is found in the *Crisis*, p. 185.

32. This is a paraphrase of a passage in an appendix to *Erste Philosophie* (Husserliana VII, pp. 40–41).

33. *Crisis*, p. 185.

34. Cited in René Toulemont, *L'Essence de la société selon Husserl* (Paris: Presses Universitaires de France, 1962), p. 57.

35. Toulemont, *ibid.* pp. 55 ff., mentions Husserl's use of "comparisons" with perception and recollection, but confuses the issue by calling these modes of experience the "indispensable foundation for the higher associations" (p. 56), i.e., those of *Fremderfahrung*. But Husserl is quite clear on the fact that *Fremderfahrung* is not *based*

less paradoxical or self-contradictory the idea of a stream of consciousness as object. In order to make this comparison fruitful, it is necessary, again, to be clear on the ways in which the two forms of experience are *not* alike. While recollection is an act in which one stream of consciousness is given to another, clearly both streams of consciousness are actually segments of one and the same stream, and past acts are constituted as standing in a continuum which leads up to the very recollective acts in which it is constituted.[36] While the recollected act can never be simultaneous with the recollection, the prime case of *Fremderfahrung* is precisely that in which the object-act is simultaneous with the subject-act. It belongs precisely to *another* stream of experience by virtue of this difference, and stands in relation to its own retentions, recollections, expectations, habitualities, etc. Furthermore, what is remembered has a kind of evidence and certain procedures of verification (*Bewährung*) which differ from those connected to the experience of another: in the one case "reactivation," simply by virtue of *having* been experienced in living presence and thus retained; in the other case analogy, "empathy," through the mediation of the other's body.

But there is another important sense in which the comparison holds; and it leads from the theory of *Fremderfahrung* to the theory of objectivity in the strong or intersubjective sense. In recollection, as we have noted, there is an inseparable correlation between the experience and the experienced, whichever may be the primary object of recollection. To recall a musical performance is to recall hearing it, and to recall hearing it is to recall the performance itself, even if the correlate is remembered in each case only indistinctly. Similarly, being aware of another person as a stream of experience implies being aware to some extent of *what* he experiences, if only "by analogy." When I am face to face with another person, I am aware not only of him but also that I am an object for him and that our surroundings are given to him as they are to me—or rather, as they *would*

---

on recollection; the latter simply offers an "instructive comparison" (*CM* p. 115).

36. Cf. § 25, "The Double Intentionality of Recollection," in *Zur Phänomenologie des inneren Zeitbewusstseins*, Husserliana X, pp. 53–54 (*PITC*, pp. 77 ff.).

be given to me if I were in his place.[37] In other words, what is *appresented* is not only the other consciousness, but also his body, my body, and our whole surroundings, as they are for him. From this central core of the alter ego, given to me by analogy in *Fremderfahrung*, the other is a stream of experience extending more or less determinately (in the case of a stranger almost totally indeterminately) into the past, together with all its objects. In short, the other is given as a complete monad in his own right.

The fact about the experience of another that makes comprehensible the full-fledged notion of objectivity is that, as monad, he is thus constituted as having "his own" world just as I do. But these two "own" worlds are construed in intersubjective experience as *appearances* or modes of givenness of one and the *same* world which is intended by both of us and indeed by all, and from which such appearances can at times differ.[38] The objective, or the transcendent in the strong sense, can thus be understood by analogy to the transcendent in the weaker or "solipsistic" sense: just as the latter is given as one by relation to a multiplicity of *my* acts, actual and potential, so the intersubjective object has the same status in relation to a multiplicity of acts by different subjects. My act and that of the other "are so fused that they stand within the *functional community of one perception,* which simultaneously presents and appresents, and yet furnishes for the total object a consciousness of its being itself there." [39]

Such is Husserl's *phenomenological* account of the alter ego, which in turn makes possible his phenomenological account of the objective world. "I *experience* the world . . . *not* as (so to speak) my *private* synthetic formation" because I experience it as given to others as well. That is, it is given as exceeding my actual *and possible* consciousness, having the full sense it does only because it is referred in part to the consciousness of another. Thus the other consciousness is *"the intrinsically first other* (the first 'nonego')" [40] because it is by being given to him that anything else is objective for me. But this is possible only because the consciousness of another, as an alien locus of givenness, itself has sense for me, i.e., it can be given to me in its

37. *CM*, p. 117.
38. *Ibid.*, pp. 107, 123.
39. *Ibid.*, p. 122.
40. *Ibid.*, p. 107.

own peculiar way. What Husserl has done, using the comparisons we have mentioned, is to point to and elucidate the form of consciousness through which *this* givenness is realized. Through appresentation and the peculiar "analogizing apprehension" involved in *Fremderfahrung,* I am confronted with an object which is a subject, a *cogitatum cogitans.*

What must be understood about this whole account is that, while the alter ego makes it possible that the "rest" of the world exceeds my actual and possible consciousness, the alter ego does not *himself* exceed my actual and possible consciousness. That is, he is described in the Fifth Meditation in the same way that everything else was described before the problem of "solipsism" was raised, namely, as transcendent only in the weaker sense: not reducible to the particular act or acts in which he is given to *me*. He is not so reducible only because he is the objective unity of actual and possible acts of my own in which he can be given. Or, if the other is himself given as objective (transcendent in the stronger sense), it is only by reference to another possible alter ego (or the same alter ego) which is transcendent only in the weaker sense. The objective is what it is *for me* because it is given to a possible stream of experience that is not my own. But this can make sense only because that stream of experience, not my own, can in turn be experienced by me—though "experienced" must now be understood in a broad enough sense to include the appresentative or "analogizing" apprehension.

In other words, Husserl's account up to this point is strictly egological; it is contained wholly within the schema *ego-cogitatio-cogitatum.* It can even be called "solipsistic" if the *solus ipse* is now understood at a higher level. This is necessary because the *cogitatum* in the broadest sense—the world—has been provided with an added dimension. The "objective world" has been explained by reference to other subjects who are not in it but are transcendental in relation to it. In this narrow sense the other ego as transcendental is not *part* of my world at all. But he and his total "contribution" to the make-up of the world— which comprise a full-fledged monad in its own right—do belong within the range of my actual and possible experience. That is, I distinguish between what is directly given to me and what is directly given only to him; but it is within my own experience that I do this. Now "my own experience" in this broadest sense can itself be considered a monad which contains and constitutes his (and also "my own" in the narrower sense). While the other does not strictly belong to my world, as we said above, he certainly belongs to my monad. Thus what has been shown is "how I can constitute in myself another Ego or, more radically, how I can constitute in my monad another monad. . . ." Furthermore, it has been shown "how I can identify a Nature constituted in me with a Nature constituted by someone else (or, stated with the necessary precision, how I can identify a Nature constituted in me with one constituted in me *as* a Nature constituted by someone else)." [41]

Thus, while everything in this framework is understood by reference to *my* actual and possible experience, the Fifth Meditation introduces into this framework an important distinction that was not articulated in the first four: the distinction between my actual and possible experiences in the strict or narrow sense (what Husserl calls the "sphere of ownness")—those which give an object directly; and those of my experiences in which what is given is another stream of experience and through which an object is given *indirectly*. The so-called "reduction" to the sphere of ownness is not another phenomenological reduction at all, but simply a focus on the first or narrow sense of givenness so that the role and nature of the second sense can emerge. [42] The two senses correspond, respectively, to the narrower and the broader concept of a *monad*.

Thus Husserl can say at the end of his account that "at no point was the transcendental attitude, the attitude of the transcendental epochē, abandoned." What has been provided is a "'theory' of experiencing someone else, [a] 'theory' of experiencing others, [which] did not aim at being and was not at liberty to be anything but an explication of the sense, 'others,' as it arises from the constitutive productivity of that experiencing. . . ." [43] It was not "at liberty" to be anything more because the alter ego is simply another, though privileged, *cogitatum*, and even though he is not "of the world" in the strict sense his givenness is dependent on that of perception. *Fremderfahrung* is tied to the perceptual givenness of the other's body, and the alter ego is thus given, "not originaliter and in unqualifiedly

41. *Ibid.*, p. 126.
42. Cf. Toulemont, *L'Essence de la société selon Husserl*, p. 40; "La nature des deux réductions est différente: la première consiste en un changement d'attitude du sujet, la seconde est un rétrécissement de son champ de vision."
43. *CM*, p. 148.

[*schlichter*] apodictic evidence, but only in an evidence belonging to 'external' experience." [44] This is certainly incompatible with any notion of "proof" that others exist with a certainty comparable to that of one's own ego. In fact it is no proof at all. In this sense the alter ego is treated as any other object is treated in Husserl's philosophy, i.e., purely as "phenomenon." The being of the other subject is at issue only in the sense that the being of anything at all is at issue in phenomenology up to this point, namely, in the sense of his being-for-me. Husserl's theory seeks to show the experiential conditions under which the other exists for me as transcendental other.

In Husserl's "solution to the problems of solipsism," then, the alter ego is not posited *outside* my own experience; rather, he is brought *into* the sphere of my own experience through the broadening of the concept of experience and the concept of a monad. That is, Husserl shows *how*—i.e., through what form of experiences—the other is given to me as subject, as *cogitatum cogitans*. This places Husserl's project in the Fifth Meditation in a context wholly different from that of the usual problem of solipsism, a context dictated by the approach of Descartes' *Meditations*.

INTERSUBJECTIVE PHENOMENOLOGY

BUT ONCE he has "solved" the problem of solipsism in this way, Husserl does not regard his work as done. Rather, he makes use of his solution to add a completely new dimension to his phenomenology. The phenomenology of the other ego's givenness provides the basis for what Husserl calls "intersubjective phenomenology." [45] Let us consider the transition from one to the other. We noted that the intersubjective object, the transcendent object in the strong or "objective" sense, can be understood by analogy to the transcendent object in the weaker or "solipsistic" sense: just as the latter is given as a unity in relation to a multiplicity of my acts, so the intersubjective object is given as a unity in relation to a multiplicity comprising my act and that of another. This multiplicity, Husserl says, is fused in the *"functional community of one perception."* [46] Now,

44. *Ibid.*, p. 149.
45. *Ibid.*, p. 155.
46. *Ibid.*, p. 122.

one might ask, whose perception is this? A perception of my own, as Husserl had seen in the lectures on time-consciousness,[47] can be considered the functional unity of various temporal phases, not all of which are strictly presentations. Here the presented and the nonpresented are not simultaneous—the non-presented is not *appresented* but retained as just past.[48] But they form a "functional unity," because their status in consciousness is the *function* of a "meaning intention" which aims at "the whole [temporal] object," e.g., an enduring tone or even a melody. The perception as such, which is "relative" [49] to this whole object, whatever it may be, cannot be reduced to any of the particular acts of presentation that make it up, not even the one that is presently "having its turn." The perception which is constitutive of the object is an act that is *itself constituted* by the "living present" of each of its temporal phases.[50]

Returning to the "one perception" of which Husserl spoke in reference to the intersubjective object, it can be seen as likewise constituted by reference to the presentations that make it up. *For me* it is the functional unity of presentation and appresentation, and, to the extent that it is for me, it can be considered my act. The unified act is constituted by the other as well, with the difference that the content of presented and appresented are reversed. But from the point of view of *either* presentation— mine or the other's—it is the *same* act that is constituted. And, if we take the concept of sameness seriously here, the perception "as such," which corresponds to "the whole *intersubjective* object," can only be considered *our* perception. The perception is a constituted act that cannot be ascribed totally to either of us, but only to both of us, to the *we*. The establishment of the *we* in common perception is the simplest form of what Husserl calls the "communalization of monads": [51] when two subjects confront one another and stand in relation to the same objects, they form, to that extent, a rudimentary community that can itself be considered as performing an act (*cogitamus*) through

47. Husserliana X, p. 38 (*PITC*, pp. 60–61).
48. And, one might add, is given in "protention" as that which is just about to come.
49. Husserl speaks of "Relativierung," Husserliana X, p. 39 (*PITC*, p. 61).
50. Cf. *CM*, p. 134.
51. *Ibid.*, p. 120.

"its" diverse (and in this case simultaneous) presentations.[52]

For Husserl, this leads to a whole theory of experience, constitution, and the world; here, his point of departure is no longer individual consciousness but such a community at whatever level it may be found. The community now becomes the "zero member"[53] about which the objective world is oriented. From this point of view the community is a *"community of monads,* which we designate as *transcendental intersubjectivity."*[54] It is transcendental because it makes "transcendentally possible the being of a world,"[55] in this case the intersubjective world. As roughly sketched at the end of the *Cartesian Meditations,* beginning with § 56, Husserl's theory follows the general lines of the theory of constitution at the solipsistic level; i.e., it bases its divisions on the ontological distinctions among the formal and material regions, on the difference in analysis between the static and the genetic, etc. Parallel to the solipsistic level, it is necessary to provide a theory not only of the community's world but also of the community's own being-for-itself, that is, a theory of its givenness to itself. A community, in other words, like an ego, must be considered as self-constituting even as it constitutes its world.

Husserl does not spell out in great detail the paths his "intersubjective phenomenology" is to follow. Clearly, in spite of its many parallels to the theory of self- and world-constitution at the individual level, it cannot be a mere repetition of every detail with merely a "change of sign" or of attitude. While it is possible to talk of the *eidos* community in relation to the world, etc., it is also necessary to take account of the much greater complexity of the intersubjective problem. For one thing, any community is composed of individuals while the individual obviously is not. We have seen that the "presentations" united in a communalization (*Vergemeinschaftung*) can be simultaneous, which is not the case in an individual. Communities not only contain individuals but also encompass smaller communities and are parts of larger ones. Furthermore, the community itself

52. Cf. Husserliana IV, p. 191: "Wir sind in Beziehung auf eine gemeinsame Umwelt—wir sind in einem personalen Verband: das gehört zusammen."

53. *CM,* p. 134.

54. *Ibid.,* p. 130.

55. *Ibid.,* p. 129.

can be conceived as a monad, and the problem of *Fremderfahrung* can be seen to arise between communities—where it clearly must be solved in a way very different from, or at least more complex than, the theory of "appresentation." [56] Finally, communities dissolve and reconstitute themselves in a way not ascribable to the individual. In general, Husserl's intersubjective phenomenology does not follow the Hegelian path of considering the community as a kind of macroperson[57] and endowing it with a life of its own of which the individual is only an abstract moment. Any community can be treated as a concrete "subject" in a phenomenological analysis, but, as our previous exposition makes clear, it must be seen in its specificity as constituted by its members.

This might lead us to think that the intersubjective level, and the phenomenological analysis that goes with it, is of merely secondary importance for Husserl. On the contrary, in his view it complements the "solipsistic" dimension of phenomenology and is a significant requirement, as the original "objection of solipsism" suggested, if phenomenology is to be a full-fledged *transcendental* philosophy. " 'Solipsistically' reduced 'egology' " is only "the . . . first of the philosophical disciplines. . . . Then . . . would come intersubjective phenomenology, which is founded on that discipline. . . ." But priority in the order of inquiry does not imply priority in the order of being. Husserl even goes so far as to say that while solipsistic phenomenology is the intrinsically first (*die an sich erste*) discipline, "the intrinsically first being [*das an sich erste Sein*], the being that precedes and bears every worldly Objectivity, is transcendental intersubjectivity: the universe of monads, which effects its communion in various forms—[*das in verschiedenen Formen sich vergemeinschaftende All der Monaden*]." Announcing the problem in the Second Meditation, Husserl puts it this way:

Perhaps reduction to the transcendental ego only *seems* to entail a *permanently* solipsistic science; whereas the consequential elaboration of this science, in accordance with its own sense, leads over to a phenomenology of transcendental intersubjectivity and, by means of this, to a universal transcendental philosophy. As a matter of fact we shall see that, in a certain manner, a transcen-

56. *Ibid.*, pp. 134–35.
57. In spite of his use of the term "personalities of a higher order," *ibid.*, p. 132.

dental solipsism is only a subordinate stage philosophically; though, as such, it must first be delimited for purposes of method, in order that the problems of transcendental intersubjectivity, as problems belonging to a higher level, may be correctly stated and attacked.[58]

It is clear from these passages that what is referred to as the "phenomenology of transcendental intersubjectivity" is not the investigation that makes up the largest part of the Fifth Meditation—the theory of how (through what forms of *individual* experience) the alter ego is given to the *ego*—but rather the "intersubjective phenomenology" that takes transcendental intersubjectivity, instead of individual subjectivity, as the point of departure for a constitutive theory in relation to the world.

INTERSUBJECTIVITY AND GENETIC THEORY

BUT WHAT IS OF IMMEDIATE INTEREST for our particular problem is not so much intersubjective phenomenology itself as the implications of this theory (and of the theory of *Fremderfahrung* on which it is based) for the notion of *individual* consciousness. Husserl begins with a concept of individual consciousness in order to develop his theory of *Fremderfahrung*, but when he is finished, the original concept is considerably enriched, if not actually changed.

Consciousness has thus far been pictured as a life of acts and attitudes through which the world is given. It is the act conceived as the living present, with its horizons of retention and protention, which is "responsible" for the original or primary givenness of anything. But in the flow or stream of consciousness what is given is retained in nonactual form and finally sedimented as something that can be reawakened; thus the act through which it is given is also an act of acquisition. In fact such acquisition is for Husserl an essential characteristic of self-evidence: to the extent that true givenness is present, acquisition occurs. As something originally lived through, the given becomes an "abiding possession" to which I can "always return." [59] In the form of knowledge, beliefs, opinions, "habits,"

58. *Ibid.*, pp. 30–31.
59. *Ibid.*, p. 60.

such sedimented evidences form the larger background against which the present life of consciousness stands out.

The theory of *Fremderfahrung* now adds some refinements to this picture. Among the things that are given in the world are persons who are not mere objects in the world but other subjects as well. What does this mean for me, the individual consciousness? It means that the world, in the sense of the objective or transcendent, is what it is not only in relation to my actual and possible conscious life, but also in its existence "for all," for other possible simultaneous consciousnesses or monads. Even in the factual absence of others, this is the *sense* of the world as given. Now the *actual* encounter with other persons, as we have seen, establishes a more or less enduring "community" of subjects whose simultaneous acts "constitute" the objective world, or some part of it. Conceived as member of a "community of monads," each subject's "own world"—in the narrowest sense —is downgraded to the status of appearance in relation to reality in the broader, intersubjective sense.

What is important to remember about this theory is that it is in part a description of the constitution of the objective world and the community *for* the individual. That is, it is not from some removed "metaphysical" point of view that the individual's own world is thus "downgraded," but rather from *his own* point of view, insofar as he is and considers himself to be a member of the community. Husserl is not asserting that what is given to the individual *is* a "mere appearance" of reality; he is stating that the individual, self-constituted as belonging to a community, *considers* it to be such. The objective is precisely *meant as* being more than what is present to me in the strict sense. We quoted in the last section Husserl's remark that the meant always exceeds what is explicitly given; as the horizon of what is given, *das Mitgemeinte* is not something merely conjectured or imagined in addition to the given but rather belongs *with* the given, forms a continuum with it. With the introduction of genetic analysis *das Mitgemeinte* was related to the previously and the potentially given in my own stream of experience. Now, in the context of the community, *das Mitgemeinte* can be seen as that which, while not explicitly given to me, is meant by me *as* being given to my fellows. In the act through which others are given as fellow subjects, through which the world becomes *our* world, I perform a synthesis some of whose elements are not *mine* in the strict sense. One might put it this way: in order to make up or fill in the world, I take over from others what is lacking in my own direct experience. It is through such an act of "borrowing" that the world-for-us comes to exist for me. This act is, in Husserl's sense, the origin of its givenness.

Now such a case of givenness naturally has the same function within the flow of my own experience as those discovered in the context of phenomenological genesis. That is, by virtue of retention and sedimentation the act is one of acquisition. What is significant is that, in the social context, much of the content of what becomes acquired is thus traced not to an act of direct experience on my part but to one of "borrowing" or appropriating the insights of others. My own experience (in the narrow sense) must dovetail or form a continuum with what I take over from others; to the extent that it does not, conflict develops and my own experience is, up to a point, taken as standard. But it must be recognized that in the large areas where such conflict is absent, the world as it is for me—as it is represented in my beliefs, attitudes, "habits," etc.—owes its origin not to acts of direct intuition, but to what can only be called acts of *communication*.

Basically Husserl's whole theory of intersubjectivity is a theory of communication, as indeed any such theory must be. To encounter another person is not only to encounter an object but also to be offered indirect access to "another world." Such access is the act of communication, the forming of a community (*Vergemeinschaftung*) through which at the same time the "worlds" merge. Instead of another world—an impossibility in any strict sense—it is another perspective on *the* world which is communicated or made available. Such "communication" in Husserl's sense takes place prior to language and even prior to any explicit desire to express something to another. The basic community for Husserl, as outlined in the Fifth Meditation, is the simple spatial encounter of two persons involving, as it does, mutual and intersubjective perception. That is, each becomes for himself an object for the other, and their surroundings become, for each, the surroundings of both. Insofar as such an encounter takes place there is communication: I am confronted with the reality of a perspective on the surroundings which is not my own, and which, simply by being what it is for me, gives my own view itself the status of a mere perspective.

The other's perspective is only indirectly given; yet it is the surroundings for both of us (including the two of us) that make up the content of my experience and which are retained and sedimented.

This model serves as a basis for understanding communities and communication in the usual, more complex sense, even though it must be said that on the whole Husserl rather takes for granted the role played by language. A community or society of persons in the normal sense of these terms is simply a more enduring and complex version of the perceptual encounter discovered above. Again, what is essential is the common world, though the shared character of the physical environment may extend beyond the immediately perceived surroundings and the particular encounter to encompass a larger terrain with which the members of the community are familiar; or at another level, the common physical surroundings may be almost totally replaced by a common "world" of highly abstract objects and events, as in an international chess or mathematical society whose members need never see one another in order to sustain their community. It is easy to see that, at least factually, communication in the linguistic sense plays an important role at any level of society which is more complex and enduring than the mere perceptual encounter. In a late manuscript in which he is concerned with an ideal science like geometry as an activity of a community, Husserl himself seems to become convinced of the essential role of language, even written language.

This manuscript, which, as we noted, has come to bear the title "The Origin of Geometry," is important because it emphasizes the role of communicative "borrowing" at the linguistic level and places such borrowing in the context of the theory of phenomenological genesis. Calling into play his whole theory of intuition, sedimentation, and reactivation, Husserl returns to the notion, discussed in the previous chapter, that judgments as "finished products" are the deposit of a genetic process of insight and can be called into play without the revival of the original activity that produced them. Now, clearly, much of what goes on in the understanding of the spoken or written word is the appropriation, for one's own use, of the results of conscious activity without the corresponding activity itself. But such results can in turn become the elements of "a kind of activity, a thinking in terms of things that have been taken up merely receptively, passively, which deals with significations only passively understood and taken over. . . ." [60] The individual's life in the community, from childhood to maturity, Husserl says, is increasingly dominated by "the realm of things that are bound together and melt into one another associatively, where all meaning that arises is put together passively." [61] He gives as an example the superficial reading of the newspaper, in which we simply passively receive the news, appropriating what we read as our opinion. Sentences, propositions, like other cultural goods, take on the form of a tradition; as such "they claim, so to speak, to be sedimentations of a truth-meaning that can be made originally self-evident." [62]

What Husserl has in mind here can best be understood by reference to a passage already quoted from the *Cartesian Meditations*. "Every evidence 'sets up' or 'institutes' for me an *abiding possession*." But clearly, not every abiding possession is the result of a self-evidence or intuition on my part. "I can 'always return'," Husserl goes on to say in the passage, "to the itself-beheld actuality." Yet I also return to and use "actualities" that have not been "themselves beheld" by me but have been borrowed or appropriated in the senses described above. In other words, a large part of the "substratum of sedimented prominences which, as a horizon, accompan[y] every living present" [63] is, for the individual in the community, the result not of intuition but of communication. Yet it plays the role of and has precisely the same significance as that which is intuited, i.e., it makes up part of the "habitualities," "abiding possessions," "beliefs" to which I in fact return and which form the background of my present conscious life.

Husserl's aim in "The Origin of Geometry" is to reveal the role of such communicative appropriation in conscious life and show its unavoidability and importance for the existence of a science like geometry—the activity of a certain kind of community. At the same time he wishes to point out its dangers. After all, what is taken over merely passively is often a meaning that can by no means make good on its "claim" "to be the sedimentation[s] of a truth-meaning that can be made originally self-evident." Hence Husserl speaks of the "seduction of

60. *Crisis*, p. 361.
61. *Ibid.*
62. *Ibid.*, p. 367.
63. *FTL*, p. 319.

language" of which we are all victims to a greater or lesser degree. To be sure, when he points out the "dangers" of passive appropriation, as in the case of reading the newspaper, he is raising the distinction between the uncritical reception and the critical examination of what is encountered in the community. And it can be said that it is the characteristic of all responsible thinking, of which science is the exemplary case, that every claim is critically examined and tested before it is accepted.

Still, Husserl does not believe that the ultimate rigor of even the most exact of our sciences is secured by "critical thinking" in the usual sense of that term. The criticism of any particular claim within a given sphere, scientific or otherwise, involves invoking, in an uncritical way, the standards against which the claim in question is measured and the purposes it is supposed to serve. And these standards and purposes, no less than particular claims and beliefs, are often absorbed into one's conscious life by virtue of membership in a community. In the last chapter[64] we quoted Husserl's remarks in a late manuscript about *Zwecksetzung* and its function of marking out a "world" horizon of actualities and possibilities. Speaking of the overriding goal of such a project, Husserl writes that it "can be a goal that we have elected for ourselves as a life-vocation, to be the dominant one in our active life, or it can be one that we have somehow drifted into through our upbringing." [65] In *Ideas* II, at a much earlier period, Husserl also speaks of social subjectivity as setting goals for the individual.[66]

By now it should be clear that Husserl's theory of intersubjectivity adds a social dimension to every aspect of his notion of individual consciousness that we have encountered so far. As *transcendental* subjectivity, my consciousness stands in relation to a world which fully transcends it because it is a world-for-all, and not just for me. And by the same token I stand in relation to the "all," i.e., to other subjects with whom I enter into communities of greater or lesser scope and permanence. By virtue of such communalization (*Vergemeinschaftung*) with others, the particular context or nature of *my* world—the world as meant by me—is in part borrowed from others; and the "sedi-

64. Cf. p. 79 above.
65. *Crisis*, p. 379.
66. Husserliana IV, p. 197.

mented prominences" that form the background of my encounter with the world are in large measure the "deposits" not of original experiences but of communication. Now the self-constitution of the ego, as we saw in the last section, consists not only in the accumulation and unification of such experiences; the ego as self-constituted is also a unity of interests and goals. As we have just seen, Husserl holds that these longer-range characteristics of consciousness can also be viewed from a social perspective.

5 / Historical Reduction and the Critique of the Philosophical Tradition

IN CHAPTERS 3 and 4 we have dealt with developments in Husserl's phenomenological theory which, as we claim, motivate and make understandable the novel historical approach of the *Crisis* described in Chapter 2. In Chapter 3 we treated the transition from the static to the dynamic or genetic theory of consciousness; a theory that originated in the lectures on time-consciousness, was omitted, for purposes of simplicity, from the general program of phenomenology in the *Ideas,* and was fully integrated into that program only in the *Cartesian Meditations.* In this dynamic theory, the transcendental life of consciousness is revealed in its flowing, cumulative, and projective character, so that the *Erlebnis* or *act* (the original focus of phenomenological investigation) is placed against its temporal background of "sedimented prominences" and its "foreground" of anticipation. As we saw, it is not only the horizons of *das Mitgemeinte,* essential to the static analysis of the act, which receive a temporal interpretation; but the concept of attitude, so important to the static stage, is also grounded in the temporal concept of *Zwecksetzung.* The sense of the genetic analysis as a whole is summed up by Husserl when he says that "the ego constitutes himself for himself in, so to speak, the unity of a 'history.'"[1]

The concept of the historicity "so to speak" of conscious life was linked with the concept of history "proper" through the theory of intersubjectivity considered in Chapter 4. The first

1. *CM,* p. 75.

stage in this theory involved a return from the dynamic to the static, drawing upon the dynamic as an "instructive comparison" or analogy. The temporally spread "depresentation" in the flow of consciousness (in the form of recollection) was used to understand the simultaneous depresentation of *Fremderfahrung*. The analysis of the givenness of the alter ego through appresentation and "analogizing apprehension" is essentially a static horizon-analysis revealing the communicative or partially "borrowed" character of *individual* conscious experiences. If the social dimension of the individual's experience is then combined with the dynamic analysis of his conscious life, the full-fledged "historicity" of transcendental subjectivity comes to light: its cumulative and anticipatory character is, at least in part, of a social or intersubjective nature. Individual conscious life may be said to be essentially historical in the sense that every *Erlebnis* takes place against the background of, and is thus mediated by, a past which is both its own past and a social past. At the same time, the anticipating structure of consciousness, in the sense of *Zwecksetzung*, is also socially mediated.

How do these developments motivate the historical approach of the *Crisis*? We have asserted that the notion of historicity was already fully developed prior to its writing. But the full *implications* of this notion seem to become clear to Husserl only in the *Crisis* itself. What we shall try to show in this chapter is that these implications strike at the very heart of Husserl's philosophical enterprise because they concern his key methodological concept, that of the epochē. In particular, they affect the distinction already mentioned between the philosophical and the phenomenological epochē.[2]

THE IDEA OF HISTORICAL REDUCTION

As we remember from Chapter 2, the *Crisis* is distinguished from Husserl's earlier works by the fact that "historical and critical reflections" belong to the very business of phenomenology and are required for its establishment as "first philosophy." They are required by the fact that as philosophers we are "historical beings," that "we . . . not only have a spiritual heritage but have become what we are thoroughly and

2. Cf. Chap. 2, p. 63.

exclusively in a historical-spiritual manner." [3] We are now in a position to understand what Husserl means. We are historical beings because we are conscious beings: our conscious life consists in constituting itself "in the unity of a history," such that each intention stands out against the background of sedimented "abiding possessions" or *habitus*. This past, as we have seen, is a social past; whatever our particular historical situation, the background of present conscious life is at least partially derived from it. Because of the peculiar character of communal intentionality, this background of possessions consists, for the individual, not only of prior evidences but also of pseudo- or quasi-evidences which nevertheless "influence" or give form to his ongoing conscious life. Moreover, not only evidences, in the sense of beliefs, are social acquisitions: attitudes and goals, marking out the spheres into which conscious life directs itself and the activity it undertakes in those spheres, are, or can be, socially derived as well. Such is the fundamental *historicity* of conscious life.

We must emphasize again that this is a characteristic of consciousness conceived as *transcendental,* i.e., in its purely intentional relation to the world. To say that we are historical beings is not merely to say that we are *in* history, that we arrive on the scene and disappear at a certain point in objective historical time. Each of us indeed conceives of himself as such an empirical ego within the world. But Husserl is concerned here not with this or any other particular aspect of the transcendental ego's self-objectification in the natural attitude, but with a universal characteristic of its intentional conscious life. Being *in* history does not imply being historical in the transcendental sense described above, for even nonconscious beings are in history; nor does being transcendentally historical necessarily require that consciousness construe itself objectively as a being in history, since Husserl's thesis is that consciousness is historical in all its aspects, not just when objectifying itself. This is what we meant in Chapter 2 when we said that as philosophers we could be "historical beings" in one sense (i.e., as being objectively in history) without thereby having to engage in historical reflection in order to do philosophy. [4] It is only be-

3. *Crisis,* p. 71.
4. Cf. Chap. 2, p. 66.

cause we are historical beings in the sense of the historicity of consciousness that historical reflections are required.

But what, precisely, is the nature of this requirement? It derives from the application of the concept of historicity to philosophers in particular. As conscious beings we are "heirs of the past," whatever our beliefs, attitudes, and goals; and if we happen to be philosophers we are obviously "heirs of the past in respect to the goals which the word 'philosophy' indicates, in terms of concepts, problems and methods." [5] Clearly, the philosopher is no less historical than anyone else. When, as a natural subject living in the social world, he turns to and engages in something called "philosophy," he is not inventing it for himself but is taking up something which existed in his society before he came along. Now philosophy exists in the social world as a more or less clearly defined set of works. These works belong to culture as a whole, and are part of the meaning of the term "philosophy" for any member of society; they form part of the definition of the term without which he could not learn what it means. But the incipient philosopher, one who considers the task seriously enough to take it up himself, will not be content with this generally accepted definition of philosophy: it is only natural that he should approach the task by reading or otherwise learning about the work of philosophers. It is thus that, both implicitly and explicitly, he is "heir to the past" in his peculiar capacity as philosopher.

There are two things to be noted about this train of thought. The first is that Husserl is not concerned with the non- or extra-philosophical motives of natural life which may determine that one becomes a philosopher rather than, say, a tailor or a doctor. Whatever the nature or importance of these motivations, Husserl is concerned rather with philosophy itself as a pregiven set of motivations and with the presuppositions *it* involves as such. Whatever may lead one to philosophy, it is itself a socially given "task" which exists primarily in the form of certain "problems" to be solved. This leads us to the second point. The peculiar historicity of the philosopher is not his simple acceptance of and self-identification with the philosophers he reads. For most, taking up philosophy does not mean simply learning the "truth" that someone else has written. Such is often

5. *Crisis,* p. 17.

the attitude of one who is not himself engaged in philosophy, who does not adopt the task as his own. It is frequently one's very dissatisfaction with traditional doctrines which constitutes one's assumption of the philosophical motivation. It is the very *task* of philosophy that Husserl has in mind; and its adoption may even involve a conscious, total rejection of the entire philosophical tradition. But even such a philosopher, Husserl is saying, is "heir to the past" in accepting the *problems* which his predecessors, in his view, have failed to solve. Yet his awareness of his indebtedness to the past rarely penetrates to this level; his acknowledged relation to the past consists in his rejection, or even his eventual critical acceptance, of what he finds there. It is the level of the *unacknowledged* heritage which interests Husserl at this point and which constitutes the peculiar historicity of the philosophically engaged consciousness.

Needless to say, the idea of the unacknowledged heritage of the individual in society is not new. It is the essential message of the "historical consciousness" which reached its peak in the late nineteenth century and was best articulated philosophically in the work of Dilthey. Now Husserl had always respected Dilthey, but it must be emphasized that he arrives at the articulation of the above view of historicity not simply by taking it over from that philosopher but because his own theory of transcendental consciousness now requires it. In fact, Husserl's respect for Dilthey was most often expressed in connection with the latter's attempt to reform psychology;[6] it was Dilthey's "historicization" of the task of philosophy, on the other hand, which Husserl had most emphatically rejected in "Philosophy as Rigorous Science." In this polemic against "historicism and *Weltanschauungsphilosophie*," he was willing to accept the *fact* that the philosophical systems of the past contradict one another and that philosophers have often served the finite aim of developing a *Weltanschauung* rather than the infinite goal of science. Furthermore, even the strict sciences that already exist are "cultural formations" whose "intellectual content is definitely motivated under given historical circumstances."[7] But pointing this out is a matter of empirical history and has nothing to do with the assumption of the task of science or of philosophy itself. Hus-

6. Husserliana IX, pp. 3 ff.
7. *PRS,* p. 124. I have occasionally made some slight changes in Lauer's translation.

serl's argument culminates in the statement quoted in Chapter 2: *"The impulse to research must proceed not from philosophies but from the things [von den Sachen] and from the problems . . ."* [8] To be sure, we somehow become aware of what the *"Sachen"* and the "problems" of philosophy are, but to busy ourselves with the empirical question of how this awareness comes about would only divert us from the pursuit of the *Sachen* and the solving of the problems. "Of course, we need history too," but only as a source of "inspiration" for the undertaking.[9] Also, the philosopher can turn to history as a *theme* of investigation, for he must deal with the problem of the "spirit" (*Geist*), and indeed that of the "common [or communal] spirit" (*Gemeingeist*), as well as that of nature.[10] But here there is no question of historical questions affecting the very method of philosophy in approaching these or any other problems.

Yet this is apparently precisely what is proposed in the *Crisis* under the title of "historical and critical reflections." Not that the skeptical conclusions of historicism are drawn. But it is obvious that, given the historicity of all consciousness and hence of that of the incipient philosopher, his relation to the past becomes much more problematic than it was originally thought to be. When he proposes the "philosophical epochē" in the *Ideas*, Husserl refers to the "doctrinal content" of all preexisting philosophy and is obviously thinking of the philosopher's acknowledged identification with and acceptance of a particular doctrine or doctrines. And this presents no special problem, since what is recognized as accepted can just as easily be bracketed. This is why there is such an immense difference between the "philosophical epochē" and the "phenomenological epochē" which "shapes philosophy itself as a method." [11] For the *Vorurteile* or "natural prejudices" set aside by the latter epochē are initially *unacknowledged,* i.e., *as* prejudices or *Vor-urteile,* and the whole laborious effort of philosophy, which runs against the very current of natural conscious life, is precisely to bring them to recognition as such.

But now, if one's relation to past philosophy also contains such an initially unacknowledged level of prejudices, and if

8. *Ibid.,* p. 146.
9. *Ibid.*
10. *Ibid.,* p. 129.
11. Husserliana III, p. 40 n. (This note is not included in the English translation.)

such a level can involve not only "doctrinal content" but even the very task of philosophy, the very conception of the problems to be solved, then the philosophical epochē becomes a much more serious affair. Not that the distinction between "natural prejudices" and "historical prejudices" is thereby undone, for the former presumably belong to the essence of consciousness (they are "natural" to it) while the latter derive from a particular historical situation. To be sure, it is essential to consciousness that it be embedded in *some* historical situation, but the particular set of prejudices belonging to any one philosopher could differ widely from those of another, while the natural prejudices would be the same for any instance of consciousness. It is the particular prejudices of the philosopher that Husserl has in mind in the philosophical epochē, and these are now seen as lying hidden and unacknowledged; they have to be dredged up and brought to light. They are *Selbstverständlichkeiten,* they are "taken for granted." In this sense they occupy the same status in phenomenological endeavor as the natural prejudices.

Granted the newly problematic character of the philosophical epochē, how is it to be accomplished? Perhaps it will suffice, now that we have become aware of the hiddenness of our historically derived prejudices, simply to be more attentive to them, more resolute in not allowing them to affect our philosophical thinking. But what do we mean by "them"? How do we find out what, in particular, they are? Here it is wise to remember a characteristic of the phenomenological reduction emphasized in Chapter 1. This reduction is not, as we saw, simply the overthrow of all natural prejudices or *Selbstverständlichkeiten* so that one can proceed from there. In a sense there is nowhere else to proceed, because the essence of the reduction is the very discovery of that which is overthrown. The natural attitude itself has to be "discovered" in order to be overthrown; or the overthrow *is* the discovery. Hence the peculiar relationship between the natural attitude and its suspension: since the natural attitude is really the subject matter of phenomenology, it must be relived at the same time it is being overthrown-discovered. The result is what Husserl describes as a "splitting of the self" and a pattern of inquiry that involves a zigzag movement between the two.[12] Is something similar possible, or even required, in regard to those prejudices which are "historical" rather than "natural"?

12. *CM,* p. 35.

To be sure, we must not forget that we still have an important distinction between the two types of prejudice, in spite of their similarities. The one is "accidental" and the other "essential" to consciousness; if we maintain the relation set forth in the *Ideas* between philosophical and phenomenological epochēs, the two types are very different in terms of philosophical significance. While phenomenology does not set aside natural prejudices in order to proceed somewhere else, this is the case with the historical prejudices: we set *them* aside in order to proceed to the natural ones. Whereas the natural prejudices do constitute, in a sense, the subject matter of phenomenology, and whereas their discovery and description constitute its aim, this is perhaps not the case with the historical ones.

Nevertheless, the similarity between historical and natural prejudices, their similar role in the life of consciousness, dictates a similar procedure. Whatever is to be done once they are brought to light, their discovery is now recognized as essential to the phenomenological program. They have to be discovered because they are not immediately recognized; their very distinguishing character is their *Selbstverständlichkeit,* their being taken for granted. Now we recall the characterization of the phenomenological reduction as the explicit, self-conscious, and universalized practice of the phenomenological epochē. Is there a similar, self-conscious practice of the philosophical epochē which will raise it to the level of method? What suggests itself, here, by analogy to the phenomenological reduction, is a reliving of our philosophical prejudices, a repetition of the philosophical *Selbstverständlichkeiten* under which we turn to philosophy in the first place. Of course, such a repetition is not a *mere* repetition: for it is undertaken under the explicit guidance of the epochē. What is relived is relived for the purposes of its discovery-overthrow. Just as the phenomenological epochē is explicitly practiced in the form of a method called phenomenological reduction, so the philosophical epochē must be systematized and universalized to become a *philosophical* reduction, or what might better be called a *historical* reduction.

Though Husserl nowhere uses this term in the *Crisis*,[13] this is, we maintain, precisely what he has in mind in that work and

13. Gerhard Funke uses the term, also in connection with the *Crisis* but in a different sense, in *Phänomenologie—Metaphysik oder Methode?* (Bonn: H. Bouvier, 1966), pp. 149–50.

is the initial key to his historical procedure. Husserl says of that procedure:

> This manner of clarifying history by inquiring back into the primal establishment of the goals . . . is to make vital again, in its concealed historical meaning, the sedimented conceptual system which, as taken for granted, serves as the ground of [the philosopher's] private and nonhistorical work. . . . If he is to be one who thinks for himself [*Selbstdenker*], an autonomous philosopher with the will to liberate himself from all prejudices, he must have the insight that all the things he takes for granted *are* prejudices, that all prejudices are obscurities arising out of a sedimentation of tradition . . .[14]

Elsewhere he writes:

> There is no doubt . . . that we must engross ourselves in historical considerations if we are to be able to understand ourselves as philosophers and understand what philosophy is to become through us. It is no longer sufficient to grasp . . . at certain working problems we have run up against in our naïve development, to treat of them with our working partners, with those who, in the same course of a living tradition, have run up against the same problems.[15]

This is why even the "theory of knowledge" has to become a "peculiarly historical task," as Husserl says in "The Origin of Geometry," and why the failure to see this is "precisely what we object to in the past." [16] It is not enough simply to proceed "naïvely" to the *Sachen* and *Probleme* of philosophy as we find them in our own present; rather, as we have put it elsewhere, the *history* of those *Sachen* and *Probleme,* their very *Selbstverständlichkeit* as part of the tradition, is now seen to count preeminently among the very *Sachen* to which philosophy must turn.[17]

And this is indeed remarkable: for it seems to demand of the philosopher, as an essential part of his method, a serious consideration of his particular historical time and place, a consideration previously declared irrelevant to phenomenology by the *eidetic* reduction. Under that reduction, facts and particular

14. *Crisis*, pp. 71–72.
15. *Ibid.*, pp. 391–92.
16. *Ibid.*, p. 370.
17. *Ibid.*, p. xxxii.

events, even and especially those revealed in transcendental reflection, serve only as examples of the patterns which are ultimately sought. Now, by contrast, facts and events become important in their own right. To be sure, we have argued that the very requirement of "historical reduction" is suggested to Husserl by what is indeed a general or eidetic theory of the historicity of consciousness as such, developed in the years prior to the writing of the *Crisis*. Certain texts of the late period form a kind of transition by applying the notion of historicity to scientific consciousness, again in the form of a general theory: It might be thought that consciousness is historical only in those spheres generally termed cultural (religion, mores, values, etc.), whereas the scientist, while he is objectively *in* history, does not exhibit the sort of historicity associated with these spheres. On the contrary, says Husserl, engagement in a scientific undertaking is also historical in the sense that certain pregiven tasks are taken up and the work of one's predecessors is presupposed. The elucidation of the historicity of science in general, as shown in the example of one type of scientific inquiry, is one aspect of "The Origin of Geometry." [18]

But when this insight is applied to philosophy in particular, and when it is a question not of talking about philosophy but of doing it, it is no longer a general theory that is required. For, as we have seen, the awareness of the prejudice-laden character of the scientific and hence the philosophical endeavor affects the method of philosophy itself, insofar as its task is to liberate itself from precisely whatever prejudices it has. It becomes a matter of method, and hence of a special sort of reduction, because, as we have seen, it is not enough simply to admit that as philosophers we have certain prejudices and then to declare them null and void. For we must discover what they are. Their existence may be suggested by a general theory, but this is only a vague presentiment if those prejudices are not actually laid bare. Hence, when explaining the need for historical reflections in order to obtain clarity on the task of philosophy, Husserl says that we can obtain such clarity "not through the critique of some present or handed-down system, of some scientific or prescientific '*Weltanschauung*' (which might as well be Chinese, in the end)"—that is, not through the study of just *any* history—"but. only through a critical understanding of the total unity of history

18. Husserliana VI, pp. 495–96.

—*our* history." [19] It is no longer the case that any example will serve as well as any other, as in the search for essences. The historical reduction, unlike the phenomenological reduction, is not and cannot be coupled with an eidetic reduction. In order to penetrate to the previously unacknowledged historical prejudices that determine the *Sachen* and *Probleme* of philosophy, we must turn not to the essence of history generally, or the essence of consciousness, but to the particular tradition of which we are a part.

THE CRITIQUE OF THE TRADITION: OBJECTIVISM

AND THIS IS EXACTLY what Husserl proceeds to do in the *Crisis*. After his brief introduction, he embarks upon what he calls the "Clarification of the Origin of the Modern Opposition between Physicalistic Objectivism and Transcendental Subjectivism." [20] His discussion of modern philosophy constitutes a "historical reduction" because it is, above all, as he says, an "inquiry back [*Rückfrage*] into the primal establishment of the *goals*" of modern philosophy, not simply a rehearsal of the "doctrinal content" of certain theories. It tries to show in detail how we are "heirs to the past in respect to the goals which the word 'philosophy' indicates, in terms of concepts, problems, and methods." It is an attempt to relive the tradition of which we are a part for the purpose of liberating us from the prejudices that are inherent in that tradition. There is no doubt that for Husserl this *Rückfrage*, at least in part, accomplishes such a liberation, for ultimately it exhibits the hidden, historical prejudices attaching to one of philosophy's most fundamental *problems*, the problem of the *world*. Through his "historical and critical reflections," Husserl discovers how this problem originated and was handed down, how philosophers addressed themselves to solving it and never to questioning it as a problem. By discovering it *as* a problem, Husserl is able to discover that it was falsely cast and is able to arrive at a new conception of the problem under the rubric of the life-world. But the relation of the "historical reduction" to Husserl's own endeavor, its significance for phenomenological procedure, is even more fundamental and striking

19. *Crisis*, p. 71.
20. *Ibid.*, p. 20.

than this preliminary sketch would indicate. In order to see this, it is necessary to follow the path of Husserl's "historical and critical reflection."

Not surprisingly, Husserl traces the origin of modern philosophical problems to the rise of modern natural science, whose decisive feature is its *mathematical* character. It is primarily to Galileo that we owe the transformation of the science of nature into a mathematical science, and as soon as this science "begins to move toward successful realization, the idea of philosophy in general (as the science of the universe, of all that is) is transformed." [21] In order to understand this transformation of the idea of philosophy, then, we must turn first to what made it possible: Galileo's "mathematization of nature."

Husserl asks: *"What is the meaning of this mathematization of nature?"* and he rephrases the question as: "How do we reconstruct the train of thought which motivated it?" [22] Then he begins his attempt to relive the modern tradition in terms of its underlying goals and problems. His answer is prefigured in the next paragraph.

"Prescientifically, in everyday sense-experience, the world is given in a subjectively relative way. Each of us has his own appearances," Husserl says, and he points out that these may be at variance with one another, a fact with which we are all familiar. He goes on:

> But we do not think that, because of this, there are many worlds. Necessarily, we believe in *the* world whose things only appear to us differently but are the same. [Now] have we nothing more than the empty, necessary idea of things which exist objectively in themselves? Is there not, in the appearances themselves, a content we must ascribe to true nature? Surely this includes everything which pure geometry, and in general the mathematics of the pure form of space-time, teaches us, with the self-evidence of absolute, universal validity, about the pure shapes it can construct *idealiter* —and here I am describing, without taking a position, what was "obvious" to Galileo and motivated his thinking. [23]

Here Husserl has described in a few words both the brilliant insight upon which modern science rests and the key to the various attempts at its *philosophical* interpretation. Galileo

21. *Ibid.*, p. 23.
22. *Ibid.*
23. *Ibid.*, pp. 23–24.

inherits "pure geometry" from the Greeks as a science which affords exact, intersubjectively valid knowledge for its domain of objects. In our encounters with the real world we have the problem of the subjective relativity of what appears, and it is the task of a science of the world to overcome this relativity. Now pure geometry is not unrelated to the world; in fact, as a science it can be seen as originally arising out of the practical needs of accurately surveying land and the like, and its theoretical formulation has always found application back to the real world. Galileo sees that this is because the real world as it presents itself to us in experience contains, somehow embedded in it, examples of what is dealt with so successfully in geometry. Galileo's proposal is that exact and intersubjectively valid knowledge of the real world can be attained by the method of treating *everything about this world* as an example of a geometrical object or relationship. If every physical shape, trajectory, vibration, etc., is seen, after being measured as accurately as possible, as a version of a pure geometrical shape, geometrical statements about the properties and relationships among these pure shapes will turn out to provide us with information about nature which shares in the exactness and universality of pure geometry. "Galileo said to himself: Wherever such a methodology is developed, there we have also overcome the relativity of subjective interpretations, which is, after all, essential to the empirically intuited world." [24] This leaves untouched, of course, certain properties which do not seem directly measurable in geometrical terms: color, warmth, weight, tone, smell, etc. Galileo notes, however, that changes in some of these properties correspond exactly to measurable changes in geometrical properties—even the Greeks had known of the relationship between the pitch of a tone emitted by a vibrating string and its length, thickness, and tension. In his boldest move of all, Galileo proposes to treat all such "secondary qualities," as they were later called, exclusively in terms of their measurable geometrical correlates with the idea that *all* will be thereby accounted for.

Thus is accomplished, according to Husserl, the mathematization of nature, and such is the origin of mathematical physics. It can be broken down into two steps, actually: Galileo's *geometrization* of nature, and the *arithmetization* of geometry

24. *Ibid.*, p. 29.

accomplished by Descartes and Leibniz. Nature becomes a mathematical manifold, and mathematical techniques provide the key to its inner workings. In mathematics we have access to an infinite domain, and if nature is correlated with that domain we have access not only to what lies beyond the scope of our immediate experience, but also to everything that could *ever* be experienced in nature, i.e., to nature as an infinite domain.

Husserl's interest is not directly in the method of science itself, but in the manner in which, through it, the task of *philosophy* was defined. The philosophical interpretation of Galileo's mathematization, in Husserl's view, becomes involved in a series of equivocations. In order to overcome the vagueness and relativity of ordinary experience, science performs a set of abstractions and interpretations upon the world as it originally presents itself. First it focuses upon the shape-aspect of the world, to the exclusion of so-called secondary qualities; then it interprets these shapes as pure geometrical shapes in order to deal with them in geometrical terms. But it forgets that its first move is an abstraction *from* something and its second an interpretation *of* something. Its first move is an abstraction because, no matter how successful we may be in correlating secondary with primary qualities, the world we are trying to explain still presents itself to us as having both kinds of properties, one of which we systematically ignore or declare "merely subjective." Its second move is an interpretation because, in order to treat the spatial relationships of the world with geometrical exactness, it must consider these relationships as the ideal ones with which pure geometry deals, whereas the real shape-aspect of the world, no matter how accurately measured, can never present us with anything but approximations to these ideal relationships.

In forgetting these moves, science forgets what remains at the basis of its activity. It forgets that *from* which it abstracts and *of* which it is the interpretation, the world of objects possessing both primary and secondary qualities, the world of spatial aspects belonging to vague and approximate types rather than a world describable in geometrical-ideal terms. Husserl calls this the "world of sense-experience," [25] the "intuitively given surrounding world [*Umwelt*]," [26] and, finally, the "prescientific

25. *Ibid.*, p. 24.
26. *Ibid.*, p. 25.

life-world." [27] This life-world is "the forgotten meaning-fundament of natural science." [28]

Overlooking the abstractive and idealizing role of scientific
thought, the philosophical interpretation comes up with an
ontological claim: *to be is to be measurable* in ideal terms as a
geometrically determined configuration. Thus it happens, says
Husserl, "that we take for *true being* what is actually a *method*." [29]
Mathematical science is a method which considers the world
as if it were exclusively a manifold of idealized shape-occur-
ences; the ontological interpretation simply states that it *is* such
a manifold. With this, the modern philosophical concept of
being and of the world is established, and any problems which
arise—problems of the scope of the world, of its beginning and
end, of its ultimate ground or cause, of man's place in it, and
above all of his knowledge of it—are henceforth determined as
problems by the character of this concept.

It is to be noted that by distinguishing between the fundamental method of science and its philosophical interpretation,
Husserl is not simply distinguishing between two groups of men,
the original scientific practitioners and their philosophical heirs.
It is well known that the distinction between philosophy and
science was not a sharp one in the early modern period, and that
the men we call philosophers were also practicing and theorizing
scientists. Furthermore, Galileo doubtless considered himself a
philosopher and would probably not have recognized the Husserlian distinction between his methodological "proposal" and an
ontological claim.[30] But Husserl is convinced that there is such a
distinction to be made, and this reveals something about the
character of his historical reflections, namely, the fact that they
are critical as well. Or, as we put it before, the attempt to relive
the tradition is conducted under the guidance of the epochē,
which is meant to uncover the *hidden* presuppositions of whatever "doctrinal content" may emerge. It is a matter not of
consulting documents and discovering what philosophers and
scientists thought they were doing, but of striking "through the
crust of the externalized 'historical facts' of philosophical history,
interrogating, exhibiting, and testing their inner meaning and

27. *Ibid.*, p. 43.
28. *Ibid.*, p. 48.
29. *Ibid.*, p. 51.
30. *Ibid.*, p. 39.

hidden teleology." [31] The point is "to understand past thinkers in a way that they could never have understood themselves." [32]

We have just pointed out that the ontological interpretation of Galileo's concept determines the problems of subsequent philosophical inquiry. But the Galilean concept was itself interrogated by Husserl with reference to the problem it was meant to solve. Its guiding problem was that of arriving at knowledge about the real world which is comparable in its exactness, universality, and intersubjective agreement to the knowledge obtained in pure mathematics. But this problem is surreptitiously confused with another problem—coming to know the real world in its true nature, coming in contact with "true being"—and the solution to the first problem is taken for the solution to the second. Husserl asks whether what we learn about the world through mathematical science is simply to be identified with the "true being" of that world and even whether such knowledge is, strictly speaking, about that world at all. By distinguishing between the two problems, Husserl has not yet provided an answer to these questions, but he has made it possible for them to be posed at all. At the same time he has revealed the "shifts and concealments of meaning" [33] through which the problems of one generation, and their solutions, determine the problems of the next.

The ontological interpretation of the Galilean method—to be is to be measurable—gives rise to a course of philosophical developments whose motivation can be traced, i.e., which can be interrogated in terms of the problems to which they are addressed. In an understandable sequence, modern philosophy proceeds from the mathematical realism of the rationalists to the subjectivism, and ultimately the skepticism, of the empiricists. For rationalism, the scientific method is treated as a kind of instrument, like the microscope, which allows us to *see* the world as it really is, which pulls back the curtain of appearances and puts us into contact with reality. Empiricism, also accepting the fundamental Galilean conception of the nature of the real, makes the point that all we ever *see* is the causal effect of the real world upon the mind. Then it raises the ultimately insoluble question of whether what we *see* accurately informs us about

31. *Ibid.*, p. 18.
32. *Ibid.*, p. 73.
33. *Ibid.*, p. 58.

what *is*—a question raised briefly, but supposedly quickly solved, by Descartes. Refusing to accept Descartes' too-hasty solution, the empiricists lower the curtain of appearance again, apparently for good.

Now, most of Husserl's critical reflection on this development is hardly new or unexpected. He shows the relation between the ontological interpretation of Galileo's "proposal" and the rise of psychophysical dualism. If the true being of the world is characterized *more geometrico* by depriving it of the "merely subjective," so that it constitutes a self-enclosed, homogeneous sphere of mathematically determined entities, it has to be recognized that what has been separated off, the merely subjective "appearances," are not nonbeing but constitute a sphere of being in their own right (§ 10). Dualism is then characterized by Husserl as responsible for the incomprehensibility of the problems of reason (§ 11). The psychic sphere, though conceived as nonspatial, is nevertheless considered as analogous to the physical sphere and susceptible of a similar treatment. Its relation to the physical realm is one either of causal derivation or of strict parallelism or harmony. When the relation of harmony is skeptically challenged, only the possibility of causal relation is left, a relation that is at best external and accidental. As soon as it is conceived as a self-enclosed realm of causally interrelated events, with no *essential* reference to anything transcending it, subjectivity itself becomes incomprehensible, along with the problem of knowledge, because that reference was precisely what was to be accounted for. Husserl's meaning is clear: without the insight into the essential intentionality of consciousness, no solution to the problem of knowledge is forthcoming. And as long as the sphere of subjectivity is conceived by analogy to that of nature, this insight is made impossible. Again a hidden "shift of meaning" has been revealed: a method that is perfectly appropriate to an idealized (geometrized) nature is taken as the method for arriving at knowledge of anything whatever, including the subjective sphere, and this theoretical prejudice distorts our view of the subjective, causes us to ignore its true nature in favor of a false interpretation.

So far, it might be objected, Husserl's historical-critical reflections are disappointing at best. They seem to add up to a supplement that is not even very valuable, let alone essential, to the phenomenological method, and can thus hardly be described as constituting a special and necessary "reduction." For, after all, these same criticisms of the modern tradition are found scattered throughout Husserl's writings, where, as we have claimed, they are not regarded as essential to phenomenological method. And if the concept of intentionality is all that emerges from this historical critique, then the latter is hardly necessary for Husserl's method: this concept had been arrived at before by purely nonhistorical means, i.e., simply by reflecting on consciousness. Or perhaps, contrary to what we have said, the historical reflections were somehow necessary to what Husserl was doing all along, and his own claim to go directly to the *Sachen* was in fact mediated by history. If such is the case, the *Crisis* hardly exhibits the novelty we have claimed for it.

Now it may very well be that Husserl's earlier theories were in fact facilitated by his critiques of other philosophers, but this does not count against the novelty of the *Crisis*. For Husserl's constant reference to the role of historical reflections, from which we have drawn the concept of the "historical reduction," reveals that he is now *conscious* of the necessity of this historical mediation and practices it explicitly, which was certainly not the case before. Furthermore, as we have seen, the *Crisis* follows a pattern of "depth analysis"—its search for hidden motivations in terms of underlying problems to be solved—that is more than a mere critique of this or that doctrine. The whole modern tradition is interrogated with a view to finding a unity of motivations running through it.

But most important, the historical reflections of the *Crisis* amount to more than a historical justification *post hoc* of theories Husserl already held. Their result is a questioning of his own procedure and his own theory, which does not directly emerge from the critique of "physicalistic objectivism" which we have followed up to now, but derives from the fact that this critique is tied to an equally penetrating account of what Husserl sees as the other dominant strand in the modern tradition, "transcendental subjectivism." This account centers not on Descartes, Spinoza, Leibniz, and Locke, who could be recognized in our discussions up to now, but on Descartes, Hume, and Kant.

THE CRITIQUE OF THE TRADITION: TRANSCENDENTAL SUBJECTIVISM

DESCARTES BELONGS to both groups of philosophers because for Husserl he has a double significance in modern philosophical history: he is "the primal founder not only of the modern idea of objectivistic rationalism but also of the transcendental motif which explodes it." [34] The genuine opposition in modern philosophy is not rationalism versus empiricism but objectivism (which includes both rationalism and empiricism) versus transcendentalism. Transcendental philosophy, in the broad sense in which Husserl uses this term, goes back not merely to Kant but to Descartes, at least in the form of a preliminary sketch. For it was he, in his search for the grounds for our knowledge of the objective world, who inaugurated the idea of a *radical reflection,* an explicit and universal examination of the entire life of consciousness, under suspension of all preconceived ideas as to its relation to the world. According to the basic conception of Descartes' epochē, consciousness is not conceived as a part of the world, as in natural reflection; the status of the world, even its very existence, and thus the question of the mind's relation to it, are left undecided. Husserl even attributes to Descartes an unrecognized and undeveloped concept of the intentionality of consciousness[35] and possibly even a correlative concept of the intentional object or *cogitatum qua cogitatum.*[36]

To be sure, Descartes did not appreciate the significance of the possibility contained in his fundamental work. Formulated as a method of systematic doubt, the radical reflection of the first two *Meditations* was conceived as merely provisional, and the point was not to develop it as a philosophical tool in its own right but to get beyond it. Descartes' aim was not to understand objectivity from the subjective point of view, i.e., to provide it with a transcendental grounding, but to produce an objective justification for the claims of mathematical science to put us in contact with the real world. Understandably, such a justification could not be found in the subjective sphere itself and had to be sought in the acceptance of a transcendent God as guarantee of objective truth. This guarantee, taken for granted by subsequent rationalists, was thought to have restored the epistemological security that had been briefly uprooted by Descartes' methodical doubt. But such security was Descartes' goal to begin with, says Husserl, and "his haste to ground objectivism and the

34. *Ibid.,* p. 73.
35. *Ibid.,* pp. 82–83.
36. *Ibid.,* pp. 77–78.

exact sciences" [37] caused him to "let slip away the great discovery he had in his hands," [38] the idea of a transcendental critique of objective knowledge. In the end Descartes' "obtrusive interest in objectivism" [39] determines his whole procedure, and the intentionality of consciousness is ignored in favor of a psychological interpretation of it as analogous to the natural world and as causally related to it. In this way he became the predecessor of Locke's "physics of the mind" and of most modern psychology.

Hume demonstrated the ultimate futility of the quest for the sort of objective justification sought by Descartes, and objectivism was thereby *"shaken* to the foundations." [40] But it was Kant who turned this apparent "failure" of philosophy to positive advantage. He did this, according to Husserl, precisely by restoring to a place of central significance that radical reflection which Descartes had considered only provisional.[41] The objectivity of knowledge is given not an objective but a subjective grounding, through an examination of the forms of thought in which it announces and establishes itself. Far from a failure of philosophy, such a grounding is the only genuine grounding our knowledge can receive. Philosophy is no longer conceived as an objective science, on the same footing as the positive sciences but simply more comprehensive; henceforth objective science and philosophy are separated, and the latter reflects upon the former as subjective accomplishment.[42] The world is now understood *qua cogitatum:* Kant's "is a philosophy which, in opposition to prescientific and scientific objectivism, goes back to knowing subjectivity as the primal locus of objective formations of sense and ontic validities, undertakes to understand the existing world as a structure of sense and validity, and in this way seeks to set in motion an essentially new type of scientific attitude and a new type of philosophy." [43] This new type of philosophy is nothing other than transcendental philosophy, no longer merely sketched and intimated, as in Descartes, but rather seriously attempted as "a truly universal transcendental philosophy meant to be a

37. *Ibid.*, p. 82.
38. *Ibid.*, p. 75.
39. *Ibid.*, p. 81.
40. *Ibid.*, p. 90.
41. *Ibid.*, p. 95.
42. *Ibid.*
43. *Ibid.*, p. 99.

rigorous science in a sense of scientific rigor which has only now been discovered and which is the only genuine sense." [44]

Even at this stage Husserl's historical interpretation is not new. He had always given Kant credit for inaugurating transcendental critique not merely *faute de mieux* but as the central task of philosophy. And at the same time Husserl had been critical of Kant on many points, some of which are mentioned in the *Crisis* exposition. But now Husserl enters upon a critique of Kant which is substantially new and which, above all, reveals its indebtedness to the whole historical approach of the *Crisis*. For now, as he proceeds to the third part of the work, Husserl criticizes Kant not so much for his emphasis on categories to the neglect of subjective activity (a critique connected with Husserl's preference for the discarded first-edition version of the "transcendental deduction"); not so much for his "psychologism of faculties" or for his concept of the thing-in-itself; not so much for his regressive or deductive rather than intuitive procedure, all of which had been central to his Kant-critique before; but rather for the Kantian concept of the objective *world* that is in need of a transcendental grounding. This turns out to be a much more decisive critique and, what is most important, one which affects not only Kant but Husserl himself. His new Kant-critique opens with a section entitled "Kant's unexpressed 'presupposition': the surrounding world of life, taken for granted as valid." [45]

The link between Husserl's new Kant-critique and his foregoing historical reflections can be easily traced. Kant is credited with conceiving of the idea of a transcendental grounding after recognizing the futility and absurdity of the realists' demand for objective grounding. The objectivity of the objective world must be understood *through* subjectivity, not independently of it. But what is the *nature* of that objective world that is susceptible of and requires such a grounding? What marks Kant's adherence to the *Selbstverständlichkeiten* of the tradition is that this world is conceived in exactly the same terms as it was by the realists, even though it is subjected to a different treatment and seen under a new attitude. That is, it is the mathematized world of the natural scientist which constitutes Kant's problem. For Kant, what needs to be understood transcendentally, and *all* that needs to be understood, is the givenness of the world as interpreted

44. *Ibid.*
45. *Ibid.*, p. 103.

scientifically, i.e., the objective validity of scientific and mathematical judgments. For Kant, the world *is* the scientifically interpreted world. The result is that while Kant indeed recognizes the objectivity of the objective world as a "subjective accomplishment," he misjudges the nature of that accomplishment because he overlooks the abstractive and interpretative character of science at the most fundamental level. What has emerged from Husserl's examination of Galileo is that such an interpretation-abstraction operates not upon meaningless sense-data but upon a "world of life" that is already rich in meaning before the scientist comes along. The scientific conception must be regarded as a view of the world, a certain way of looking at it and dealing with it which serves certain purposes. It is in this sense that the pregiven life-world constitutes a "hidden presupposition" in Kant's philosophy: that from which scientific abstractions are made, that of which scientific theory is an interpretation, is simply taken for granted as needing no transcendental critique. The "subjectively-relative" sphere, which science is at pains to transcend, is "merely subjective" and "merely relative" only by contrast to the intersubjective agreement (i.e., objectivity) obtained by the scientific view. Because of this contrast, modern objectivism banished it entirely to the interior of the mind, where it could be interpreted, by analogy to the physical world, as mental material subject to its own causal laws and could give rise to the bastard notion of "sense-data." Yet, considered in its own right, without reference to the world of scientific objectivity, this sphere is anything but merely in the mind. It, too, constitutes a world of its own—indeed, the world we live in most of the time, with its own structure, its own sort of intersubjectivity, and its own objectivity. And most important, the scientific world and the life-world do not simply coexist, alongside one another; it is precisely on the foundation of the life-world, in virtue of its structure and thanks to motivations that arise within it, that the scientific view is able to arise. This is why Husserl calls the life-world the "forgotten meaning-fundament of natural science." [46] But in the modern philosophical tradition, the life-world was never considered "in its own right" because of the overriding preoccupation with science. Once this consideration is inaugurated, the philosophical *problem of the world,* and thus of its transcendental grounding, must be seen

46. *Ibid.,* p. 48.

in a new light. It is not only the scientific world that is in need of such a grounding, but the life-world as well, indeed pre-eminently so.

Thus, while Kant succeeded in one sense in overthrowing the naïve objectivism of his predecessors, his philosophy contains a hidden presupposition inherited from them: the transcendental problem of the world, for Kant, is predetermined by a concept of the world borrowed from modern science, and he does not penetrate to the depths of the transcendental problem. Though he does not simply assert the ontological Galilean thesis, "to be is to be measurable," it is still this concept of being alone that is subjected to transcendental inquiry. In fact, Hume was more alive to the true problem of the world than Kant, even though the idea of a transcendental grounding was foreign to him. For Husserl, Hume had a much clearer awareness than Kant of "the world-enigma in the deepest and most ultimate sense." [47] Far from limiting his problem to scientific and mathematical judgments, Hume questioned "the *naive obviousness* of the certainty of the world, the certainty in which we live—and what is more, the certainty of the *everyday* world as well as that of the sophisticated theoretical constructions built upon this everyday world." [48]

So we see that Husserl's discussion of Galileo, in which the concept of the life-world emerges, reveals its ultimate significance not in his critique of objectivism, which directly follows it in the text, but rather in his critique of the transcendental turn through which objectivism is supposedly overthrown. But whose transcendental philosophy is actually being criticized? Is this merely a critique of Kant? The strange fact about the Kant-critique of the *Crisis* is that, while Husserl takes Kant to task for not recognizing the significance of the life-world, this is the first time, in Husserl's own writings, that the life-world emerges as a topic in its own right and is accorded this significance. If the life-world concept in its present form is lacking not only in Kant's but also in Husserl's previous work, it is hard to avoid the conclusion that his Kant-critique is really a Husserl-critique in disguise, that the inadequate notion of transcendental philosophy that is attacked here is not Kant's but Husserl's own. If this is so, and if the life-world problem is really not only new but

47. *Ibid.*, p. 96.
48. *Ibid.*

also of crucial importance, as Husserl claims, and if it emerges directly, as it seems, from the "historical reduction," then the latter procedure, far from simply continuing what had been accomplished without it, brings about a significant shift in the whole phenomenological enterprise.

6 / Husserl's New Concept of the World: The Life-World

AT THE END of the previous chapter we suggested that Husserl's critique of Kant is actually a critique of Husserl in disguise. In the present chapter we shall try to show how this is so, pointing to the novelty of the concept of the world, as it emerges in the *Crisis,* not only in contrast to Kant but also in contrast to Husserl's own earlier views on the subject.

To be sure, even the new critique of Kant contains one element that had always been part of Husserl's objection to his philosophy. This concerns Kant's emphasis on natural science and (material) mathematics. Husserl had always insisted that these disciplines alone do not define the transcendental problem in its totality. In *Ideas* I the transcendental problem is posed by reference to the natural attitude and its world, and in *Ideas* II Husserl is careful to note that this natural attitude must be distinguished from the narrower *naturalistic* attitude of the scientist.[1] What Husserl saw in *Ideas* II and III is that, quite apart from the problem of the *Naturwissenschaften,* the *Geisteswissenschaften* and the sciences of life pose quite peculiar transcendental problems of their own. They, too, treat of a certain kind of objectivity in a theoretical way, and one of the great problems of modern philosophy and science is that all scientific theory is conceived according to the model of natural science. Husserl had always insisted, as we have seen, that other domains of objectivity must be approached according to methods and concepts appropriate to them, not with tools borrowed from

1. Husserliana IV, pp. 180 ff.

somewhere else. Another standard Husserlian objection to Kant is that he had erroneously conceived of the transcendental problem only in connection with the material disciplines, where the so-called synthetic a priori is at work, and had taken the formal mathematical and logical disciplines for granted. In this way, too, Kant had incorrectly limited the sphere of transcendental inquiry.[2] In *Formal and Transcendental Logic* Husserl insists that formal disciplines, no less than material sciences, stand in need of a transcendental critique.

But Husserl's new Kant-critique, conducted in the *Crisis* under the general rubric of the life-world concept, is of a much more radical nature than this. It is true that he has concentrated throughout on the modern preoccupation with natural science and on the difficulties caused by this preoccupation. But even in the early account of Galileo, Husserl's point is not so much that the emphasis on nature causes us to overlook other domains of objectivity and the peculiar character of the sciences corresponding to them. The idea of mathematization, and that of its correlate, the scientifically interpreted world, is opposed not to other forms of theoretical accomplishment and other worlds or domains as interpreted by them, but rather to a form of consciousness which is totally free of theory, completely unengaged in the theoretical *interest* in any of its possible forms. The life-world is not the correlate of scientific consciousness directed toward the spirit or the psyche, as opposed to nature; rather, it is the world of *pre*-theoretical, *pre*-scientific experience, and it must be approached according to the ways it is given in such experience.

These points are of course not unrelated. If the world is identified with the mathematized world, then any discipline which claims to be scientific, even if it concerns man's spiritual nature, must be grounded in it. Hence the nineteenth-century attempts to ground all *Geisteswissenschaften* in psychology, which in turn needed a physiological and ultimately physical grounding. On the other hand, if nonphysical sciences are accorded some degree of autonomy, and if the mathematized sphere is seen as merely a particular domain of the real, then the general concept of the world must be broadened. But the notion of the life-world derives not so much from a broadening as from a deepening of the concept of world. The life-world is the realm of what is pregiven to consciousness not only prior to natural

2. *FTL,* pp. 260 ff.

science but also "before anything that is established scientifically
. . . in physiology, psychology, or sociology." [3] These disciplines,
as well as the *Geisteswissenschaften* in the usual sense (history,
the study of literature, etc.), are guided by a *theoretical* interest
even if they proceed according to appropriate rather than inappropriate methods. What Husserl has recognized, by way of his
historical critique of the rise of modern (natural) science, is
that human beings are not necessarily theoretical all or even
most of the time. Yet they are still conscious, and they still live
in a world. It is *this* consciousness and *this* world that must be
understood before we can adequately understand the particular
forms of consciousness that give us the theoretically interpreted
world, whether physical, psychological, or spiritual. "For the
human being in his surrounding world there are many types of
praxis, and among them is this peculiar and historically late
one, theoretical praxis." [4] The problem that arises from Husserl's
historical-critical reflections is that of understanding consciousness not according to the model of scientific or theoretical consciousness, but in such a way that theoretical consciousness can
be seen as only one of its possible forms.

THE CONCEPT OF THE LIFE-WORLD

HUSSERL'S ACTUAL DESCRIPTIONS of the life-world at
this stage in his argument proceed primarily by way of contrast
to the mathematized world of the scientist. The scientific method
is not an instrument for improving our *sight*, something invented
during the Renaissance along with the telescope, which enables
us to put aside the world of appearances for good. It was and
remains an idealizing construction *based upon* what is seen, and
what is *seen* remains ever the same whether or not we are
scientists who are engaged in such idealization. Above all, the
life-world is a world of objects having both primary and secondary qualities, a world whose spatial features fall into vague
and approximate types, not a world of geometrical idealities.
While science operates with abstractions, the life-world is the
concrete fullness from which these abstractions are derived;
science constructs, and the life-world provides the materials of

3. *Crisis*, p. 105.
4. *Ibid.*, p. 111.

construction; the ideal character of scientific entities precludes their availability to sense-intuition, while the life-world is the field of intuition itself, the "universe of what is intuitable in principle," the "realm of original self-evidences," to which the scientist must return in order to verify his theories.[5] Science interprets and explains what is given; the life-world is the locus of all givenness. The emphasis here is on the *immediacy* of life-world experience in contrast to the mediated character of scientific thought. The life-world is prior to science, prior to theory, not only historically but also epistemologically, even after the advent and rich development of scientific theory in the West.

Much of what Husserl says in this regard is simply a recapitulation of the phenomenology of *perception* with which readers of the *Ideas* and the *Cartesian Meditations* are already familiar. The life-world is first and foremost a world of perceived "bodies." "For everything that exhibits itself in the life-world as a concrete thing obviously has a bodily character. . . ."[6] He speaks of the perspectival character of perception, of outer and inner horizons, placing more emphasis than before, perhaps, on the role of the living body and its kinesthetic functions and on the oriented character of the field of perception around the body. His descriptions are similar to those centered about the concept of the "world of pure experience" in the lectures on Phenomenological Psychology.[7] The critique of the distinction between primary and secondary qualities, in which Husserl follows Berkeley, is of course not new, nor is his insistence on the ideal character of pure geometrical structures as opposed to the realities of the experienced world. Above all, Husserl is concerned with the sphere of passive synthesis and of prepredicative experience referred to in the *Cartesian Meditations* and in *Formal and Transcendental Logic* and developed in *Experience and Judgment*. The "pregiven" character of the life-world— pregiven, that is, for the active synthesis of predicative, scientific consciousness—is actually the result of a flowing, synthetic conscious activity in its own right, whose study is neglected by Kantian transcendental philosophy, and which Husserl had earlier proposed to examine in detail under the borrowed Kantian title of a "transcendental aesthetic."[8]

5. *Ibid.*, p. 127.
6. *Ibid.*, p. 106.
7. Husserliana IX, pp. 55 ff.
8. Cf. *FTL*, pp. 291–92; CM, p. 146.

But if this is so, to what extent is the concept of the life-world new? Those who seek to minimize the novelty of the *Crisis* point out the close relationship mentioned between many of Husserl's discussions of the life-world and these earlier investigations or projected investigations. It is also to be noted that even the *term* "life-world appears quite early in Husserl's writing, e.g., in a manuscript dated 1917 by the Louvain archivists.[9] All of this is true, but it does not suffice, in my opinion, to deny our claim that the life-world theory of the *Crisis* is an implicit criticism of Husserl's earlier views concerning a fundamental dimension of this thought. For one thing, as we shall see, the concept of the life-world extends beyond what we have discussed so far, and it is not limited merely to the theme of a "transcendental aesthetic" or phenomenology of perception. But even if we restrict ourselves to this theme as presented in the *Crisis*, we find that it represents a significant step beyond earlier, superficially similar investigations. For none of these earlier investigations is carried to the point of requiring such a thorough reconstruction of the *world*-concept. It is true that the term "world" is used in earlier investigations; and that the "world of immediate experience" bears a founding relationship to the domains of entities that appear in theoretical science. But it is precisely this relationship to the problem of science that distinguished the earlier view of perception and the perceptual world from the later. The fact is that the earlier treatments are always oriented toward an understanding of judgment in general and scientific judgment in particular. The borrowed term "transcendental aesthetic" suggests that, though Husserl expressly wishes to enlarge on the Kantian conception, he still sees his own project as oriented, like Kant's, toward a theory of judgment and ultimately toward the nexus of interrelated judgments which make up a theory. In other words, Husserl is *led to* the problem of the transcendental aesthetic by his interest in accounting for theoretical judgment, and he treats of this problem almost exclusively in these terms. This is evident in *Formal and Transcendental Logic* in the way in which the concept of transcendental aesthetic is introduced and in the manner in which it is investigated. In *Experience and Judgment* this orientation is indicated in the very title of the work.

Now, it is true that in the *Crisis*, too, Husserl originally

9. Husserliana IV, p. 375.

approaches the concept of the life-world from a consideration of science, indeed natural science. But one of the most significant developments in this work occurs after the concept has been announced and treated in these terms. "The manner in which we here come to the life-world as a subject for scientific investigation makes this subject appear an ancillary and partial one within the full subject of objective science in general." [10] Science has become incomprehensible, and in order to understand it in keeping with the "transcendental turn," we must treat it as a theoretical accomplishment, turning to the cognitive character of this accomplishment in conscious subjectivity. In doing this, we must consider "the scientist's constant recourse . . . to the life-world with its ever available intuitive data." [11] The general problem is that of "the relation between objective-scientific thinking and intuition." [12] But intuition is not as simple a matter as earlier epistemologists had thought. When the problem of intuition becomes the problem of the life-world, the latter takes on a significance of its own.

> It is clear . . . that prior to the general question of its function for a self-evident grounding of the objective sciences there is good reason to ask about the life-world's own and constant ontic meaning for the human beings who live in it. These human beings do not always have scientific interests, and even scientists are not always involved in scientific work; also, as history teaches us, there was not always in the world a civilization that lived habitually with long established scientific interests. The life-world was always there for mankind before science, then, just as it continues its manner of being in the epoch of science. Thus one can put forward by itself the problem of the manner of being of the life-world; one can place oneself completely upon the ground of this straightforwardly intuited world, putting out of play all objective-scientific opinions and cognitions, in order to consider generally what kind of "scientific" tasks, i.e., tasks to be resolved with universal validity, arise in respect to this world's own manner of being. [13]

Of significance in this passage is the mention of what "history teaches us." We shall return to this later on. For the

10. *Crisis*, p. 122.
11. *Ibid.*
12. *Ibid.*, p. 134.
13. *Ibid.*, p. 123.

moment, let us consider only what the passage proposes. The problem of the life-world is deliberately and explicitly severed from its relation to the problem of a transcendental grounding of science and is set up as a problem in its own right. To be sure, once the concept of the life-world is properly worked out, it will, among other things, also function as clarificatory in relation to the sciences. Why, then, should it be separated from that problem, the very problem that led us to it in the first place? For one thing, presumably, because it will also function in the clarification of other dimensions of consciousness which, like science, are "higher" than, and are founded upon, the life-world. But there is an even stronger and more important implication in the passage quoted above. It is that a focus upon the life-world purely in terms of its relation to science might lead us to mistake both its own nature and its role in the life of consciousness. If the consideration of the life-world by the phenomenologist is merely a preliminary step in clarifying scientific consciousness, he might be misled into believing that for natural consciousness as such, in its own nature, the life-world has only a preliminary status. Even in the *Crisis*, Husserl gives expression to this belief by frequently referring to the life-world as "merely subjectively relative," as if it were correctly characterized as something less than real *for* consciousness, something essentially in need of the sort of *dépassement* which is carried out by the scientist. But, commenting on the term "merely subjective relative," he says: "For us, of course, this 'merely' has, as an old inheritance, the disdainful coloring of the δόξα. In prescientific life itself, of course, it has nothing of this; there it is a realm of good verification and, based on this, of well-verified predicative cognitions which are just as secure as is necessary for the practical projects of life that determine their sense." [14] The life-world is intended as "merely subjectively relative" *only* for the scientist *qua* scientist insofar as the vagueness and indeterminacy of life-world experiences is at variance with the exactness he demands. The same may be true for the nonscientist who adopts a scientific frame of mind. But, for nonscientist and scientist alike, when neither is engaged in science, the life-world is *lived* as anything but "merely subjectively relative." Far from being in any sense less than real, the life-world here *is* the real. Furthermore, even for the scientist in his work, namely, where

14. *Ibid.*, p. 125.

unquestioned perception of instruments, intercourse with colleagues, etc., are involved, the life-world has a real status that is not undone by his theoretical beliefs. It is necessary to distinguish between beliefs motivated by theoretical considerations—fundamental ontological presuppositions, theoretical hypotheses confirmed by scientifically interpreted experience—on the one hand, and the kind of belief involved in the scientist's perceptual experience on the other hand. It is in the latter case that the life-world is involved. It is only at this level of theory that the scientist or anyone else would be led to consider the life-world *as a whole* as "merely subjectively relative." At the level of practice, whether scientific or otherwise, it is of course possible to regard an individual experience as questionable if there are good motives for doing so. But this is not the same as considering all perceptual experience as somehow defective, much less considering the domain to which it gives access, the life-world itself, as something less than real. All theoretical activity, whatever its outcome in terms of beliefs, and all other activity, theoretical or otherwise, rests upon a foundation of belief which can never be destroyed on its own terms, though it may be questioned or even denied theoretically. At this level there is no distinction between the life-world and the real world. In fact the life-world is *the world itself*.

Hence the great importance of freeing our considerations of the life-world from the question of its role in science. For we run the risk of confusing the life-world as we *live* it with the life-world *as considered* from the point of view of a theory which relegates it as a whole to a "merely subjectively relative" status. But had Husserl himself fallen prey to this confusion, and is he now, as we suggest, implicitly criticizing himself for having done so? The fact is that, from the perspective of the *Crisis*, it is hard to see exactly where the concept of the *world* really belongs in Husserl's earlier philosophy. Not that such a concept is lacking in importance. We have seen, in fact, in Chapter 1, that the phenomenological "discovery of the world" went hand in hand with the discovery of the natural attitude and that this dual discovery led not only to an expansion of the subject matter of Husserl's investigation in the *Logical Investigations*—the correlation between intentional experience and intended object—but also to the basic conception of the phenomenological reduction in its original form. But if we look closely at what Husserl says about the world in the *Ideas* and subsequent works, we find some ambiguity surrounding this fundamental concept.

THE EARLIER CONCEPT OF WORLD: THE *Ideas*

IN CHAPTER 1 we stressed, as the crucial concept of world that emerges in the *Ideas*, the world as *horizon*. The world is the horizon, in fact the ultimate horizon, of anything given in an act of perceptive consciousness. Let us consider again what this implies for an understanding of the *givenness* of the world as such. Husserl begins by saying that in the natural standpoint "I am conscious of a world." But what does it mean to be conscious of the world? "Above all [*vor allem*]," it means that "I find it before me [*ich finde sie vor*] immediately, intuitively, as existing; I experience it [*ich erfahre sie*]." [15] But this description is considerably refined as Husserl goes on. "Through sight, touch, hearing, etc., in the different ways of sensory perception, corporeal things somehow spatially distributed are for me simply there [*einfach da*], in the literal or figurative sense 'at hand' [*vorhanden*], whether or not I pay them special attention. . . ." [16] In sense-perception it is first of all *things* that are immediately given. These are, however, surrounded by a "perceptual field" which is given both as background and as potential focus of attention. But the perceptual field is in turn surrounded and permeated by what is more or less clearly copresent [*mitgegenwärtig*]: "actual" and "determined" objects, which are nevertheless not perceived, are "there for me." Here Husserl mentions the portion of the room behind my back, the children in the garden; and one should also mention the hidden sides and aspects even of the perceptual field itself. [17] Now, the more or less determined sphere of reality is itself given as a mere *segment* of the real as a whole, which forms a horizon extending indeterminately in all directions. Not only is it extended in space but it is also extended in time, though obviously in a completely different sense of "extension." [18] As we saw, if we did not recognize the presence of this proximate and then ultimate

15. Husserliana III, p. 57 (*Ideas*, p. 101).
16. *Ibid.*
17. *Ibid.*, p. 58 (*Ideas*, p. 101).
18. *Ibid.*, p. 59 (*Ideas*, p. 102).

horizon, we would overlook an important character of the individual perceptual act.

It is in *this* manner, then, that the world is *"bewusstseins-mässig vorhanden,"* consciously present, "in every waking moment." [19] Thus Husserl explicates what he means by saying that I "experience" the world "immediately, intuitively." The emphasis on the immediacy of this experience is important: as in the analysis of the perceived object, it is not some image or picture of the world, or some sign for it, which is present to my experience, but the world *itself*. Yet the world is clearly not itself a perceived object. Its givenness can be understood to some extent by analogy to an object only part of which is the direct focus of our perception; or better, by analogy to some object too large to be included in our perceptual field, like the earth, but which stands behind and forms the background to what we see. But these are still *potential* objects of perception: given the right position, as we now know from space travel, the earth can be taken in by the perceptual field—in which case it has its horizon, which is ultimately the world. For Husserl, obviously, the world can never be a perceived object; yet it is directly experienced in and through each perception. It is experienced, not *merely* thought about or meant; yet it is experienced *only* in the manner of a horizon, or rather *the* horizon, of any*thing* perceived or otherwise directly experienced.

Such is the conception developed in Part Two of the *Ideas* by way of an introduction to what Husserl calls "the fundamental phenomenological outlook." He is aware that he is onto something important and new. He notes quite early that the "exhaustive characterization" of the "breadths and depths" of the natural attitude is an "extraordinarily important, though up to now hardly noticed" task, but it is not one he wishes to undertake at the moment. [20] He believes that he has described the natural attitude adequately in a preliminary way, for his purposes, and he goes on to characterize all positive sciences normally so-called as "sciences of the natural attitude." [21] His purpose, of course, is to proceed to the process of "bracketing" the natural attitude as a whole.

But the question is whether Husserl remains true to this

19. *Ibid.*, p. 58 (*Ideas*, p. 102).
20. *Ibid.*, p. 62 (*Ideas*, p. 106).
21. *Ibid.*, p. 63 (*Ideas*, p. 106).

conception in other things that he says. In the first section of the *Ideas*, i.e., *before* the beginning of the section just referred to, he defines the world as "the complete totality [*Gesamtinbegriff*] of objects of possible experience and experiential knowledge, of objects which, on the basis of direct [*aktueller*] experience, are knowable in correct theoretical thinking." [22] Two things are to be noted about this definition: First, experience is directly linked to "knowing" (*erkennen*), which is in turn characterized in terms of "correct theoretical thinking." Though it is not stated, the *suggestion* is that what is experienced is experienced *as knowable*, i.e., given *as* something potentially subsumable under a theory. The later theory of the life-world does not, of course, deny that anything experienced is potentially an object of theoretical thought, or even that it is in some sense given as such; but it does deny that it is given only or even primarily in this way. Yet there is no hint of this in the above passage.

Second, there is the suggestion that the world *itself* is given *as* the complete totality of objects considered from a theoretical point of view. It is significant that the rather redundant term "*Gesamtinbegriff*" is used rather than, say, "*Gesamtheit*" or (a term often used by Husserl later) "*All*." The suggestion is that Husserl is viewing the world as the object of a concept, that he is referring to how the world is *thought*. Yet, in his description of the natural attitude, only two chapters later, he says explicitly not only that the world itself is *experienced*, as we have seen, but also that our awareness of the horizon surrounding the perceptual field is a kind of knowing (*ein Wissen*) "that has nothing of conceptual thinking in it [*das nichts vom begrifflichen Denken hat*]." The world as horizon is experienced, and as such is given as "unlimited," "indefinite," and "infinite," but not as a "totality." [23]

It might be objected that this definition of the world from Part One of the *Ideas* is given in an admittedly "prephenomenological" context, one whose point is to distinguish different types of sciences or theoretical disciplines (the factual versus the eidetic). In such a context there is nothing wrong with characterizing the objects of experience in terms of their being subsumable under theory, since they certainly are. Furthermore,

22. *Ibid.*, p. 11 (*Ideas*, p. 52).
23. *Ibid.*, pp. 58–59 (*Ideas*, p. 102).

the world *can* be thought as well as experienced, and Husserl has simply given us, in a context where it is appropriate, a definition of the world as thought *rather than* as experienced. This would suggest a discussion rather different from that of the later Part Two, since it is not yet the natural attitude itself that is being characterized, but rather a theoretical and conceptual attitude built upon or inscribed within the natural attitude. But this interpretation is not borne out by the text. The natural attitude is not introduced first in Part Two, where the thesis of the natural attitude is suspended, but rather in the very context we have been discussing. And the *world* is also introduced as corresponding directly to the natural attitude. The world is not merely defined as quoted above, i.e., in terms of theory: the natural attitude itself—Husserl calls it "this original attitude"—is explicitly described as a "theoretical attitude." [24] Husserl does use the term "horizon" (*Gesamthorizont*) to describe the world corresponding to this attitude, but he characterizes it as the total horizon of possible *Forschungen,* a term linked, of course, with *scientific* investigation. Again the suggestion is that the world as horizon is encountered in the natural attitude *as* or in terms of its possible theorization through *Forschung.*

It is clear that, especially from the perspective of the *Crisis,* there is some discrepancy between the two accounts, in the *Ideas,* of the natural attitude, its objects, and its world. But which one is dominant? To be sure, Husserl never, even in Part One, characterizes the objects of natural experience as being themselves theoretical entities, e.g., such as those of physics. In fact, he takes pains in several places throughout the *Ideas* to show the secondary, constructed, and nonexperiential character of theoretical entities in relation to experienced things given beforehand.[25] His main adversaries in these discussions are those scientific realists who begin by assuming the "real" physical object to have mathematically determined properties and take this to be the "hidden" or "unknown" cause of experienced objects which are "mere appearances." Husserl is concerned to show that the concept of the physical object grows out of a prior natural attitude that does not originally contain it, and that such entities can hardly be unknown—even if it is

24. *Ibid.,* p. 10 (*Ideas,* p. 51).
25. *Ibid.,* §§ 40, 52.

true that they are "hidden," i.e., never experienced—since they are precisely objects of scientific knowledge. Yet, because of the very frequency of these discussions, Husserl's own description of the natural attitude and its objects concentrates on the relation these bear to their own possible theoretical interpretation by the physicist. Throughout the *Ideas,* and not just at the beginning of Part One, objects of experience are characterized predominantly as "objects which, on the basis of direct experience, are knowable in correct theoretical thinking." Later, in the chapter entitled, "The Natural World As Correlate of Consciousness," Husserl says that "the factual course of our human experience is such that it forces our reason to go beyond the intuitively given things (those of the Cartesian *imaginatio*) and to place beneath them a 'physical truth.' " [26] No doubt Husserl's preoccupation with scientific realism explains this, but there is no indication that he is aware of stressing only one aspect of natural experience because of this preoccupation.

Then there is the question of the manner in which the world itself is given in the natural attitude, as distinguished from the objects of this world. In § 46 Husserl notes that *"existence in the form of a thing . . . is never demanded as necessary by virtue of its givenness,* but in a certain way is always *contingent.* That means: It can always happen that the further course of experience will compel us to abandon what has already been posited *with empirical justification."* [27] Thus "everything which is there for me in the world of things . . . is in principle only *presumptive reality [präsumptive Wirklich-keit],"* [28] i.e., it is real "until further notice," whereby it is easy to imagine what such "further notice" might be like. But Husserl then transfers this notion of givenness from what is *"there for me in the world of things"* to the *world itself,* in order to argue for the "contingency" *(Zufälligkeit)* and even the "dubitability" *(Zweifelhaftigkeit)* of the latter! But does this not contradict the very thesis of the natural standpoint itself? "All doubting and rejecting of the data of the natural world changes nothing of the *general thesis of the natural attitude.* 'The' world is as reality *[Wirklichkeit]* always there; it is at most here or there 'other' than I took it to be, this or that under such names as

---

26. Husserliana III, p. 110 (*Ideas,* p. 147).
27. *Ibid.,* p. 108 (*Ideas,* p. 144).
28. *Ibid.* (*Ideas,* p. 145).

'illusion' or 'hallucination' and the like, must be struck *out of it,* so to speak; but the 'it' remains forever, in the sense of the general thesis, the existing [*daseiende*] world." [29] Here *all* doubting and rejecting of the data (*Gegebenheiten*) leaves the general thesis intact; whereas, in the other passage, Husserl seems to suggest that we can conceive of circumstances in which the very existence of the *world,* like that of some particular object, might be cast into doubt. Yet would not such doubts have to arise, as in the case of a particular object, from some *experience* which conflicts with earlier ones, and would not such an experience itself presuppose the existence of the world? Can we really, as Husserl claims, conceive of an experience in which the *existence* of the world as such is cast into doubt? To be sure, what he probably has in mind is a set of experiences in which our expectations about the order and harmony of things are continuously and consistently frustrated.[30] But would this not be merely a limiting case—extreme, admittedly—of the world being "*other* than I took it to be"? Here Husserl seems to have the *Sosein,* not the *Sein* of the world in mind. But even the world's *Sosein* is an infinitely distant idea, as far as our knowledge of it is concerned;[31] and just as no set of experiences is imaginable which would ever *establish* the *Sosein* of the world once and for all, so no set of experiences, however chaotic, could ever suffice to *deny* the presence of some ultimate order in things. At best Husserl is asking us to imagine an *infinite* chaos of experiences, but by the same token the emergence of order could be infinitely postponed, i.e., it could be infinitely distant.

"The reflexions just carried out . . . make it clear that no proofs drawn from the empirical consideration of the world are conceivable which could assure us with absolute certainty of the world's existence," says Husserl.[32] *This* much is true and is a perfectly legitimate and important point to make: no experience can ever prove the world's existence, since experience presupposes the world's existence. But by the same token, as we have seen, no proofs drawn from empirical considerations could ever *deny* the world's existence. And if confirmation or

29. *Ibid.,* p. 63 (*Ideas,* p. 106).
30. *Ibid.,* p. 115 (*Ideas,* p. 151).
31. Cf. *ibid.,* § 143 and the notion of Idea in the Kantian sense.
32. *Ibid.,* p. 109 (*Ideas,* p. 145).

denial are ruled out, doubt as a rational procedure has no place. Saying that the nonexistence of the world is conceivable is not the same as saying that there ever could be doubts as to its existence.[33]

More important than Husserl's apparently faulty reasoning in these passages is their implied description of the manner in which the world is given in the natural attitude. "Let us think of the possibility of non-being which belongs essentially to every thing-like transcendence." [34] Referring in the next breath to the "nullification of the thing-*world*," Husserl unavoidably leaves the impression that the world is given as a kind of transcendent *thing*, the *totality* of all things rather than the horizon of all things. And this conception is involved in the faulty reasoning we described previously. The world is itself not experienced, as in his description of the natural attitude, but posited as the ultimate order of things, an order which lies at the end of an infinite process of consciousness whose aim is the grasping of that order. But this grasp cannot be conceived as itself something experiential. It is only conceivable as *thought* which goes beyond experience, generalizes from it, and proceeds inferentially to general conclusions. In other words, it is only conceivable as *theory*.

This conception is borne out in the later parts of *Ideas* I which form a transition to *Ideas* II and III. The last section of the first volume is entitled "Reason and Reality." How is "reality" constituted in consciousness? As Husserl frames the question, "When . . . is the noematically 'meant' identity of the X 'something real' [*Wirkliches*] rather than something 'merely' meant, and what does this 'merely meant' mean?" [35] The real, he answers, is that which is "rationally demonstrable" (*vernünftig ausweisbar*). It is true that here he qualifies "the real" as the real "in the logical sphere, in that of assertion [*Aussage*]," but there is no mention of any other sort of reality, and indeed anything not rationally demonstrated is relegated here to the sphere of the "merely meant." Now what counts as rational demonstra-

33. This point is apparently recognized by Husserl in *CM*, p. 17. Evidence for the world's existence is not tied to the coherence of experience, since experience could still be a "coherent dream." But he also mentions the idea of the coherent dream in Husserliana III, p. 108 (*Ideas*, p. 144).

34. Husserliana III, p. 115 (*Ideas*, p. 151).

35. *Ibid.*, p. 332 (*Ideas*, p. 378).

tion is determined not only by formal-logical norms for objects of any sort, but also by the "material a priori" of the region of reality to which the object belongs. "An object determined through the regional genus has, as such, so far as it is real, its modes of being perceivable . . . , thinkable, demonstrable [*ausweisbar*], which are prescribed *a priori*." [36] The theory of the constitution of "reality" must therefore be differentiated according to the different material regions. The "phenomenological investigations on constitution," then, which form Volume II of the *Ideas*, take their clue from these material regions, which in turn correspond to the main divisions of (material) science: the natural, the psychic, and the spiritual (*geistig*). This procedure not only confirms the identification of the real with what is actually or potentially established theoretically in the sciences; it also effects a curious fragmentation of reality whereby the notion of world as the *unitary* domain of the real somehow gets lost. Husserl's world-concept here falls prey to an ambiguity which the text does not clear up. At one point he speaks of "the opposition between the naturalistic world and the personalistic world," [37] but the question is: What has become of *the* world of the natural attitude? One possibility is that it could be understood in a sort of additive sense, as the sum of the three regions of reality put together. It is true that Husserl places much emphasis at every turn on the manner in which the different regions are intertwined, but he is also at pains to deny that any of them can be reduced to any other. He is careful to note that the regions he is describing correspond to the theoretical attitudes or "interests" of the natural and psychological sciences and the humanistic disciplines.[38] This might suggest, as a second possibility, that the "fragmentation" is the result of such theoretical attitudes, and that there is a unitary phenomenon—"world"—which corresponds to a pretheoretical attitude, and from which the different regions are singled out. But in this case, given the identification of the real with the "rationally [i.e., scientifically] demonstrable," and the division of the notion of reason according to material regions, such a unitary, pretheoretical world begins to sound like something less than real, i.e., like something "merely meant." This

36. *Ibid.*, p. 364 (*Ideas*, p. 411).
37. Husserliana IV, p. 173.
38. Husserliana V, p. 1.

description, which seems to follow from the dominant conception of reality in *Ideas* I–III, suggests that scientific *Ausweisung* comes to the aid of natural, prescientific experience by providing something which it lacks, namely, the sense of the reality of its objects. But this is obviously at variance with the original description of the natural attitude in which the world is *experienced*, in the manner of a horizon, as reality (*Wirklichkeit*) itself, rather than thought, or "merely meant," as the horizon of subsequent *Forschung* which will procure for it a reality it lacks.

There is some question as to whether this same theoretical conception is not contained even in Husserl's chapter on the natural attitude, or rather in what he says about the *thesis* of the natural attitude. The "general thesis," he says, "does *not* consist of course *in an act proper,* an articulated judgment *about* existence." [39] That is, our *Erfahrung* of the world is not ordinarily expressed in a judgment; such expression would be an *Erlebnis,* indeed a judgmental and not a perceptual *Erlebnis,* or even an *Erlebnis* of experience (*Erfahrungserlebnis*), in the broad sense, though it would of course be *based* on experience. Nevertheless, Husserl suggests that our experience of the world *can* be expressed in such a judgment; he does this by expressing it himself ("the world is as reality [*Wirklichkeit*], always there," etc.). Does the utterance of such a judgment, which somehow converts the world into an object judged about, really express adequately our relation to the world when it is experienced in the manner of a horizon?

AFTER THE *Ideas*

IF THIS QUESTION is to be answered negatively, it has far-reaching implications. However, we shall postpone discussion of these for the moment. It suffices for now to have shown considerable ambiguity in the *Ideas* regarding the world and the givenness of the world in the natural attitude. We have suggested that the world is conceived on the one hand as experienced in the manner of horizon, on the other as intended in the manner of theoretical thought, and that the latter of these two conceptions is dominant. This is not to say that the former

39. Husserliana III, p. 63 (*Ideas,* p. 107).

conception is henceforth dismissed from Husserl's mind. But it does seem to retain the subordinate position suggested by our analysis of the *Ideas*. In the lectures on phenomenological psychology of 1925, for example, Husserl makes considerable use of the term *"natürlicher Weltbegriff,"* a term that had long been in his vocabulary and was clearly borrowed from Richard Avenarius' *Der menschliche Weltbegriff.*[40] Husserl had never used the term in the sense used by Avenarius for his positivistic purposes; and he never credits Avenarius with its invention. But the term had somehow caught on in his mind. Now (1925) he speaks of a "science of the natural world-concept,"[41] a "great" science whose full execution he puts off as not necessary for his purposes, as he had put off full treatment of the natural attitude in the *Ideas*. But what he says about this *natürlicher Weltbegriff* is significant. The term "world-*concept*," of course, suggests a distinction between an "idea" of the world and the "real" world, as it had for Avenarius, but perhaps this distinction should not be attributed to Husserl since the term is borrowed. (It is interesting, however, that this particular terminology is *not* used by Husserl in the *Crisis*.) Husserl describes this science as "the universal descriptive science of the invariant essence of the pregiven as well as of any possible experienceable world."[42] Certainly this is a precursor of the science of the life-world in the *Crisis*. But the science of the natural world-concept is described as marking out "the universal framework which must contain within itself the a priori of any possible mundane science. All possible goals which such sciences set for themselves superficially (*äusserlich*), all problems ever to be posed within them, have an a priori type. They stand, that is, under essentially general problems of which the sciences in question must be conscious in order to be able to work with ultimate clarity on goals and methods, i.e., in order to be sciences in the strict sense."[43]

In this brief programmatic description two aspects of the ambiguous world-concept of the *Ideas* are preserved. On the one hand, the "natural world-concept" is correlated with a domain which is defined in terms of its relation to the sciences. The world emerges as a field of problems which the sciences

40. 3d ed. (Leipzig: O. R. Reisland, 1912), § 1.
41. Husserliana IX, p. 93.
42. *Ibid.*
43. *Ibid.*

come along and solve. It is not, of course, stated that this is *all* there is to the "natural world," but, again, nothing else is mentioned. On the other hand, this world is described as a unitary phenomenon which precedes in consciousness the fragmentation deriving from the adoption of scientific interests.

> Nature and spirit as scientific themes are not there from the start [*vorweg*]. Rather, they first take shape in a theoretical interest and in theoretical work guided by this interest, upon the substructure [*Untergrund*] of a natural, pretheoretical experience. There they appear in an original, intuitive interpenetration and coexistence [*Ineinander und Miteinander*]. We must begin from this concrete, intuitive unity of the prescientific world of experience and then make clear which theoretical interests and directions of thought it prescribes, and how, thereby, nature and spirit can become unified, universal themes, henceforth inseparably related to one another.[44]

To this extent, then, something like the world of the natural attitude, as described so briefly in *Ideas* I, is preserved here. It should be noted, too, that what Husserl says is in keeping with a very important remark in *Ideas* III, whose general title is "Phenomenology and the Foundations of the Sciences": "It is not what calls itself 'modern science,' and not those who call themselves 'specialists' who make [scientific] method: it is the essence of the objects and the corresponding essence of possible experience [*Erfahrung*] of objects in the appropriate category . . . which prescribe everything fundamental about the method. . . ."[45] These essences, then, are somehow available to consciousness, presumably to a prescientific consciousness, before the adoption of scientific interests, and these interests dictate that such pregiven evidences are to be followed in the pursuit of science. Furthermore, later on in the *Phenomenological Psychology*, we find Husserl insisting that the world itself is *experienced*: "Now Kant teaches explicitly that the world is not an object of possible experience [*Erfahrung*]. . . . [But] I cannot accept the Kantian assertion. . . . For us, real particulars are experienced, but the world is experienced too, indeed the two are inseparable."[46]

These passages might conceivably be taken as implicit

44. *Ibid.*, p. 55.
45. Husserliana V, p. 22.
46. Husserliana IX, p. 95.

criticisms of the doctrine of the *Ideas,* or at least as attempts to clear up some of its ambiguity. In some of Husserl's notes on the *Ideas,* made as he reread it in later years, we find such criticisms made explicit.[47] One such note, written in 1927, bears the title "Objection to the whole first chapter of the first section," i.e., to the chapter in which the natural attitude is described as "theoretical" and the world is defined as the correlate of "correct theoretical thinking." Husserl notes that this chapter takes its point of departure from the natural attitude and that it proceeds to discuss the sciences as following certain formal and regional essences. Then he asks:

> Can I know that all being [*alles Seiende überhaupt*] fits into [*einfügt*] such a regional distribution, that sciences are to be grounded on this? Are the regions not universal structures of the world, whereas the concept of world-structure is not treated at all, since the world as a unitary universe [*einheitliches Universum*] is not placed at the beginning?
>
> Also, the great error that [the chapter] takes its point of departure from the natural world (without characterizing it as world) and then goes immediately to the eidos—as if one already arrived directly [*ohne weiteres*] at the exact sciences.[48]

A second critical remark is much briefer. Next to the passage on the first page of the *Ideas* which describes the natural attitude as a theoretical attitude, Husserl wrote in the margin of one of his copies, apparently sometime around 1928: "And what about the natural practical attitude?" [49]

A third criticism dates from 1929 and relates to the notion of the world as the presumptive reality corresponding to experiential harmony. Commenting on the second chapter of Part Two, where the idea of the dubitability of the world is presented, Husserl remarks that he has limited himself too much to individual experiences of individual things, and has neglected the all-important concept of horizon.

> Things and world have constant validity for me, and not merely through a limited perception of individual things, even if we

47. These notes are included as appendixes to the Husserliana edition of *Ideas.* See Hans-Georg Gadamer, *Wahrheit und Methode,* 2d ed. (Tübingen: Mohr, 1965), p. 232, who also refers to some of them.
48. Husserliana III, p. 390.
49. *Ibid.,* p. 463.

consider these as having their horizons, but rather through a validity-consciousness [*Geltungsbewusstsein*] in the manner of a universal horizon-consciousness [*Horizontbewusstsein*]. This consciousness too, then, requires a critique insofar as I deal with questions as to what kind of validity [*Recht*] the experience of the world has for me. . . . *All this points indeed to complicated and difficult investigations* whose adequate concrete execution has only lately been successful. In the first version of the *Ideas* they were not yet carried out in a satisfactory way.[50]

Thus we find Husserl himself, in the late twenties, criticizing the very conception of the natural attitude and the world of the natural attitude which we found to be dominant in the *Ideas* and to be at variance with the description of the first chapter of Part Two: the idea of the natural attitude as theoretical attitude and of the world as a horizon which is not so much experienced as it is *thought* as the ideal end-point of theorization.

THE *Cartesian Meditations*

IN VIEW OF THESE CRITICISMS from 1927–29, it is all the more remarkable that the *Cartesian Meditations* (1929–30) takes so little account of them. Of crucial importance is the manner in which the *world* is presented there. After the early, Descartes-inspired argument for the nonapodicticity of the existence of the world in the First Meditation, which differs in some respects from that of the *Ideas*,[51] the problem of the world does not receive much treatment throughout the Second or much of the Third Meditation. When the all-important schema *ego-cogito-cogitatum* is introduced, the *cogitatum* is treated almost exclusively in terms of the particular object of consciousness; it is never broadened to the point of invoking the world as the universal *cogitatum* or horizon. "Each cogito, each conscious process, we may also say, '*means*' *something or other* and bears in itself, in this manner peculiar to the *meant*, its particular *cogitatum*."[52] The concept of horizon is, to be sure, important, but is used almost exclusively in a limited way, to indicate the

50. *Ibid.*, p. 400.
51. *CM*, pp. 17–18. See above, n. 33.
52. *Ibid.*, p. 33.

" 'predelineated' potentialities" [53] attaching to every conscious process pointing from one particular object to *other* particular objects. In the presentation of the notion of intentional analysis, much emphasis is placed on the intentional object as "transcendental clue" for the analysis, and upon the material regions of reality. Here, as in the later parts of the *Ideas,* the world is mentioned as a kind of summation of the material regions of reality: ". . . transcendental theories of constitution arise that, as non-formal, relate to any spatial things whatever . . . to any psycho-physical beings, to human beings as such . . . to any social communities, any cultural objects, and ultimately to [an] objective world [as such] . . ." [54] presumably as comprising these regions. This conception leads into the Third Meditation on *"Wahrheit und Wirklichkeit,"* which corresponds to the *"Vernunft und Wirklichkeit"* section of *Ideas* I. *Wirklichkeit* is explicitly defined as the (ideal) "correlate of evident verification [*Bewährung*]." [55] As before, the "presumptive evidence of world-experience" is invoked, and the world itself is described as "an *idea* correlative to a perfect experiential evidence." [56]

This conception, outlined in the *Cartesian Meditations,* brings out in an even stronger way the view found in certain pages of the *Ideas* of which we have already spoken. To speak of the world as merely presumptive reality in this way amounts to asserting that *for* consciousness, *for* the natural attitude itself, the reality of the world is somehow forever left undecided until some infinitely distant, unattainable moment of complete verification. But does the *world itself* have this status in our experience? Again Husserl seems to be confusing the world as horizon with what is given within this horizon at any given moment. The concept of presumptive reality has an important application here: no matter how vividly or undoubtedly an object or state of affairs is present to consciousness in external perception, the possibility that such evidence may be undone by later experience is always open; and indeed, in some implicit sense we are aware of this possibility. That is, the merely

53. *Ibid.,* p. 45.
54. *Ibid.,* p. 52. Cairns's translation of "eine objektive Welt überhaupt" as "any objective world whatever" seems slightly misleading here.
55. *Ibid.,* p. 59.
56. *Ibid.,* p. 61; emphasis mine.

presumptive character of any particular evidence or conviction is something that belongs to the natural attitude itself. And, of course, at a higher level, such a presumptive character belongs as well to convictions based on generalizations from experience, even convictions about the whole objective order of things. The question, as we saw before, is whether this presumptive character can be said to attach to our conviction *that* the world exists and even that there is an order to be found (whether or not it ever is). A negative answer seems to be implied by the notion of the world which is itself experienced in the manner of a horizon in the natural attitude, a notion developed early in the *Ideas* themselves but somehow lost in what followed. The difference is between the experience we *actually have* of the world in the natural attitude, and the *idea* of an experience, which in principle we can never have, which would ultimately verify our *conception* of the world. To which does the world correspond: is it *given* in actual experience, or is it merely *thought* in the *idea* of an (unattainable) adequate experience? The fact is that both ideas make sense, and are even compatible with each other, but they belong to different levels of conscious life. Husserl seems not to see this, not to be able to keep them apart or to see their relation to each other. The result is that the characteristics belonging to one conception of the world (as idea) seem to be applicable to the other, such that the world as experienced has a merely presumptive character always in need of further verification.

One explanation for the dominance of the theoretical and ideal conception of world in the *Cartesian Meditations* is the fact of Husserl's preoccupation, during the same period, with the problem of logic. According to Landgrebe, *Formal and Transcendental Logic* was written "in a few months during the winter of 1928–29," [57] and Strasser writes that Husserl seems to have begun preparing the Sorbonne lectures at the end of January, 1929.[58] Though he adopts different approaches in the two works, the close connection between them is obvious. But this connection only underscores something that can be said about Husserl's career as a whole. It was his concern to clarify logic, after all, which had led him to phenomenological investigations in the first place, in 1900–1901, and this concern was

57. *EU* p. viii.
58. Husserliana I, p. xxiii.

bound to remain prominent in his mind as the phenomenological method was developed as a universal method of philosophy. It is not surprising, then, that the conception of the world which is dominant in Husserl's work, up to this time, should be one that correlates directly with his approach to logic. From the very beginning, Husserl had characterized logical concerns as arising from a *critique* directed at straightforward experience and judgment. In the *Logical Investigations* he writes:

> If we perform the act and live in it, as it were, we naturally refer to its object and not to its meaning. . . . This latter first becomes objective to us in a reflex act of thought, in which we not only look back on the statement just made, but carry out the abstraction (the Ideation) demanded. This logical reflection is not an act that takes place only under exceptional, artificial conditions: it is a normal component of *logical* thinking. What is characteristic of such thought is the context of theory, and the theoretical consideration of the latter, which is carried out in step-by-step reflections on the *contents* of the thought-acts just performed. A very common form of thoughtful pondering may serve as an instance: "Is *S* *P*? That could very well be. But from this proposition it would follow that *M* is the case. This cannot be, and so what I first thought possible, *that S is P,* must be false, etc." [59]

Such "logical thinking" is of course not yet the thinking of the logician, who makes a further ideational jump from propositions as ideal objects to propositional forms and their purely formal interrelations. But the "logical thinking" described by Husserl in this passage is still a step above the precritical, "prelogical" consciousness which affirmed or at least considered the judgment "*S* is *P*" in the first place. As such it presupposes such a precritical level of consciousness as that which it criticizes in its special way. Such logical thinking is oriented toward truth in "the context of theory," i.e., it is interested in the truth not just of one proposition but of a whole nexus of propositions which are consistent with one another. Given this orientation or interest, it is natural that the evidence (e.g., perceptual) on which the proposition is based would be "merely presumptive" pending the integration of the proposition into a theoretical nexus. Such is the "caution" which the theoretical interest imposes upon the naïve evidences of the natural attitude. To be sure, "logical thinking" itself belongs to the natural attitude.

59. *LI,* p. 332.

It is one aspect or type of what we have called "natural reflection" and thus is by no means "exceptional" or "artificial." Still,
it is necessary to recognize that it *is* precisely reflection and
presupposes a prereflective level of consciousness upon which it
operates. At any point in the critical-reflective process, certain
particular propositions or beliefs are subjected to criticism and
in the process become "merely presumptive." But to what extent
does this make the natural attitude itself a mere presumption,
to what extent does the *world* of the natural attitude have merely
presumptive reality?

Furthermore, we can ask whether the theoretical orientation or interest itself is essentially or necessarily characteristic
of the natural attitude. Granted that, *given* such an orientation,
not only particular beliefs but a whole system of beliefs can
become merely presumptive for consciousness. But is such an
orientation necessarily given with the natural attitude itself?
Is it not the case that the theoretical interest, with its concom-
itant "logical thinking," is merely one possible orientation among
others within the natural attitude? It appears that by describing
the *world* as having merely presumptive reality, and as an *"idea*
correlative to a perfect experiential evidence," Husserl has described not the world of the natural attitude itself but a conception of the world that corresponds to a particular interest
within the natural attitude.

Of course, the idea that logical-critical reflection presupposes
a preexisting "naïve" level of consciousness on which it operates
is not lacking from Husserl's work during this period. On the
contrary, it is something on which he places great emphasis in
both the *Cartesian Meditations* and *Formal and Transcendental
Logic*. In *Ideas* I he had already asserted that the modalities of
belief (the possible, the probable, the doubtful, the questionable)
such as might arise from logical criticism presuppose a primary
level of belief (*Urglaube* or *Urdoxa*) upon which such criticism
does its work.[60] In the later writings, this notion is crucial in
the introduction of the idea of genetic analysis and in the transition from formal to transcendental logic. Logical thought can be
treated with a view to extracting the formal principles it presupposes, and the system of such principles can be articulated
as a formal axiomatic system (*mathesis universalis*). But if we
wish to understand the place of logical thought in the life of

60. Husserliana III, p. 258–59 (*Ideas*, pp. 299–300).

consciousness, we must grasp its relation to the level of consciousness that it presupposes, and this is none other than the level of experience. Logic has always concentrated on judgment (*apophansis*) but "*the intrinsically first thing in the theory of evident judgments* (and therefore in judgment theory as a whole) *is the genetical tracing of predicative evidences back to the non-predicative evidence* called *experience* [*Erfahrung*]."[61] The evidence of judgment presupposes the evidence or self-givenness of objects (*gegenständliche Evidenz*), and it is in experience that objects are given.[62] To the distinction between predicative and nonpredicative (or prepredicative) evidence corresponds the distinction, prominent in the *Cartesian Meditations*, between active and passive genesis. "In active genesis the Ego functions as productively constitutive, by means of subjective processes that are specifically acts of the Ego [*durch spezifische Ichakte*]."[63] This expression confirms the self-conscious or reflective character of active genesis. "Here belong all the works of *practical reason*, in a maximally broad sense. In this sense even logical reason is practical."[64] This is none other than the "logical thinking" of the *Logical Investigations*, involving reflection, ideation, and appeal to formal rules. But "anything built by activity presupposes, as the lowest level, a passivity that gives something beforehand; and when we trace anything built actively, we run into constitution by passive generation."[65] Such "passivity" is of course, for Husserl, a limiting form of conscious activity; it can be called "passive" because it does not involve reflection (it does not consist of *spezifische Ichakte*) and the explicit appeal to rules. Nevertheless, it follows its own implicit rules. At this level of consciousness, in the flowing unity of time, "things," "objects" are given or pregiven. This is the level of evidence of objects (*gegenständliche Evidenz*) presupposed by predicative evidence. Here, too, consciousness proceeds by synthesis, bringing together the changing, flowing modes of appearance to constitute the things of everyday perception.

Husserl devoted a great deal of time and effort, especially throughout the 1920s, to the analysis of passive synthesis. It is this analysis, incidentally, to which he gave the name

61. *FTL*, p. 209.
62. *EU*, p. 11.
63. *CM*, p. 77.
64. *Ibid.*
65. *CM*, p. 78.

"transcendental aesthetic." [66] What is remarkable is that the notion of *world* plays almost no role at all in these analyses.[67] They follow from the phenomenology of perception begun in the *Ideas*, broadened and deepened through the additional consideration of the time-dimension. They pursue the problem of how perceptual objects take shape before us as directly experienced. But what has become of the notion we found in the *Ideas* that in every peception the *world itself* is directly experienced as reality in the manner of a horizon? To be sure, the notion of horizon is prominent, but, as in the *Cartesian Meditations* themselves, its use is restricted to describing the cointended surroundings of a given object in terms of what it implies for possibilities of continuing experience. In the section of the *Cartesian Meditations* where passive genesis is introduced, Husserl writes: "Thanks to the aforesaid passive synthesis . . . the Ego always has an environment [*Umgebung*] of 'objects.'" [68] But there is no mention of the fact that this *Umgebung* is itself surrounded by a "horizon of undetermined reality" of which I am "obscurely conscious," which is "present" (*vorhanden*) for consciousness "in every waking moment," as stated in § 27 of *Ideas* I.[69] Part of the heading of that paragraph is *Ich und meine Umwelt,* but Husserl immediately makes it clear that for the natural attitude the *Umwelt* or *Umgebung* cannot stand alone. It is experienced *as* a segment of the world as such (*Welt*) which extends "into the limitless beyond." [70] Yet in the period of the *Cartesian Meditations* the world figures only as an "idea" which owes its significance for consciousness to the presence of the theoretical or logical interest.

An indication of the importance accorded to prereflective, nonlogical experience is found in the late pages of the Fifth Meditation. In the context of explaining the role of ontology within the phenomenological program, Husserl speaks of a "universal ontology of the objective world" and remarks: "As regards this, nothing prevents starting at first quite concretely with the human life-world around us [*menschliche Lebensumwelt*], and with man himself as essentially related to this our

66. Husserliana XI, pp. xv–xvi.
67. This is borne out throughout the investigations published in Husserliana XI.
68. *CM* p. 79.
69. Husserliana III, p. 58 (*Ideas*, p. 102).
70. *Ibid.*

surrounding world [*Umwelt*], and exploring, indeed purely in-tuitively, the extremely copious and never-discovered Apriori of any such surrounding world whatever, taking this Apriori as the point of departure for a systematic explication of human existence [*menschlichen Daseins*]." [71]

This passage is interesting in several respects. Most obvi-ously, perhaps, it represents Husserl's first public hint of his reaction to a first reading of Heidegger's *Being and Time*. The project of exploring the *menschliche Lebensumwelt* is linked with other attempts at a "new ontology" based on phenomeno-logical insights, such as those of certain earlier phenomenolog-ical "schools" (e.g., Munich) which had failed to make the "tran-scendental turn" of the *Ideas*. All of those attempts have their validity, Husserl is saying, but they are only "philosophically intelligible" when their a priori results are "related back to the ultimate sources of understanding, [i.e.], only when problems of constitution . . . become disclosed and the natural realm of knowledge is at the same time exchanged for the transcenden-tal." [72] If these remarks are indeed aimed at Heidegger, we find Husserl admitting that the former's investigations are com-patible with phenomenology, but claiming that they are not yet themselves phenomenological or ultimately grounded. The im-plication, however, is that they could be, if only the transcen-dental turn were taken.

But there is no indication that, given this development, the *phenomenology* (as opposed to the ontology) of the *menschliche Lebensumwelt* would be able to claim any priority over the phenomenologies corresponding to the other ontologies he men-tions ("pure grammar, pure logic, pure jurisprudence, the eidetic theory of intuitively experienced Nature, and so forth" [73]), that is, that such phenomenological theories would themselves be fully intelligible only when grounded in a phenomenology of the life-world. Rather, the *menschliche Lebensumwelt* seems simply to stand alongside other domains, and we can, if we wish, explore it as well as the others. "Nothing prevents" our starting here, but nothing seems to require it either. Yet it is precisely the doctrine of the *Crisis* that the phenomenology of the life-world must precede all others.

71. *CM*, p. 138.
72. *Ibid.*
73. *Ibid.*

7 / Life-World, Historical Reduction, and the Structure of the *Crisis*

WE HAVE ARGUED that the theory of the life-world in the *Crisis* is developed in and through a criticism which is directed not only at past philosophers, Kant in particular, but also, even primarily, at Husserl's own earlier views. In the foregoing chapter we have tried to demonstrate the ambiguities and lack of clarity surrounding the concept of *world* which the theory of the *Crisis,* in our view, is designed to rectify. Let us now summarize our account of Husserl's earlier views in order to contrast them with the later theory.

It is in his early statement of "the fundamental phenomenological outlook" (*Ideas* I, second section, first chapter) that Husserl comes closest to the view which ultimately prevails in the *Crisis*. Here the world itself is directly experienced as a horizon "in every waking moment," in every perception. And it is experienced *as reality (Wirklichkeit)*. But Husserl's interest in grounding the sciences ultimately leads him away from this conception. On the one hand, in the further development of the *Ideas* (including Volumes II and III) and in the later period of the *Cartesian Meditations* and *Formal and Transcendental Logic,* the notion of the world as *experienced* horizon is simply neglected, and the world becomes identified with the *thought* horizon of a theoretical investigation which is ideally (though perhaps impossibly) completed.[1] What is assumed here is the

1. Frederick J. Crosson makes a very similar criticism in "Phenomenology and Realism," *International Philosophical Quarterly,* VI, no. 3 (1966), 455–64, esp. p. 458.

presence in consciousness of a scientific or theoretical interest. But such an interest, when considered materially rather than formally, envisages not a unified world but rather a particular region of reality. At this level the concept of *reality* is not concrete except as correlated to the material a priori of some region. Reality is "fragmented," and the only remaining concept of the world-as-such as reality is that of a summation or *Inbegriff* of the various material regions. Thus, because of Husserl's preoccupation with the theoretical interest, the world is conceived as neither an experienced nor a unitary horizon.[2] And when he does consider in those works the level of experiential consciousness underlying the theoretical interest (in the theory of a "passive genesis"), the concept of world seems not to figure at all.

On the other hand, we have seen that the idea of the world as an experienced, unitary horizon is not entirely neglected in all of Husserl's writings prior to the *Crisis*. In his remarks on the *natürlicher Weltbegriff* and the "world of immediate experience," especially in the lectures on phenomenological psychology, Husserl seems to have just such a world in mind and to remain true to the early conception of the *Ideas*. But even here, Husserl does not go as far as he obviously wishes to go in the *Crisis*. For one thing, the "world of immediate experience," though it *is* a unitary horizon prior to the adoption of scientific interests, is discussed almost exclusively in terms of its relation to those very interests. Husserl's only reason for mentioning this horizon seems to be his own interest in discovering how the sciences arise out of the natural attitude and take their basic concepts from the pregiven structures of its world. These structures, and the attitude that relates to them, tend to be described as proto-scientific, i.e., as tending toward science even if they are not yet scientific themselves. Furthermore, we find here no emphasis

2. Only at the level of formal ontology, which abstracts from material differentiations, is the world maintained as a unity even for thought in the natural attitude: formal ontology deals not with a region of reality but with the whole of reality from a formal point of view. Thus its domain is not a region but only a "quasi-region" (Husserliana III, p. 140 [*Ideas*, p. 175]; see also Husserliana III, p. 27 [*Ideas*, p. 67]). But since the concept of *experience* is irrelevant here (experienceability only enters in when differentiated materially), there is some question as to whether the "horizon"-sense of reality has any relevance at this level. Reality becomes a formal manifold (*Mannigfaltigkeit*) given all at once in the unity of a system, rather than something presenting itself by horizons.

on the *reality* of the world of immediate experience. If such a world is given *merely* as something to be surpassed by scientific consciousness, and if the point of science is to get at "reality," the pregiven world, though it is a unitary and experienced horizon, seems still to be something less than *real*.

THE OLD AND THE NEW CONCEPTIONS OF WORLD

THE STRIKING CONTRAST between these earlier views and that of the *Crisis* is made evident in a manuscript not included in the latter text, but added as a *Beilage* and tentatively traced by the editor to the winter of 1936–37 (*Crisis*, Appendix VII). "Consciously we always live in the life-world," Husserl begins; "normally there is no reason for making it explicitly thematic for ourselves universally *as* world." Then he notes that, living the life-world and always conscious of it "as a horizon," we pursue particular ends, either as fleeting and changing ones or as long-term, perhaps lifetime projects in the sense of "vocations" (*Berufe*). Through such projects "a self-enclosed 'world'-horizon is constituted. Thus as men with a vocation we may permit ourselves to be indifferent to everything else, and we have an eye only for this horizon as our world and for its own actualities and possibilities—those that exist in this 'world'. . . ." [3] What Husserl has in mind here actually corresponds to what, in his earlier terminology, he termed an *attitude*.[4] He is dealing with consciousness not as an act or a flow of acts, but as a frame of mind (*Geisteshaltung* or *Einstellung*) whose correlate is not a particular object or state of affairs, but a whole domain of possible objects of concern. Such a domain could conceivably be as narrow as the "world" of postage stamps for the collector, and need not correspond in the literal sense to a vocation as determined by the conventions of a society.[5]

In any case, the point is first to distinguish such a "world"-horizon from the "always obviously existing world in the most universal and full sense of the life-world." The world in this sense always "lies outside our interest" when we are engaged in some particular vocation; it is not "thematic" for us and we

3. *Crisis*, p. 379.
4. Cf. Chap. I, pp. 20–21.
5. Cf. Husserl's note in the *Crisis* text itself (p. 138), which is very similar to the text under discussion here.

have no reason to make it so. Nevertheless, says Husserl, it is always there, indeed *bewusstseinsmässig,* that is, for consciousness, precisely as horizon. And the particular "world"-horizon outlined by some attitude is "held within," enveloped by the larger horizon, Husserl says, presupposing it.[6]

"The goal-directed life which is that of the scientists' life-vocation clearly falls under the generality of the characterization just made, together with the 'world' that is awakened therein . . . as the horizon of scientific works."[7] Having said this, Husserl goes on to discuss how the scientist's "world" differs in important ways from other "worlds" within the horizon of the life-world. For one thing, at the level of fundamental physical theory (as opposed to some specialized branch) the scientist would deal not merely with a class of objects, like postage stamps, but with one of the highest genera (i.e., a region) of reality. But the important thing in this characterization is that the scientist's world is placed alongside other possible "particular worlds" in relation to the life-world and is not given a privileged position. Many different horizons can be carved out of the broadest horizon of the life-world, and the world of the scientist is only one of them. Any such horizon contains "its own actualities and possibilities—those that exist in this 'world'—i.e., we have an eye only to what is 'reality' here (what is correct, true in relation to this goal) or 'unreality' (the incorrect, the mistaken, the false)."[8] "Reality," then—in quotation marks—is a concept defined by a particular goal or task, and the scientist's "reality" is not the only one. Rather, all such "realities" have their place within and presuppose the "always obviously existing world" in the sense of the life-world.

It is clear what makes for the radical distinction here. The life-world is the world that is constantly pregiven, valid constantly and in advance as existing, but not valid because of some purpose of investigation, according to some universal end. Every end presupposes it; even the universal end of knowing it in scientific truth presupposes it, and in advance; and in the course of [scientific] work it presupposes it ever anew, as a world existing, in its own way [to be sure], but existing nevertheless.[9]

6. *Crisis,* p. 379.
7. *Ibid.,* p. 380.
8. *Ibid.,* p. 379.
9. *Ibid.,* p. 382.

We can see how Husserl's earlier theory of the sciences would fit into the new conception. The particular region of reality focused upon by the scientist—physical nature, for example—is the "self-enclosed 'world'-horizon" constituted by the scientist's vocation. According to that vocation, furthermore, his attitude toward that horizon is *theoretical* rather than something else. Those who pursue other vocations may focus upon the same horizon but approach it in nontheoretical ways: the technologist, the farmer, the landscape or still-life painter. But the scientist does not *live* in this horizon in the fullest sense, for two reasons we have already discussed: first, he is not always engaged in the practice of his vocation, and second, even when he is so engaged, his acceptance of the world about him is always prescientific to some degree. Both within and outside his "working hours" as a scientist, the life-world is always given as a horizon even though it is never thematic as such. This is where he *lives* in the most fundamental sense, i.e., both in the sense that he is always, and not merely sometimes, to some degree within this horizon and also because the particular horizon of his work is built upon the life-world and takes it for granted.

It is necessary, then, to distinguish two senses of "world"— the first as the horizon of some particular vocation, and the second as the life-world which encompasses all such horizons in the first sense. But Husserl points to yet a *third* sense of "world" in this manuscript, namely, the "theoretical 'universe'" of "philosophy in the old sense." [10] If we begin with the various branches of science, each with its own, theoretically treated region of reality, it is possible to ask questions concerning "reality as such," the "whole" of reality, the "universe." How do the various regions relate to one another? Are they, for example, not so much "regions" of reality but rather, in each case, the whole of reality seen from a particular perspective? Or is the distinction among regions only apparent, such that all reality can ultimately be dealt with according to the principles governing one of them, e.g., physical nature? Is it possible to come up with a simple *material* (as opposed to formal) theory of "being," or are the conditions for "being a physical thing," "being an organism," "being a person (*Geist*)" essentially different? These

10. *Ibid.*, p. 381.

are, of course, some of the traditional questions of philosophy
in the sense of ontology or metaphysics. Just as one does not
have to be a scientist in order to ask scientific questions or assume a scientific attitude toward the world, so one does not
have to be a "professional" philosopher in order to think philosophically. For example, the physicist may be of the *opinion*
that all reality can be reduced to physical reality, even though,
in his work, he simply excludes from his consideration animals
as animals, persons as persons, cultural objects as cultural. In
other words, his scientific work does not itself accomplish the
reduction that he thinks is possible. Rather, it is *qua* philosopher
that he thinks about "the whole of reality" or "reality as such."
Perhaps everyone does this to a certain extent, either from the
perspective of his particular vocation or in abstraction from it.

But is this truly the philosophical problem of the world, in
the sense of the most fundamental and original problem? Husserl's answer is negative. *"Does there not arise here a necessary
and at the same time dangerous double meaning of 'world,' of .
the domain of philosophy,* which is after all supposed to have
the full and complete world, together with all the particular
worlds mentioned above, as its subject matter?" [11] The fact is
that the "world" of traditional philosophy, in the sense of the
"universe," even though it encompasses other particular theoretical horizons, is still a particular world staked out by a particular
interest. Even though it is the broadest possible one of its
kind, the philosophical interest is still particular if only because
it is theoretical; and the particular material domains it takes
for granted and tries to bring into harmony with each other (the
regions of the various sciences) are themselves theoretical domains. As a particular interest, the philosophical attitude is one
which asserts itself *within* the pretheoretical world-life with its
all-encompassing life-world horizon, the horizon which sur-
rounds and underlies all particular interests, both theoretical
and nontheoretical. Like scientific and other interests, though
it may be only fleetingly and occasionally present, it is also
capable of constituting a "habitual" attitude to which one can
return in a consistent way, making of it a vocation. And this has,
of course, happened historically. But to paraphrase what Husserl says about science: human beings do not always have

11. *Ibid.*

philosophical interests, and even philosophers are not always engaged in philosophical work.[12] Perhaps we can even say in addition that "history teaches us" that there was not always in the world a civilization that lived habitually with long-established philosophical interests. In any case, there arises the problem of understanding the life-world which underlies the traditional philosophical world or universe, and this too is a problem for philosophy. The philosophical approach to this problem, needless to say, would have to be radically different from that of traditional philosophy; otherwise the same problem would simply arise again.

It is not surprising, of course, to find Husserl advocating an approach to the world which differs radically from that of traditional philosophy. But we should be clear on the fact that what is proposed in this manuscript of Appendix VII is radically different in a new sense, even for Husserl himself. The point here is not simply to distinguish the straightforward ontological approach to the world—that of traditional philosophy—from the transcendental phenomenological reorientation in which the world is treated as meant, as phenomenon. The question rather concerns the *nature* of the world that is ultimately to be subjected to this treatment. As in the case of Husserl's critique of Kant, it is not the transcendental turn itself that is in question—as we have seen, Kant made such a turn and is given credit for doing so—but rather the point at which such a turn is applied. It is easy to read Husserl's Kant-critique into this manuscript: Kant took for granted the material ontology of Newton's physics, then made the further, philosophical move of assuming that all reality could be subsumed under such an ontology. He then asked the question under what condition it was possible to know reality in this sense. But Husserl's critique is much broader than this, and significantly it is not directed only at Kant. Rather, it is directed at philosophy generally—"which is after all supposed to have the full and complete world, together with all the particular worlds mentioned above, as its subject matter"— and at its tendency to derive its conception of the world from the ontology of the sciences. The critique applies, whether, as with Kant, this conception derives from a reduction of all ontology to the ontology of physical science, or whether the world-concept is a sort of summation of the ontologies of the several

12. *Ibid.*, p. 123.

branches of sciences, which are related to one another but not reduced to one.

It is in this latter sense that the critique applies to Husserl himself. The implicit self-criticism can be seen to have two aspects. The first point is that Husserl had derived his conception of reality from the existing sciences. This shows the closeness of his earlier work, in the matter of the relation of science to philosophy, to the concurrently developing neopositivism. It is true that he did not share the belief of neopositivism in the reducibility of all empirical science to physics. But he did believe that physics, unlike psychology, the humanistic disciplines, and perhaps even biology, had finally achieved a truly scientific status within its own domain. He thought that the other sciences could achieve such a status, with the help of phenomenology, though it is not clear whether such help was necessary: physics had, after all, somehow made the grade without it. He never criticized the actual division of scientific domains or regions; reality was simply taken to be essentially differentiated according to the physical, the psychic, and the human. Once all the sciences were able to stand on their own, they would supply us with an essentially adequate (though not a complete) picture of the world, both a priori (through their respective ontologies) and empirically. The only task left for philosophy was to interrogate scientific knowledge itself and, as we saw in Chapter 1, to discover the hidden *Selbstverständlichkeiten* that it naïvely invokes but never makes thematic. To be sure, this was much more important than the merely ancillary and critical task envisioned by the positivists. Since Husserl, like Kant but unlike the positivists, held a version of the "synthetic a priori" view, there was much more to be said on this score. Husserl even went beyond Kant and argued that philosophical analysis, as phenomenology, could claim the highest status of science. But still philosophy was not on the same level as the sciences in the positive sense; it was not competing with them, but in a sense took their conclusions for granted.

This resulted in another aspect of Husserl's earlier approach, and one which is now implicitly under criticism. Because his notion of reality had taken the existing division of science for granted, and because unlike the positivists, he refused to reduce all sciences to one basic one, Husserl had never explicitly posed the problem of an *ontology* of the *world as such* at all. In this manuscript he distinguishes between the sciences, which take some region of reality as their domain, and (traditional) philosophy, whose domain is the world as such. Of great importance to his whole critique of modern philosophy, as we have seen, is the notion that an ontology of nature was surreptitiously substituted for ontology *tout court,* that the solution to certain scientific problems was taken for the solution to the philosophic problem without the full realization that this is what had taken place. Then he accuses modern philosophers of overlooking the distinction between the scientific and the philosophic task even at the level of ontology, quite apart from the question of the transcendental turn. Now it is true that, apart from dealing with the material ontologies underlying the sciences, especially in *Ideas* II, Husserl also addresses himself to the problem of their "intertwining," [13] to the problem of how some are founded on others, etc. And he had certainly argued against reductionism, which is a *philosophical* ontological strategy or attempt to make a particular material ontology into an ontology of the world. But throughout his writings on these subjects, it never appears to be clear to Husserl that in arguing against a certain ontology of the world, he must face up to the task himself of providing such an ontology, even, indeed especially, in the context of his phenomenology. Husserl is thus himself guilty of the very confusion with which he reproaches the whole tradition, though in a slightly different sense: others took the ontology of natural science to be an adequate ontology of the world; he took the ontology, or ontologies, of the several branches of science to be an adequate ontology of the world.

Now, by contrast, Husserl recognizes that the ontology of the world constitutes a problem in its own right, and if the transcendental turn is to be made correctly, such an ontology must be properly carried out.[14] But at the same time he realizes that such an ontology cannot simply be a summation or combination of the ontologies of the sciences, since these are the results of an explicitly theoretical attitude. It is necessary to move not merely from the world of a particular science to the world of the sciences as a whole, but rather from the world of the sciences as a whole to the world which they all, both separately and together, take for granted. There emerges "the

13. The problem is announced at the end of *Ideas* I: Husserliana III, p. 374 (*Ideas,* p. 421).

14. Cf. Iso Kern, *Husserl und Kant* (The Hague: Martinus Nijhoff, 1964), p. 218.

task of an 'ontology of the life-world,' " a task which could even
be carried out independently of the phenomenological project.
"Even without any transcendental interest—that is, within the
'natural attitude' . . . —the life-world could have become the
subject matter of a science of its own, an ontology of the life-
world purely as experiential world (i.e., as the world which is
coherently, consistently, harmoniously intuitable in actual and
possible experiencing intuition)." [15] Such an ontology, though
it could have its "own sense of an a priori science," "contrasts
sharply" with any ontology in the tradition, since these concern
a mathematized, not an experiential world.[16] Husserl does not
spend much time discussing this project of such an ontology
of the life-world, because, as always, he is concerned with moving
from ontology to phenomenology and avoiding any temptation
to confuse the two. But even in mentioning it, a very important
point has been made. Phenomenology is not itself ontology, but
it does have an ontological component on its objective or
noematic side. This is simply to say that consciousness is always
interrogated with respect to its objects, which are intended
within some horizon of being. The phenomenological clarification of the sciences, with their corresponding material regions of
being, is by no means discarded as a task. But henceforth these
regions must be understood as standing within, being derived
from, and presupposing the broader horizon of the life-world,
which is more than a merely prescientific and deficient domain.
Scientific activity, by the same token, must be understood as one
possibility, among others, for a consciousness whose essential
and never-lacking domain is the life-world. The ontology, then,
which must figure within a phenomenological theory of consciousness as the most fundamental ontology is that of the
world-as-such in the sense of the life-world. To be conscious
is to be first and foremost, and indeed always, within a horizon
of pregiven being. Every case of active genesis, of the focus of
consciousness on some objectivity within the world, whether for
practical, theoretical, or other purposes, at the same time intends
that objectivity as standing within a domain or region, a "self-
enclosed 'world'-horizon" to which it belongs. Such a particular
horizon, then, no less than the particular objectivity itself, corresponds to a "frame of mind" or attitude which abstracts from

15. *Crisis,* p. 173.
16. *Ibid.*

or selects from the full concreteness of the pregiven world. Such an attitude, like the conscious act itself, is not a creation *ex nihilo* of its domain, but operates on a horizon given beforehand. Any phenomenology of such conscious acts and attitudes, then, must trace such operations from their sources in the life-world. We cannot speak of the world of science, or of any other particular activity, as if it simply stood alone, and then introduce the world of immediate experience as if it were merely another such particular world. Rather, all particular worlds must be related to the pregiven life-world that encompasses and underlies them all.

Is the Life-World Compatible with Transcendental Phenomenology?

OUR DISCUSSION THUS FAR of the concept of the life-world in the *Crisis*, and of the contrast between it and Husserl's earlier views, should convince us that the introduction of this concept is indeed, as many have argued, a significant new development in Husserl's philosophy. It is clearly more than a new emphasis on something that had been present in his thought all along. As we have seen, the life-world is not merely an interesting noematic domain of consciousness which, in the interests of completeness, should be investigated phenomenologically alongside others—in this sense the life-world had indeed been involved, to a limited extent, in earlier works. Rather, insofar as it involves a transformation of the concept of *world*, the concept brings with it nothing less than a radical revision of the over-all guiding scheme of phenomenological investigation.

A question which has often been raised, in view of the novelty of the life-world concept, is whether the phenomenological program can sustain this innovation and remain intact. We have ourselves argued, of course, that the procedure of phenomenology is profoundly altered by the introduction of historical considerations. But it is sometimes asserted that phenomenology in its classical sense is dealt a deathblow by the concept of the life-world outlined above. This may seem to be a strange suggestion in light of our own presentation, since we have argued, in effect, that the life-world concept *was* grasped, if only fleetingly, in the early pages of the *Ideas*, only to be neglected thereafter. What is more, our presentation in Chapter 1 would seem to imply that it was that early grasp which made possible the formulation of the methodological foundation of transcendental phenomenology, the reduction. It would seem that the manuscript from the *Crisis* period discussed above would fit well with the second section of the *Ideas*. The notion of various "world"-horizons marked out by particular attitudes is certainly compatible with that section, since, as we argued, it is precisely there that the concept of attitude is introduced. Crucial to the presentation of the *Ideas*, of course, is the *natural* attitude itself, on which all particular attitudes are based. But is this not the equivalent of the fundamental form of consciousness described in the *Crisis* manuscript, whose horizon is the life-world prior to its differentiation into particular domains?

Nevertheless, certain questions may be raised. What is crucial to the inauguration of phenomenology, it must be remembered, is the suspension of the natural attitude, the special form of epochē through which the natural attitude as a whole is bracketed so that it can become an object of investigation. But let us recall one feature of the presentation of the epochē in *Ideas* I. Husserl first envisages the bracketing process only after the natural attitude has been articulated as a *thesis*. "We can treat the potential and unexpressed thesis [which by now, however, has been expressed by Husserl] exactly as we do the thesis of the explicit judgment," he says.[17] One such treatment, he goes on to say, is Descartes' attempted doubt, from which he then "extracts" the element of bracketing. Hence it is, as Husserl says in the title of the chapter, the *thesis* of the natural attitude that is *ausgeschaltet*, suspended. Now it might be argued, as we suggested earlier,[18] that the *thesis* of the natural attitude is not the natural attitude itself—or better, that the expression of this thesis is not the natural attitude. Rather, it is the utterance of a judgment, which would be a certain type of *Erlebnis,* not an *Einstellung* upon which all *Erlebnisse* are based. In this particular judgment, the world is an object that is judged about, and is no longer a horizon which is experienced in and through individual perceptions. Is this not, in fact, the equivalent of that traditional *philosophical* approach to the world "as such" or "as a whole," the approach of traditional ontology as metaphysics, which takes the world as an object to be known theoretically

17. Husserliana III, p. 63 (*Ideas,* p. 107).
18. Cf. p. 150 above.

in keeping with the accomplishments of the sciences? It would seem that, as soon as we articulate the *thesis* of the natural attitude, we leave the natural attitude itself behind; or rather (since we never actually leave it behind), the world-*as-meant* in the expression of such a thesis is no longer the world-*as-experienced* "in every waking moment." It is henceforth something like "an idea correlative to a perfect experiential evidence." [19] i.e., correlative to a progression of experiences extended to infinity, rather than "reality" directly experienced through such perception in the manner of a horizon.

Now if this difference really exists between the natural attitude and the thesis of the natural attitude, the question is: does the *bracketing* process apply only to the latter? It has been argued by one commentator, in fact, that "the necessity of the epochē is relative to Husserl's taking his point of departure exclusively from an objective [*gegenständlichen*] world, or, to put it another way: it is relative to his conception of all human comportment as 'intentionality,' that is, as objectifying positing. . . . Only what is posited as an object [*gegenständlich Gesetzes*] can be bracketed. . . ." [20] It follows from this that the world of the natural attitude, which is experienced as a horizon and not objectified in a judgment, cannot be bracketed. Thus, if Husserl had truly grasped the sense of his original discovery of the natural attitude, i.e., seen the difference between this and its "thesis," his phenomenology would never have got off the ground, or at least not in the sense he intended.

But let us examine this objection more closely. What exactly does it mean *not* to bracket the life-world? It must be remembered that bracketing is an operation carried out by the phenomenologist in reflecting upon his own experience in a radical way. What is experienced is considered, from the point of view of such reflection, purely *as* it is experienced, *as* it is meant. In order to focus upon and understand the experience in which the meant is meant, it is necessary to refrain from simply accepting the latter as it gives itself in naïve, prereflective experience; being involved in such acceptance, taking *for granted* the meant, is incompatible with fully understanding it *as* it is meant and understanding the experience *in which* it is meant.

19. *CM*, p. 61.
20. Ernst Tugendhat, *Der Wahrheitsbegriff bei Husserl und Heidegger*, 2d ed. (Berlin: Walter de Gruyter, 1970), pp. 263–64.

Now the failure to bracket the life-world would mean nothing less than acquiescing in its acceptance, taking it for granted *rather* than focusing upon the manner *in which* it is taken for granted. And it is the philosopher himself, one who is acquainted with the idea of the bracketing operation, who does not bracket the life-world. He does not, according to the objection under discussion, because he *cannot.* The very manuscript of Husserl's that we quoted might seem to suggest this. For as a philosopher he is, after all, in pursuit of the truth about a particular domain, in this case the phenomenological domain, which might be construed as just another "self-enclosed 'world'-horizon." Like every other particular horizon, his, too, presupposes the life-world. To be conscious is necessarily to live within the horizon of the life-world, and no operation, no voluntary adoption of an attitude for philosophical purposes, can undo this. We can bracket the existence of particular objects and even particular domains within the life-world, but if we try to carry the epochē to its limits, seeking to encompass in its grasp the "world in the most universal and full sense of the life-world," we must fail. This is perhaps the meaning of Merleau-Ponty's famous dictum that "the most important lesson which the reduction teaches us is the impossibility of a complete reduction." [21] The philosopher is left, whether he likes it or recognizes it or not, with the naïve and never fully understood acceptance of the world as life-world. Many have seen this as implying the breakdown of Husserl's transcendental idealism, and as heralding the return to a kind of realism of the lived world. Whether Husserl himself saw this, or was prepared to admit it in his last work (and clearly he did not), is not important to the objection itself. The point is that he should have seen it as an implication of his own theory.

But the curious thing about this theory is that it rests upon a very definite notion of exactly how the life-world is given, and of the form of experience in which it is given. In other words, the theory develops out of an attitude in which the life-world is *not* simply accepted straightforwardly, but is interrogated with respect to the manner in which it is consciously lived. But this is nothing other than the attitude of phenomenological reduction itself, applied precisely to the life-world! Such a reduction seems

21. Maurice Merleau-Ponty, *Phenomenology of Perception,* trans. Colin Smith (New York: Humanities Press, 1962), p. xiv.

to be a presupposition of the view which declares that the reduction itself (with respect to the life-world) cannot be carried out. Not only does this theory appear contradictory: in asserting that the life-world must, in the end, simply be accepted, it does more than simply remain within the prereflective life; it makes a philosophical assertion about the world *after* having carried out a phenomenological reduction on it. Insofar as it proclaims or even hints at the revival of a philosophic realism as its result, the theory under discussion ceases simply to live in the life-world and instead transforms it into the object of an assertion, in the manner of "philosophy in the old sense." It is a matter of invoking the brackets (while not admitting to this), and then dropping them for a return to the philosophical mode which rests upon, but is not coextensive with, the natural attitude.

A little scrutiny reveals that this objection rests upon a fundamental misunderstanding of the epochē. It supposes, in effect, that to bracket the natural attitude is *simply* to drop it, to free oneself from it in order to enter a new domain. Husserl supports such a conception, of course, when he speaks of a "new region of being" opening up, thanks to the epochē.[22] It is clear, however, that the natural attitude is not simply cast aside, since Husserl insists repeatedly that in some sense or other it remains exactly as it was.[23] In fact, in some sense it must remain in effect, since the whole purpose of bracketing it is precisely to be able to focus upon *it*, not to turn one's attention elsewhere. The world of the natural attitude, too, is not simply banished from view; on the contrary, it is still under investigation precisely as the correlate of the natural attitude. What has happened, as we saw in Chapter 1, is that we now have a new way of looking at it. What is achieved by phenomenological reduction, then, is not a new domain but a new point of view on the *same* domain. As for the "region" of consciousness itself, that is, to be sure, posited as the domain of phenomenology. But this domain is not posited on the basis of the life-world, in the manner of natural reflection, as if consciousness were within the world; nor does consciousness simply become the world, encompassing all, as in the case of subjective idealism. Rather, consciousness is considered only as being intentionally related *to* the world, which is *not* thereby rendered part of consciousness.

22. Husserliana III, p. 70 (*Ideas*, p. 112); *CM*, p. 27.
23. Husserliana III, p. 65 (*Ideas*, p. 108).

It is argued, of course, that insofar as consciousness is intentionally related to something, that something must be an *object* for consciousness; and that since we are dealing with the world as horizon and not as object, bracketing is not possible. But suppose we consider a scientific consciousness focused upon some physical object. The object is given within the self-enclosed horizon of physical nature. Are we to say that, because the latter is a horizon, consciousness is not intentionally related to it? How then is it related to it? It can easily be seen that what is essential to the intentional relation is not that the intended be an *object* for consciousness, but that it transcend consciousness, that it not be collapsible into the experience in which it is meant. Is this not true, not only of the particular horizon of physical nature, but also, indeed a fortiori, of the ultimate horizon of the life-world? To be sure, insofar as it is itself a horizon and not an object, it must be a horizon *of* objects: that is, it is cointended only insofar as something particular is intended within it. It is true that Husserl conceives of "all human comportment" as intentional, and that this means that particular objects are always intended; though it does not necessarily mean that they are intended as "objective" in the scientific sense. The life-world is not something we attend to as an object, except as "philosophers in the old sense," in which case we transform it. But in the natural life of consciousness the life-world is always meant, always intended, insofar as anything at all is intended. And the life-world, *as* horizon, certainly *transcends* consciousness. Certainly, the objection in question would not include the argument that the life-world collapses into consciousness. In Husserl's theory of the life-world, and also in the theory which attacks it, consciousness moves within a horizon which transcends it, not as an object, but precisely as horizon. As we have seen, it is only by contrast to scientific "objectivity" that the life-world is "merely subjectively relative." Considered on its own terms, apart from its relation to science, as it should be, it has its own transcendence. By insisting that everything intended be an object, the objection under discussion turns its back upon a discovery of Husserl's that is at least as important as the notion of intentionality itself: the notion of horizon, with its correlative notion, that of attitude (*Einstellung*). As we saw in Chapter 1, it was this notion which enabled Husserl to move beyond a psychological theory of consciousness, based on intentionality but still rooted in the natural attitude, to the concept of reduction and to phenomenology as transcendental philosophy. The attempt to argue from this very concept related to the life-world to the impossibility of the reduction is, as I hope to have shown, based on an inadequate understanding of Husserl.

Is the Historical Reduction Compatible with Transcendental Phenomenology?

AT THE SAME TIME it is impossible to conclude that, once this fundamental revision of its concept of world has been accomplished, phenomenology can simply go on as before. For this very revision has been occasioned by a procedure which is very different from that of phenomenological reduction in its classical form. The notion of the life-world is a significant innovation in its own right, but even more significant is the manner in which it is arrived at, namely, *not* through the phenomenological reduction alone but through the historical reduction we spoke about earlier. Up to now, we have traced the origin of the idea of historical reduction and seen its application and results in the *Crisis*. What we must do at this stage is to make clear to ourselves in general terms the nature of this reduction as it affects phenomenological procedure. The concept of the life-world itself does not, as argued by the objection just discussed, render the phenomenological reduction inoperable. But what of Husserl's new historical procedure?

First, let us look again at the motivation and development of that procedure. What our discussion has revealed is that the concept of the life-world emerges only after Husserl turns to the philosophical past in order to root out its hidden *Selbstverständlichkeiten*, its handed-down conceptions of the *Sachen und Probleme* of philosophy. Such a turn is occasioned, as we have seen, by Husserl's own theory of the historicity of consciousness, which is then applied to philosophical consciousness. What results is far from a historical justification *post hoc* of theories he already held, a mere repetition of his earlier views on the shortcomings of his predecessors. Rather, he develops a wholly new critique of the tradition, especially of Kant, which, in its very newness, places the earlier Husserl himself within the tradition he criticizes. The historical investigations of the *Crisis*, both in their intentions and in their results, are first and foremost a questioning of Husserl's own assumptions and a recognition of their rootedness in their own past. Applying his notion of the historicity of philosophical consciousness to himself, Husserl recognizes himself as having taken over the *Sachen und Probleme* of the philosophical tradition in which he grew up. He enters into that tradition in the manner of "critical-historical reflections," or what we have called "historical reduction," and comes out with a phenomenological conception of the world which differs markedly from that of his own earlier work. The *Crisis* offers us important critiques of Husserl's philosophical predecessors, but, as we have seen, the most important critique it offers is that of Edmund Husserl himself. It is true that this is not explicitly stated, but, if anything, this fact confirms the new view of the historicity of the philosophical project: Husserl is under attack not as an individual but only as a particular bearer of prejudices which were common to a particular historical period and which were derived from the tradition which extends back to Galileo and Descartes. Thus we can understand Husserl's strange remark that in order to achieve clarity on the task of philosophy we must interrogate history, but not just any history; rather, we must achieve "a critical understanding of the total unity of history—*our* history." [24] The apposition of "the total unity of history" and "*our* history" may appear paradoxical, but it has a discernible and important meaning. The tradition must be interrogated as a total unity, as a coherent development, not in the manner of isolated pieces of criticism directed at this and that philosopher, as Husserl had done before. But at the same time it must be interrogated as *our* history, i.e., from the point of view of us whose task is to accomplish the project of philosophy. Thus it is understandable that the history of philosophy, and not history as a whole, should be directly relevant to such an investigation; so it is obviously not the "totality of history," in any ordinary sense, which is in question. But even more than this, the history of philosophy is not approached as it is in history proper, with a view to completeness and objectivity. Rather, it is quite explicitly and openly admitted that our view on the tradition is perspectival: everything is seen in light of the task of the present generation, and even of the particular philosopher, to start philosophy anew. The tradition is approached not as it is "in itself" (whatever that may mean) but rather in terms of how it has affected *me*—or as it has affected

24. *Crisis,* p. 71.

us as a community of philosophers sharing the same task—by way of hidden presuppositions or *Selbstverständlichkeiten*. Such an interrogation is not so much an objective history as a reconstruction or revival of one's own history. What is important is not so much what the philosophers in question "really" said as how I—or we—read them.[25] As if to emphasize how radically such a historical reflection differs from "objective" history, Husserl refers to it in one place as *Dichtung*—poetic invention[26]— and even as a kind of fiction: he speaks at one point of "the construction of the 'novel' of history for purposes of self-reflection [*Selbstbesinnung*]." [27] While such a reflection may have the character of an "invention" or "construction" by reference to objective history, however, it is still the *re*construction of something real: namely, the historical situation of the philosopher himself and his own *particular* historicity as one who is rooted in that situation. It is a reconstruction or reliving of the philosopher's own historical prejudices for purposes of overcoming those very prejudices.

The emergence of the concept of the life-world in the *Crisis* confirms the necessity of historical reduction which was only prescribed in principle by Husserl's investigations in genetic and intersubjective phenomenology. What better confirmation of the *need* for historical reduction than that such a reduction, once carried out, should bring with it an important revision of the phenomenology which thought it could get by without such a reduction? The remarkable thing about the *Crisis* is that in the course of the book itself we can see this train of thought working itself out. It must be remembered that the *Crisis* is an unfinished work and was still being revised at the time Husserl became ill and had to stop working on it. If our interpretation is correct, Husserl's earlier investigations in genetic and intersubjective phenomenology came together with his reflections on the nature of philosophy as a task to suggest the need for a historical reduction as an indispensable supplement to phenomenological reduction per se. It is remarkable enough that Husserl, in his mid-seventies, a man so apparently certain of his method and even dogmatic in his rejection of the criticisms of others, should open up his philosophy from the inside to a wholly new self-critical

25. *Ibid.*, pp. 392–93.
26. *Ibid.*, p. 394.
27. Husserliana VI, p. 556.

procedure. Doubtless he thought and hoped that, in spite of the fact that he was introducing a new methodological element into his procedure, his reflections would, as he says in the preface, "establish the unavoidable necessity of a transcendental-phenomenological reorientation of philosophy," [28] without changing the nature of that reorientation that Husserl had been arguing for all along. But the historical reflections, once carried out, have a somewhat different result. It is true that Husserl by no means sees his concept of philosophy as transcendental phenomenology being totally invalidated because of these reflections; and we have argued that such invalidation does not follow from the new developments of the *Crisis*, at least in the sense envisaged by some of Husserl's critics. But the historical reflections do lead Husserl to the new concept of the life-world, which, as we have seen, constitutes a significant revision of the whole domain of phenomenological investigation and an implicit critique of Husserl's earlier work. As such this concept establishes even more firmly than before the indispensability of historical reflection.

A NOTE ON THE COMPOSITION OF THE *Crisis*

IT MAY SEEM ODD to suggest that Husserl began the historical reflections of the *Crisis* without knowing what important developments would result from them, but this reading is confirmed by a recent reconstruction, made by Mr. Eduard Marbach of the Archives at Louvain, of the text of the Prague lectures of November, 1935, which served Husserl as a basis when he began writing the *Crisis* for publication.[29] This reconstruction, a typescript of some sixty pages based on a manuscript found in Husserl's papers, contains nothing of substance that has not found its way into the text of the *Crisis*, except for its summary and conclusion. Much of the wording is the same, and some of what is contained in the *Crisis* is simply an elaboration and extension of what had already been said in the lectures.

But the *Crisis* text contains two significant and lengthy additions to the text of the Prague lectures. The first is the long

28. *Crisis*, p. 3, n. 1.
29. Dated June, 1968. I am indebted to Mr. Marbach and the Husserl Archives at Louvain for permission to consult this reconstruction.

§ 9 on Galileo, found at the very beginning of the historical section in Part II. In the Prague lectures, Husserl mentions Galileo only in passing and proceeds immediately to a discussion of Descartes and the ensuing rationalist and empiricist traditions. Rewriting the lectures for publication, Husserl apparently decided to devote a section of the exposition to Galileo, and the result was so long (some forty pages in the published German text) that it had to be divided into lettered subsections. Now it is not surprising that Husserl should take up Galileo here as a figure of importance equal to Descartes in the modern period. In earlier texts, Husserl had often treated Galileo, as he does here, as the supreme figure and personification of the scientific revolution of the Renaissance. But never had he treated him at such length. It may be that, in the years immediately preceding the *Crisis*, Husserl had devoted more thought to Galileo than before. In any case, what is notable about the Galileo treatment of the *Crisis* is that it is here that the life-world concept begins to emerge. The emphasis, of course, is upon the idealized objects of geometry which are read into the real world, upon the contrast between perceived objects and the geometrical "interpretation" of them for scientific purposes. The treatment here does not yet achieve the radical innovation which emerges later, of which we have already spoken. The world of immediate experience is discussed exclusively in its relation to scientific idealization and theoretization, which is understandable in light of the context. This much, as we have seen, is not new. But there are nuances here which point ahead to the more radical conception, and the best evidence of this is the fact that the second major intervention into the plan of the Prague lectures is precisely Part III A, the section on the life-world itself. In the Prague lectures, the train of thought proceeds directly from the discussion of modern philosophy from Descartes through Kant into the critique of modern psychology that corresponds to Part III B of the *Crisis*. Husserl asserts that, especially because of his "constructive" and "nonintuitive" procedure, Kant had failed to make transcendental philosophy truly scientific and had resorted to "mythical" concepts of inaccessible human faculties. The tradition of German Idealism, directly inspired by Kant, though it shared his insight into the transcendental turn, was even less scientific in its procedure, dealing instead in vague and "profound" speculations. In search of a truly scientific theory of consciousness, and as a result of the famous collapse of German

Idealism, the psychology of the nineteenth century rejected the insights of the transcendental approach altogether and returned to a dualistic theory in which consciousness is again conceived as causally dependent upon, and as structurally analogous to, nature. From this point Husserl urges that a truly unprejudiced approach to consciousness would force the recognition of its intentional nature and make possible a "phenomenological-psychological reduction," which would in turn ultimately lead back to the transcendental turn and to the phenomenological reduction proper.

This corresponds exactly to the train of thought of *Crisis* III B. In fact, there is evidence that the over-all structure of the *Crisis* was meant to follow that of the Prague lectures, which led directly from the historical discussion of modern philosophy to that of psychology, until quite late in its composition. In the published version, III B seems to follow directly upon Part II and makes no reference to the intervening III A. It would seem that Husserl had this structure in mind even at the time he sent off Parts I and II, including the Galileo section, to be published as a first installment in Liebert's yearbook *Philosophia*. This was sometime late in 1936. It must be noted, too, that the title of the Prague lectures, "The Crisis of European Sciences and Psychology," is retained in the text of Part I of the *Crisis*.[30] The "way into" phenomenology, then, was apparently to be simply "from psychology," an approach Husserl had adopted in the *Encyclopedia Britannica* article written in 1927. Only after the present Parts I and II had been published, and after the present III B had been written, then, did Husserl decide to insert III A, "The Way into Phenomenological Transcendental Philosophy by Inquiring back from the Pregiven Life-World." It is even possible that III B, too, had been sent to Liebert but was called back because of the planned insertion of III A. This would accord with Strasser's remark that Husserl "demanded the return" of the third part "that he had already sent to the publisher, in order to correct it," [31] something that is not mentioned by Walter Biemel,

30. Actually there is a slight difference. The title of the Prague lecture was "Die Psychologie in der Krise der Wissenschaften," while the title mentioned in *Crisis* (p. 3) is "Die Krise der europäischen Wissenschaften und die Psychologie."

31. Husserliana I, p. xxx. Thus my conjecture in the Translator's Introduction to *Crisis* (p. xviii, n. 5) that it was III A that was sent and returned is doubtless incorrect.

the editor of the German version of the *Crisis*. This places the composition of Part III A at the very end of Husserl's productive life, in the few months of 1937 that remained to him before the onset of his terminal illness. So late was it written, in fact, that there was no time left to bring the already written version of Part III B into accord with it.[32]

To summarize, our reconstruction of the *Entstehungsgeschichte* of the *Crisis* looks something like this: First, the historical-critical reflections proceed from Descartes not only to Kant, but beyond, to the breakdown of post-Kantian transcendental philosophy and the development of nineteenth-century psychology. The latter then provides the way into phenomenology (first as psychology) and thence back to transcendental philosophy. Then, seeking to improve upon his investigations into the origins of the modern period, Husserl adds the section on Galileo, drawing upon ideas developed before but greatly expanding them and, most important, "discovering" the concept of the life-world. It is to be noted that if our theory is correct, this discovery takes place in keeping with the idea of historical reflection *as* historical reduction and *after* such a reflection had already been carried through to Kant and perhaps even beyond. Thus the "discovery" of the life-world takes place in the context of a reflection on the whole of modern philosophy, not just on Galileo. Pondering the importance of this discovery, Husserl decides to explore the life-world in its own right and sees this as providing its own way of access to transcendental phenomenology. Here, too, of course, he draws upon investigations of a much earlier date; but as we have seen, these are given a decisive new turn.

But he chooses to *insert* the section on the life-world into the historical discussion rather than place it at the end. Why break up the continuity of the work as planned? Why not simply add it *after* the "psychological way"? Because, as we have seen, the life-world is significant as a critique of transcendental philosophy itself, and not simply as a critique of the post-Kantian psychology that had rejected the transcendental turn entirely. Thus it is that Husserl interrupts the historical reflection with Kant, a philosopher who is fully in possession of the idea of transcendental

32. I have been greatly aided in this reconstruction by a carefully researched paper entitled "A Common Misunderstanding Concerning Husserl's *Crisis* Text" (forthcoming in *Philosophy and Phenomenological Research*) by Philip Bossert.

philosophy even though he has not placed it on a rigorously scientific basis. But the turn to the life-world does not simply leave the historical discussion behind; Husserl *continues* the critique of Kant, but this time in a new direction, taking Kant to task for presupposing the life-world, for failing to see its position in relation to the sciences and to subject it to an investigation in its own right. Thus, as we said earlier, the discussion of Galileo in which the concept of the life-world emerges reveals its true significance not in Husserl's critique of objectivism, but rather in his critique of transcendental philosophy; and the transcendental philosophy which is criticized with respect to the life-world is as much Husserl's as Kant's.

A Tentative Conclusion

Assuming that this reconstruction of Husserl's train of thought is correct, the text of the *Crisis* assumes almost the character of a working manuscript in which the idea of historical reduction is for the first time put into practice and in which its results gradually emerge. But because of this very character, we may well ask if this new procedure is fully grasped in a self-conscious way and whether Husserl is aware of all its implications. How, exactly, does the new historical reduction relate to the phenomenological reduction in its classical sense? Does it somehow completely replace it or does it work together with it? Through this reduction, the idea of the life-world emerges, as we have seen, as the genuine concept of the world, or as the most fundamental and pervasive sense of the world upon which all other givenness of objects is based, from which all other senses and types of objectivity derive. The phenomenological understanding of consciousness must at the same time be an understanding of its world, as always, but as Husserl sees it now, the world had always been misunderstood phenomenologically, or only inadequately understood, prior to the discovery of the life-world.

In this sense, the concept of the life-world represents the fulfillment of the aims of the phenomenological reduction. Husserl's aim had always been to describe the world just as it presents itself to us, and to describe the forms of consciousness in which this presentation is actualized. This is what was meant by going to the *Sachen selbst*. The point of the reduction was to bring about, in the form of a habitually established attitude, a direct contact with our experience, a contact which we always already have but are forever overlooking, and to guard it against our natural tendency to theorize around and about it. By bracketing all our theoretical prejudices, and finally by overcoming the prejudice of the natural attitude itself, we are able to restore and maintain this direct contact, and the result is an awareness of and an ability to describe the *genuine sense* of the world, the sense which is constantly being by-passed by the attempts of philosophers to reduce it to some simple schema, such as the "naturalism" Husserl had attacked in "Philosophy as Rigorous Science," or by attempts to assert that there is no one genuine sense, such as the "historicism" he had attacked in the same essay. As he says at the close of the *Cartesian Meditations*, "phenomenological explication does nothing but *explicate the sense the world has for us all, prior to any philosophizing . . . a sense which philosophy can uncover but never alter.*" [33] Its aim, in other words, is to be able to describe nothing other than the "natural" attitude and its world, to do so thoroughly, completely, and without distortion. The project is the same as that inaugurated in the early pages of the *Ideas*.

With the discovery and explication of the concept of the life-world, Husserl feels that he has finally arrived at the fulfillment of this project. The genuine or most fundamental sense of the world, the sense that lies before all interpretation of its objects, the "sense the world has for us all, prior to all philosophizing," is now available for phenomenological description. But the process of establishing and maintaining contact with this sense is now complicated by the concept of historicity. As we have seen, the phenomenological reduction itself is in effect a "complication" of the desire to return to the *Sachen selbst;* it results from a recognition that in order to understand our engagement in the world we must suspend it, distance ourselves from it. And this suspension is an enormous mental effort which goes against the very grain of conscious life. But the "complication" deriving from the concept of historicity is of a different nature. The point is no longer merely to overcome the *natural* tendency or prejudice of consciousness in order to understand consciousness. Now it is also necessary to overcome the *historical* prejudices of consciousness, which, no less than the natural

33. *CM*, p. 151.

ones, prevent the philosopher from grasping the *Sachen selbst.*
While Husserl's earlier "philosophical epochē" had insisted on
the need to set aside all prior philosophical views, these views
were not accorded the status of prejudices—*Vorurteile* or *Selbstverständlichkeiten*—in the fullest phenomenological sense; thus
their force in conscious life was not seen as comparable to
that of the natural prejudices themselves. Through the concept
of historicity Husserl is led to the recognition that historical
views *are* prejudices in this sense, and that a failure to recognize
this fact and to deal with it seriously may have the result that
the phenomenologist's insight into the natural state of consciousness is obscured. Historical prejudices cannot be set aside by fiat;
they must be examined and worked through in order to be uprooted. In other words, the desired contact with "the genuine
sense the world has for us all" is not to be established without a
complicated process of reliving and examining the historical-
intellectual situation of the philosopher who seeks that contact.

We have seen the form this complicated process has taken
in the *Crisis.* Primarily, it amounts to identifying and describing
a certain attitude toward the world which is bound up with the
modern tradition of physical science and showing the effect this
has had on philosophy. The strength and success of a certain
theoretical approach to reality has led philosophers to see this
as the only approach to reality and to suppose that the world as
determined by this approach is the genuine sense of the world.
What the historical reduction does is to identify this approach
as a historical phenomenon and explain philosophers' preoccupation with it as a result of their historical situation. The cir-
cumscription of the theoretical approach of physical science is
extended to include all theoretical approaches to the world, and
the theoretical attitude as a whole is contrasted with the pretheoretical engagement of consciousness in the life-world.

We could summarize Husserl's critique of the tradition by
saying that philosophers have concentrated on how we *think*
about the world to the neglect of how we *experience* and *live in*
the world, and they characterize the world primarily as an object
of thought. Indeed, the world as thought about is surreptitiously
substituted for the world as experienced, so that the latter is not
simply neglected but described in a distorted way. That is, the
description of the world as experienced is derived from theoretical thought rather than from the way we actually experience
it. This squares with our account of the ambiguities in Husserl's

own conception of world throughout his early works, a conception which, if we are correct, is itself implicitly under attack in the *Crisis*. Even the transcendental turn, to which Husserl was fully committed, did not free him of the force of historical prejudices derived from objectivism. His concept of transcendental philosophy required that he reflect upon consciousness and the world and describe the latter as it actually presents itself. Instead, like the modern tradition generally, whether transcendental or not, he had described it in terms of a certain theoretical stance. Only after identifying and examining this stance *as* historical and as purely theoretical could he see beyond it to the description of the world he had sought all along. The world as experienced or as lived, the life-world, is a world discovered only by *contrast to*—and in consequence of freeing oneself from—the theoretically interpreted world of the sciences. Only by seeing *through* and *beyond* the confines of a certain historical framework is that primitive contact with experience reestablished. Once we succeed in the arduous task of bracketing our *thought* about the world, we can recognize it as it is really lived. Only after this insight is achieved will the philosophical understanding of theory itself be complete, since the life-world is not only to be distinguished from the world of theory and described in its own terms; it must be seen as the "meaning-fundament" of all theory, the underlying soil from which the latter is derived. The theoretical approach to reality is different from pretheoretical conscious life, but it is nevertheless founded on it. Modern epistemology not only overlooked and neglected the life-world in its concentration on theory; it also misunderstood the full nature of theoretical thought because it failed to see it in its proper context, namely, in its relation to the life-world.

The contrast, then, is between the world as thought about—the world as subjected to a certain interpretation deriving from a historical tradition—and the world as lived in the sense of the pretheoretical natural attitude. The analysis of the natural attitude and its world, begun in the *Ideas* but distorted and confused precisely because of the influence of the theoretical stance on Husserl's own description, is now reinstated, its genuine significance realized. It remains only to broaden and deepen the understanding of the life-world by devoting to it as exhaustive a description as possible, one which is newly liberated from the preoccupation with scientific theory by the awareness of the historical status of that preoccupation. This seems to be the task prescribed for Part III A of the *Crisis*. Once the life-world is thus understood in its *own* terms, the problem of science can be dealt with adequately for the first time.

8 / Ambiguities in the Concept
of the Life-World

THE ACCOUNT OF HUSSERL'S PROCEDURE with which we
closed the last chapter would be satisfactory were it not for a
strange counterpoint which begins to enter into his discussion
of the life-world in the section devoted to it in the *Crisis*. Quite
early in Part III A, in the context of his critique of Kant, Husserl
writes: "Naturally, from the very start in the Kantian manner of
posing questions, the everyday surrounding world of life is
presupposed as existing—the surrounding world in which all of
us (even I who am now philosophizing) consciously have our
existence; here are also the sciences, as cultural facts in this
world, with their scientists and theories." [1]

It is odd that Husserl should count the *sciences* among the
constituents of the life-world, especially in view of the context
and the manner in which Kant is being criticized. In the very
next sentence he says: "In the world we are objects among
objects in the sense of the life-world, namely, as being here and
there, in the plain certainty of experience, before anything that
is established scientifically, whether in physiology, psychology,
or sociology." [2] Here he is speaking of the manner in which we
exist for ourselves and for one another, *not* as scientifically interpreted objects but as persons in the world who are at the same
time subjects *for* this world. He goes on to speak of the "content-
alteration" of perceptual experience and the persistence of *the*
world throughout all change. He speaks of the perspective given-

1. *Crisis*, p. 104.
2. *Ibid.*, pp. 104–5.

ness of objects, as well as of memory and expectation as fundamental modes of consciousness belonging to life-world experience. Keeping Kant in mind, he refers to "the very limited
justification for speaking of a sense-world, a world of sense-
intuition, a sensible world of appearances."[3] As opposed to the
notion of a manifold of undifferentiated "sense-data," he invokes
a phenomenological theory of the preception of bodies in space,
noting the role of the living body (*Leib*) and the function of its
sense-organs in perception. All this harks back to *Ideas* II.
"Objective science . . . asks questions only on the ground of
[the life-world's] existing in advance through prescientific life.
Like all praxis, objective science presupposes the being of this
world."[4] Appealing to the notion of passive genesis, Husserl
speaks of the "anonymity," the "taken-for-granted" character of
life-world experience and accuses Kant of having overlooked it
for this reason.[5] He proposes that it is precisely the task of
philosophy to explore this "anonymous" realm, and begins his
"exposition of the problem of a science of the life-world,"[6]
arguing, as we have seen, that the problem of the life-world
must be separated from its relation to the sciences in order to be
understood properly.

How, then, can "the sciences, as cultural facts in this world,
with their scientists and theories," be part of the life-world? In
other places, too, Husserl speaks of them in this way. Referring
to "cultural accomplishments" such as scientific theories, he
says: "Before all such accomplishments there has always already
been a universal accomplishment [i.e. that of the life-world],
presupposed by all human praxis and all prescientific and
scientific life. The latter have the spiritual acquisitions of this
universal accomplishment as their constant substratum." This
much is in keeping with the passages quoted above, but then
he goes on: "and *all their own acquisitions are destined to flow
into it [einzuströmen]*."[7] Later on he says that the life-world
"takes up into itself all practical structures (even those of the
objective sciences as cultural facts . . .)."[8] The theoretical

3. *Ibid.*, p. 106.
4. *Ibid.*, p. 110.
5. *Ibid.*, pp. 112–13.
6. *Ibid.*, p. 123.
7. *Ibid.*, p. 113; emphasis mine.
8. *Ibid.*, p. 173.

results of science take on "the character of validities for the life-world, adding themselves as such to its own composition. . . ." [9] The objective sciences are "subjective constructs—those of a particular praxis, namely, the theoretical-logical, which itself belongs to the full concreteness of the life-world." [10]

It should be clear that this use of the term "life-world" is at variance with the application of the term in our discussions up to now.[11] The distinction between the world as *thought about* and the world as *experienced* or *lived* seems to be blurred. At first it even appears that Husserl, after having insisted on the separation of life-world and scientifically interpreted world, is in these passages putting them back together again. But it is not quite as simple as that, since Husserl almost always refers to science and its theories "as cultural facts," as "subjective constructs," or as the accomplishments (*Leistungen*[12]) of persons within the life-world. Thus it is apparently not the world as described by science that is being integrated into the life-world, but scientific theories themselves and scientific practice, as cultural goods and cultural activity. The distinction is of course a valid one: there is a difference between engaging in science, i.e., interpreting the world according to its concepts and methods, and living in a cultural world of which science is a part. "If we cease being immersed in our scientific thinking," Husserl writes, "we become aware that we scientists are, after all, human beings and as such belong among the components of the life-world which always exists for us, ever pregiven; and thus all of science is pulled, along with us, into the—merely 'subjective-relative'—life-world." [13] Science is a kind of human activity, and scientific theories can be seen as something analogous to arti-facts, i.e., products of human fashioning which surround us like the man-made furniture of our social environment. Still, their peculiar nature must be recognized, as Husserl admits. He writes:

9. *Ibid.*, p. 131.
10. *Ibid.*, p. 129.
11. I have discussed the difficulties which are the subject of this chapter in an article entitled "Husserl's Problematic Concept of the Life-world," *American Philosophical Quarterly*, VII, no. 4 (1970), 331–39. It should be clear from the following that I no longer en-visage so easy a solution to these difficulties as the one I proposed there.
12. *Crisis*, p. 131.
13. *Ibid.*, pp. 130–31.

[Science's] theories, the logical constructs, are of course not things in the life-world like stones, houses, or trees. They are logical wholes and logical parts made up of ultimate logical elements. . . .

But this . . . ideality does not change in the least the fact that these are human formations, essentially related to human actualities and potentialities, and thus belong to this concrete unity of the life-world, whose concreteness thus extends farther than that of "things." [14]

The life-world, in these passages, is said to contain scientific theories as "human formations," and presumably includes other such formations as well. And yet, as the last passage indicates, it does not contain them in the same way that it contains objects, oriented around the body and perceived against a spatial horizon. Scientific theories are not objects in space; they are not perceived. Our access to them is of a much more complicated nature. Assuming that we are not ourselves the originators or developers of such theories, but rather encounter them in the world around us, such encounter first of all rests upon the kind of communicative encounter with other persons described in the Fifth Meditation. Others are experienced not as objects but as subjects with whom we share a common world. But in the present case our encounter with others must be much more than the mere sharing of a common perceptual environment. Scientific theories are ideal objects, and *language* is the medium through which such objects become public property, as Husserl recognized in his essay on "The Origin of Geometry." [15] Though he had played down the communicative function of language in the *Logical Investigations* as not being essential to meaning as such, he now recognizes its essential role in the publicity of meanings. Thus it is not merely against an intersubjective and perceptual horizon that ideal objects appear, but within a "linguistic community," what Husserl calls the "horizon of civilization [*Mensch-heitshorizont*]." [16] And here the notion of "horizon" is obviously being broadened considerably. As Husserl points out, language itself is in a sense an ideal object—"for example, the word *Löwe* occurs only once in the German language." [17] Though it is not thematic as such, except to the grammarian or linguist,

14. *Ibid.*, p. 130.
15. *Ibid.*, p. 358.
16. *Ibid.*
17. *Ibid.*, p. 357.

and must be sharply distinguished from the ideal objects, such as geometrical relationships, that it is able to disclose, it is still necessary that, in understanding what someone says to me, I grasp the *same* proposition that he utters and recognize it as the same each time it is uttered.

To exist in a world of which geometry, for example, is a part, then, is to exist within a "horizon of civilization" in which both the implicit identity of language and the explicit identity of geometric objects and relationships are fully mastered. Only in this way are theoretical truths available, by analogy to artifacts, as human products or formations. In fact, even artifacts themselves are available as such only within the human community which dictates the contexts of their applications: as tools and items of equipment they have their significance within frameworks which are always social and communal, never merely individual; and it is hard to imagine such frameworks, too, apart from the function of language which gives things their work-related names and furnishes communication among those who engage in the projects in which they are applied.

THE CULTURAL AND THE PERCEPTUAL WORLDS

TAKING ALL THIS INTO ACCOUNT, it would seem that Husserl has introduced into his discussion of the life-world some descriptions of a distinct and important level of conscious life which might be called the *cultural* or *communal*. It is not only scientific theories that "exist" and are accessible in this linguistic milieu, but also laws, institutions, customs. This level must, of course, be distinguished from scientific consciousness as such, from the forms of experience, the presuppositions and interests of the scientist *qua* scientist. To be sure, the scientist, too, lives in the community and partakes of this form of life—and indeed the particular community of scientists, of which he is a part, must also be analyzed in such terms, even if such a community exists within a larger culture containing many such "subcultures." But the scientist's own theoretical activity and observation, and the picture of the world framed by his theories, are of a very different nature from his encounter with the community of which he is a participant.

At the same time, such a cultural world can obviously not be placed on the same level with the *life-world* as it has been described in our discussion so far. For if we follow most of the descriptions of the life-world which emerge in the Galileo section and are pursued in Part III A of the *Crisis*, we must be convinced that the life-world is not only prescientific in the sense of pre-theoretical, but also precultural in the sense that it does not include those entities, relations, and horizons that require a linguistic community for their availability. The key to the life-world up to now, it will be remembered, is perception, and it is represented by the peculiar notion of a perceptually experienced horizon which is first uncovered in the early pages of the *Ideas*. Perception, according to Husserl, is not linguistic in the sense of requiring language in order to be possible. At the most rudimentary level, language as expression is the vehicle for intentions which refer to a world given beforehand.

This is not to say, then, that the cultural world is totally *unrelated* to the perceived or immediately experienced world. In fact, it is of the utmost importance to show the dependence of the cultural world upon the perceived world for its constitution. The cultural community is not something perceived, like a thing or body, but neither is it given to us independently of perceived bodies; we are acquainted with the community in virtue of perceiving other persons as members, representatives, or authorities of the community and in virtue of perceiving physical objects such as tools and books, factories and monuments as its artifacts and documents. But the cultural world is precisely *dependent* for its givenness upon the perceived world and is not *identical* with it. It represents a higher and distinct level of constitution, just as, to go back to the *Logical Investigations*, reading and understanding a sentence represents a higher level than simply perceiving the words as physical configurations on the page. The former is *founded* upon the latter, but is by no means *reducible* to it.

Thus it is by no means necessary to envisage under the titles "life-world" and "life-world experience," in the sense of perceptual horizon, a mode of consciousness in which language and culture are factually absent. Whether language and culture ever are or could be lacking from human experience is something we need not argue. The point is first to distinguish, as we have said, between levels of experience and to argue for the priority of one as the condition of the possibility for the other. There is a phenomenological distinction to be made between the world of perception and those entities and relations which exist only in the cultural milieu; the distinction is phenomenological in virtue of the question always raised by a phenomenological inquiry about any type of objects: how are they given? The point of priority is made simply in the sense that the givenness of the cultural presupposes the givenness of the perceptual and is mediated by it, while the givenness of the perceptual is not mediated by the cultural. While there are many possible linguistic and cultural communities, they represent many possible ways of dealing with and building upon a form of perceptual awareness and a perceptual world that in its structure is presumably common to all. Husserl's criticism of the Galilean developments in science as historical is not that they are wrong but that they are not necessary, that they represent one possible, and in many respects very successful, way of interpreting the pregiven life-world. The same thing could be said for any cultural structures. The point is to distinguish necessary from contingent structures of experiences and experiential objects.

In view of these distinctions, which seem so important to most of Husserl's descriptions of the life-world, it is odd that, in many other places, the term seems to cover many of the entities described above as distinctively linguistic and cultural. The only indication Husserl gives that he is aware of the distinction is his occasional use of the term "concreteness," as when he says, for example, that the "concreteness" of the life-world "extends farther than that of 'things,'" [18] or that the praxis of science "belongs to the full concreteness of the life-world." [19] Thus we might distinguish a "full" or "concrete" sense of the life-world, which includes such ideal entities and intellectual activities, from a narrower sense, namely, the one that informed our discussion previously, which does not include them. But Husserl is not always careful to make this terminological distinction—and he leaves us with a puzzle. Is Husserl introducing here, without making it clear that he is doing so, an important expansion of the concept to which he has been led by his historical reduction?

One possible source of this difficulty is the history, in Husserl's own vocabulary, of the term *Lebenswelt* itself. We have already pointed out that the term does not make its first appearance in the *Crisis*. Two earlier uses of the term which have

18. *Ibid.*, p. 130.
19. *Ibid.*, p. 129.

appeared in print should be examined. The first occurs in an appendix to *Ideas* II to which the archivists give the date of 1917. The manuscript is appended to the third part of the work, dealing with "the constitution of the spiritual [*geistige*] world," whose purpose is to work out the fundamental concepts of the *Geisteswissenschaften*. Of fundamental importance for Husserl is the concept of the person. His purpose is to distinguish the person from both the psychophysical object of psychology and the epistemological subject of philosophy. The person is related to his world not causally but through motivation. "The subject can be motivated only by what he 'experiences,' by what he is conscious of in his life, what is given to him subjectively as actual, as certain, as supposed [*vermutlich*], valuable, beautiful, good." His world is an intersubjective one made up of "things that are not mere physical bodies [*Körper*] but value-objects, goods, etc." [20] The point here, of course, is to characterize not the transcendental subject but rather the empirical subject insofar as he becomes the object for the humanistic disciplines. Even so, he must be grasped not only against the background of the "objective" or natural world, but also within the cultural world that has significance for him, and it is to this world that Husserl occasionally refers when he speaks of the *Lebenswelt*. Though no mention is made of language, Husserl is quite explicit in not wanting to limit this life-world to the perceptual horizon or to exclude cultural objects of the most sophisticated sort from it. For purposes of the *Geisteswissenschaften*, which deal with persons, their actions, their societies, and their products, no limit should be placed on the "full concreteness" of the world in which these things are found.

A second earlier use of the term *Lebenswelt* is found in the Fifth Meditation. Here the term is introduced toward the end of § 58, which deals with the "intentional analysis of higher intersubjective communities." [21] As we saw in Chapter 4, once the nature of communalization has been established in principle, the phenomenological task is to understand the community as a kind of intentional subject, and this leads to the problem of the "world" of the community. The first world of the community is the *kulturelle Umwelt* which has its own sort of "objectivity,"

20. Husserliana IV, p. 375.
21. *CM*, p. 131.

i.e., it is "accessible to everyone." Yet its objectivity is "restricted" because it is "manifestly different from that absolutely unconditional accessibility to anyone which belongs essentially to the constitutional sense of Nature." [22] "Everyone, as a matter of apriori necessity, lives in the same Nature," whereas different communities can constitute "different surrounding worlds of culture." [23] Thus such a world is accessible in the first instance only to those who belong to the community. "Each man understands first of all . . . *his* concrete surrounding world or *his* culture; and he does so precisely as a man who belongs to the community fashioning it historically." [24] Here again, the term "life-world" is applied to this cultural world, and it is significant that in this context Husserl uses the term in the plural: "concrete life-worlds." [25] The individual is brought up in the cultural world which is objective in the sense that it is not merely subjective or private; yet he can come to discover, by entering into contact with other communities, that there are other such worlds as well. At the end of the section Husserl sets as a task for phenomenological research the investigation of the world in this sense: "the transcendental sense of the world must also become disclosed to us ultimately in the *full concreteness* with which it is incessantly the *life-world* for us all. That applies likewise to all the particular formations of the surrounding world, wherein it presents itself to us according to our personal upbringing and development or according to our membership in this or that nation, this or that cultural community." [26]

Thus it would appear that, prior to the period of the *Crisis* itself, the term "life-world" was used as a synonym for cultural world, in the sense of a horizon of entities and relations that exist in virtue of the community of language. How can we interpret the appearance of this concept in the *Crisis* in connection with a notion of the life-world which seems to differ substantially from it? In the one case we have the world of "immediate experience," the "universe of what is intuitable in principle," the horizon of perceived space in which "things themselves" are given in their orientation around the living body, the horizon presupposed by all idealization, all language,

22. *Ibid.*, p. 132.
23. *Ibid.*, p. 133.
24. *Ibid.*
25. *Ibid.*
26. *Ibid.*, p. 136.

all theoretical interpretation. In the other, we have the horizon of social and institutional relations, of cultural objects, and even of ideal objects such as scientific theories. Husserl seems to be ranging under one *term* two essentially different *concepts* that need to be kept apart. Not only do the two concepts differ; they also seem to have very different positions on the phenomenological map. In the *Cartesian Meditations* the "life-world" as cultural world is introduced, so to speak, at the "upper reaches" of phenomenological investigation, as something that must be taken into account, if phenomenology is to be complete, *after* its fundamental "solipsistic" stage—with its world— has been surpassed in the direction of an *intersubjective* theory. As in the *Crisis*, the life-world as cultural world is contrasted with the objective-scientific world. But it is introduced after the objective-scientific world has been treated, and there is no suggestion that the latter depends upon the life-world or presupposes it, as in the *Crisis*. There we find the cultural world apparently combined in a curious way with the life-world as perceptual horizon, where the point is not merely to contrast life-world and scientific world, but to show that the latter is founded on the former. In the sense of the *Crisis*, the life-world belongs not to the highest or last but to the most fundamental and first stages of phenomenological investigation. By combining the two concepts in this way, Husserl seems at best to be inconsistent.

The most uncharitable interpretation of this inconsistency is that, in the *Crisis*, having arrived at the notion of the horizon of perception as pretheoretical, and having termed this the "life-world," Husserl simply forgets himself occasionally and reverts to the concept of the cultural world to which this term had previously been applied. Yet there is one passage in which Husserl seems at least to be aware of the difficulty he has created. "The concrete life-world, then," he writes, "is the grounding soil [*der gründende Boden*] of the 'scientifically true' world and at the same time encompasses it in its own universal concreteness. How is this to be understood? How are we to do justice systematically—that is, with appropriate scientific discipline—to the all-encompassing, so paradoxically demanding, manner of being of the life-world?" [27] Thus Husserl seems to raise the right question, the question we are raising here. But

27. *Crisis*, p. 131.

he provides no answer to this question, no solution to the difficulty at hand, at least not explicitly. Is there a solution to be found?

DO CULTURAL AND PERCEPTUAL WORLDS HAVE ANYTHING IN COMMON?

WE HAVE RAISED the present difficulty by pointing out the obvious and important phenomenological differences (differences in manner of givenness) between life-world as perceptual horizon and life-world as cultural world. Perhaps we should ask whether they have anything in common. One thing that must be remembered is that Husserl has arrived at the idea of the life-world in the *Crisis* by a method of *contrast*, that the life-world is consistently contrasted with the world as envisaged by the theoretical attitude of the scientist. The life-world is characterized as pretheoretical, as the horizon of being that is given before theory, to which the scientist addresses himself by adopting a peculiarly theoretical frame of mind. It is the theoretical interest—the search for a consistent and logically interrelated set of propositions about the world "in itself" —that forces the natural scientist, for example, to focus upon its measurable aspects, to measure them as approximations to entities and relationships thought of as ideal, and thus to transform his domain of inquiry into one that can be treated in mathematical terms. Husserl's life-world concept is based on the insight that the relation of consciousness to the world need not be theoretical at all, indeed has not always been so, and that, even when the theoretical attitude is present, it presupposes the world given beforehand in a pre- or nontheoretical way.

Now one thing that must be said about the *cultural* world as described so far is that its mode of givenness does not require the presence in consciousness of a theoretical stance. This is true even if the cultural world includes, as in the case of the modern world, the theories of natural science. As we said before, there is a difference between *being* a scientist, thinking in terms of theories and viewing the world in light of its concepts, on the one hand, and living in a cultural world of which science is a part, on the other. As Husserl himself points out, modern science is part of our world, even if we are not scientists and have never actively engaged in it. The scientists' theories are part of our world as "human formations," analogous to artifacts, but they are ideal, rather than physical in nature. Our mode of awareness of them is not perceptual, since they are not things to be perceived, but neither is it theoretical. Scientific theories, like other similarly ideal cultural objects, exist within a cultural horizon in which we participate by sharing a language which renders them available to us. We are acquainted with them through a form of communication, which, like perception, is not itself a "theoretical accomplishment," not something falling within the theoretical interest or frame of mind.

Thus perceptual world and cultural world are alike in being nontheoretical. A large part of Husserl's point in the *Crisis*, of course, is to mark off the theoretical attitude of modern science and show that it is precisely *an* attitude, not the only attitude of consciousness, by distinguishing it from others. In distinguishing theoretical from nontheoretical forms of consciousness, perceptual and cultural worlds together belong to the latter. Thus the term "life-world" could simply be a general term for the world as experienced in a nontheoretical way. But this is only a negative characterization and seems unsatisfactory and oversimplified. In fact, it leaves Husserl open to his own objection that the concept of the life-world is entirely derivative, even if by negation, from the notion of science. Rather than explain the life-world in its own terms, Husserl gives us only a derivative and rather blurred concept, lumping together under one term many levels of experience—like perceptual and cultural—that need to be distinguished. At the same time, the life-world thus characterized would not square with another of the points on which Husserl insists, namely, the priority and primacy of the life-world in relation to science. It is not only that there are attitudes other than that of science, and a world which corresponds to these attitudes, but also that the life-world is presupposed by scientific mental activity—continually presupposed—so that science does not simply replace it but builds upon it.

Now Husserl might mean that the cultural belongs to the life-world in this sense too. We have already mentioned the analyses of "The Origin of Geometry," in which Husserl links the "manner of being" of a science like geometry to language and culture. Perhaps he means to say that the scientist's adoption of the theoretical attitude requires that he exist beforehand not only within the perceptual horizon but also within the "horizon" of culture. He has argued, after all, that it is the mastery of language as an ideal structure that renders the objective ideal structures of geometry accessible. While the usual array of possible cultural entities and relationships—institutions, hierarchies, etc.—may not be necessary, we might want to say that language, the "medium" which renders them accessible, is. Thus we would be saying more than that science has always developed and flourished within culture—which is an obvious fact, but does not establish any necessary relationship. We would also be saying more than that man always exists within some culture or other, while he does not always engage in science. We would be saying that his existence in culture—at least to the extent of speaking a language—is a condition for his engaging in science. The life-world in the minimal sense, then, would be the horizon of perception plus the horizon of language.

Actually, however, this account is not really implied at all by the essay on "The Origin of Geometry." Although the role and significance of language receives perhaps more attention there than elsewhere in Husserl's philosophy, he does not go so far as to argue for the thesis suggested in the last paragraph. Beginning, as it were, with geometry *in medias res*, Husserl turns first to our own situation, the situation in which geometry already exists, "available to us through tradition (we have learned it, and so have our teachers), [as] a total acquisition of spiritual accomplishments which grows through the continued work of new spiritual acts into new acquisitions." [28] This is the manner in which geometry is encountered precisely as a cultural "entity" both by those who then proceed to become geometers, and add to its composition, and those who do not. But his whole point is that geometry must have had an origin, a "primal establishment" [*Urstiftung*] in order to be available to us in this way: "we inquire into that sense in which it appeared in history for the first time—in which it had to appear, even though we know nothing of the first creators and are not even asking after them." [29] Geometry comes to *us*, as it were, ready-made; even though it is an ideal structure, it is analogous to an artifact existing within our cultural space. But as such it had to be created, and it follows that there was *someone*—

28. *Ibid.*, p. 355.
29. *Ibid.*, p. 354.

"some undiscoverable Thales of geometry" [30]—for whom it did *not* already exist in this form. Whoever this was—and whether it was one person or many separated individuals does not matter—he had to make the first shift from the surfaces, lines, angles of the surrounding world to the idealized surfaces, lines, etc., that are treated in geometry. What we must say about the putative first geometer is that he existed within a world of "things," "that all things necessarily had to have a bodily character," and that these bodies "had spatiotemporal shapes and 'material' [*stoffliche*] qualities (color, warmth, weight, hardness, etc.) related to them." [31] Must we also say that he had language? This Husserl does not argue. What requires language is the process by which geometrical entities and relationships are rendered "objective," in the sense of being "there for 'everyone' (for actual and possible geometers, or those who understand geometry)." [32] The point about the originator of geometry is that before something can become objective in this sense, i.e., communicable and public, it must first be grasped "in self-evidence," i.e., "with the consciousness of its original being-itself-there [*Selbst-da*]." [33] Through the medium of language, the geometer makes publicly available what he has himself grasped privately, as it were, beforehand. Written language, furthermore, "makes communications possible without immediate or mediate personal address." [34]

If we consider the main point made by Husserl's essay on "The Origin of Geometry," we will see that he is precisely *not* arguing for the essential role of language in the theoretical accomplishment of geometry per se; rather, the contrary. When something grasped by the original geometer is rendered public or objective through spoken or written language, the reader or hearer of such communication can "reactivate the self-evidence" of its author by reproducing in his own consciousness the same insight.[35] He can thus assure himself of the truth of the other's claim. But in order to do this he must first understand that claim; and understanding it as a claim does not require that it be verified. We are back to the distinction between intention

30. *Ibid.*, p. 369.
31. *Ibid.*, p. 375.
32. *Ibid.*, p. 356.
33. *Ibid.*
34. *Ibid.*, pp. 360–61.
35. *Ibid.*, p. 361.

and fulfillment. But there is a third possibility, as we saw in Chapter 4. This is that the claim be accepted *as* fulfilled—as true—without the reactivation taking place. The recipient "can concur 'as a matter of course' in the validity of what is understood without any activity of his own." [36] This, of course, is the manner in which most of us learn of the results of science without becoming scientists ourselves. The best we can do is grasp and understand the *sense* of the scientist's claim, and we are willing to leave to him and his colleagues the assurance of its truth. They are *functionaries* for the layman in the matter of achieving scientific truth; we delegate our authority to them. *Their* attitude toward scientific claims, of course, must be different. It is their task not to admit any claim as valid unless *what* it claims is grasped in self-evidence, unless it is given exactly as it is meant.

Yet, even for the scientist, Husserl says, this is largely an unfulfilled ideal. Every scientist seeks to build on the accomplishments of his predecessors. In an advanced stage of a science, as in our own day, does he in fact reactivate for himself everything that he presupposes in order to make his own contribution? If he did, says Husserl, "a science like our modern geometry would obviously not be possible at all. . . . Even if this could have succeeded at a more primitive stage of geometry, its energy would ultimately have been too much spent in the effort of procuring self-evidence and would not have been available for a higher productivity." [37] Geometry would never have reached its present stage. Science owes its very capacity to move forward to the fact that it can take for granted something upon which to build. The position of the geometer may be like that of the layman, then, with the difference that the former accepts certain things as established for the purpose of accomplishing something new. Much of his work may involve not the reactivation but merely the "explication" of his assumptions in order to see more clearly what follows from them logically. Following this pattern, a science is capable of immense proliferation in terms of new theorems and broader applications. But at the same time it moves farther and farther from its origins in self-evidence.

Husserl's point is that the very thing that makes a science like geometry capable of forward movement is at the same time

36. *Ibid.*, p. 361 n.
37. *Ibid.*, p. 363.

a threat to its self-understanding as a science. It enters into that process of "technization" that renders it more prolific and at the same time "[empty] of meaning." [38] Husserl is, in effect, issuing a call to sciences like geometry and mathematical physics to return to their origins by reactivating the fundamental insights on which they rest. It is not clear that Husserl is actively recommending this to scientists themselves, for he is constantly pointing out the advantages—both theoretical and technological —which derive from the process of technization. But he does urge the "return to origins" on a *philosophy* which would adequately understand the *sense* of science. Thus he insists, toward the end of the essay, that *epistemology* cannot be as ahistorical an inquiry as is thought by the enemies of historicism. Geometry can be understood philosophically only through the "historical backward reference" to the supposed "Thales of geometry." [39] The cultural existence of a science like geometry, as an ongoing tradition, must be understood as an edifice resting upon an accomplishment which does not presuppose such prior existence. Geometry maintains its own sense as a science to the degree that its claims can be " 'cashed in' for self-evidence." [40] And even if the science as a cultural tradition were to vanish, through some universal loss of memory and a "conflagration of the world's libraries," it could arise again in virtue of a repetition of the same original accomplishment.[41]

Thus Husserl is again leading us back to the life-world, and this precisely in the sense of the *perceptual* horizon, not the cultural. As we have seen, all that we must say about the proto-geometer is that he existed in a world of shapes, surfaces, lines, angles, which were subjected to an idealization and grasped in original self-evidence. Geometry as a *public* phenomenon does indeed owe its existence to language, but the genuine sense of geometry is an accomplishment which does not presuppose that public status, but is rather presupposed by it. With regard to *language,* Husserl is being consistent with his views in the *Logical Investigations:* Language is a medium of communication, a system of signs which serve as indicators (*Anzeichen*)

38. *Ibid.,* p. 46.
39. *Ibid.,* p. 370.
40. *Ibid.,* p. 363.
41. *Ibid.,* p. 350. Cf. Jacques Derrida in the introduction to his translation of Husserl, *L'Origine de la géométrie* (Paris: Presses Universitaires de France, 1962), p. 93.

of our thoughts, a vehicle through which we transmit them to each other.[42] Here Husserl pays considerable attention to the role of language, not because his essay expresses a different view of its relation to thought, but because he is interested in the public and traditional status of a science like geometry. Far from elevating the status of language, he speaks of the *"seduction of language"* [43] by which publicly available meanings are made our own without the corresponding insight. Far from being essential to thought, or to insight, language is capable of leading us away from it.

We are left without an answer, then, to the question of the problematic relation of cultural world to perceptual world under the heading of the life-world. Our attempts to conceive of a sense in which the two share a community of essence seem not to accord with Husserl's meaning, in spite of several passages which suggest this. But there is another possible interpretation of Husserl's statements which we have not yet considered. Husserl says in one place, we recall, that the "spiritual acquisitions" of science have the "universal accomplishment" of the life-world as their "constant substratum," and yet at the same time they are "destined to *flow into it* [*einzuströmen*]." [44] In another place he says that they take on the "character of *validities for the life-world*." [45] In the first of these passages Husserl is not simply saying, as he says elsewhere, that a scientific theory, once it is "invented," becomes part of the life-world, is added to its composition. He says rather that it "flows into it," i.e., *into* that very substratum on which it is erected. In the second he says not that a scientific theory becomes a sort of entity or item, as an ideal structure, *within* the life-world, but that it becomes a validity *for* the life-world, or, as we might say, something *valid* for the life-world. These differences of expression, though slight, open the way to a different conception of the relation between cultural and perceptual world. Suppose we give up the attempt to expand the range of possible constituents of the life-world to include scientific theories and the like, which seems suggested by some of Husserl's remarks, and remain instead with the life-world concept that seemed implied earlier: that of the

42. *LI*, pp. 276–77.
43. *Crisis*, p. 362.
44. *Ibid.*, p. 113; emphasis mine.
45. *Ibid.*, p. 131; emphasis mine.

experienced horizon of perceived reality, the sphere of "what is intuitable in principle," etc. As we have seen, scientific theories themselves, whether as actively subscribed to or even as cultural objects, *cannot* become part of this world simply because they are not perceived; they are not "objects" in the sense of "bodies." Is there any sense at all in which they can "flow into it," become "validities *for* it"?

A POSSIBLE SOLUTION TO THE PROBLEM

THE ONLY WAY to make sense of this is to refrain for a moment from considering scientific theories as ideal cultural artifacts, as we have been doing, and turn rather to their content as theories. As theories they are, after all, about something. They make certain claims. What do they "speak" about and what do they say about it? Naturally, they talk about things and animals, man and (as *Geisteswissenschaften*) man's culture. In other words, they speak of the very world in which we live. In the case of natural science, theory speaks of the spatio-temporal world. It is the very same world which is our perceptual horizon, the same objects that we directly perceive, that are referred to in scientific theory. And what does it say about them? The point of Husserl's interpretation of modern natural science is that before it proceeds to tell us something about the real world it restricts itself severely with regard to the *kinds* of things it can say. It subjects the everyday objects around us to a certain interpretation, considering only those aspects of them which lend themselves to exact measurement and hence to description in strict mathematical terms. Everything that is going to be said about the world, about the makeup of things, the manner in which events regularly occur, etc., is going to be said in these terms. Indeed, "these terms" prescribe what is to count at all for the scientist as an event, property, relation. This "interpretation" of the everyday world, this restriction of the kinds of properties, relations, and events that *can* be dealt with in science, is not itself a theory, not a part of the content of science. Rather, it is an "attitude" corresponding to the "interest" of producing such theories, an attitude which, according to Husserl, marks off "a self-enclosed 'world'-horizon." Such an attitude is presupposed by the theories themselves, for it prescribes what kind of content they can have.

Returning now to the case of scientific theories considered as "artifacts" encountered in the cultural world, we have spoken of the manner in which these are encountered. According to the analysis of "The Origin of Geometry," it is through language that they become available to us. But there is a certain ambiguity in this. It is true that scientific theories are not perceived objects, and that we become aware of them through communication. But we might make a distinction between a weak sense of "becoming aware of them" and a stronger sense which involves becoming *acquainted* with them, actually encountering them. By being told or overhearing it, we could learn that there *are* scientific theories in the world, that such things "exist" and have been produced by certain of our fellows who are called "scientists" and whose business it is to produce such things. This could hardly be described as an encounter or a direct acquaintance, however; indeed, such hearsay might lead us to suppose that "scientific theories" were some form of artifact, like shoes. Even if we knew that scientific theories were something on the order of bodies of propositions or claims, we would not yet have encountered them. In suggesting that such theories form part of our world as cultural facts, Husserl obviously means that to some degree we encounter the theories themselves, that through our schooling or through the reading and conversation of the generally "educated," we have some acquaintance with them, however vague. Now the only way really to "encounter" a theory or a body of assertions or claims is to *understand* those claims, to grasp their meaning. And this is nothing other than having a sense of what the claims are speaking about and what they are saying about it. We need not withdraw the point we made earlier, that there is an obvious distinction between engaging in science and living in a world of which science is a part. To understand what science is about, it is not necessary to be a scientist. But we now see that if science is truly a part of our world, in the sense that we have some acquaintance with its theories, it cannot be conceived *merely* as counting among the elements of our world, as being one type of "object" within it. For, as something encountered in the sense of being understood, it is understood *as* referring to and saying something about other aspects of our world; natural science, for example, says something about the perceived objects and events around us. And even if we are ignorant of, or have forgotten, most of the detailed content of scientific theory—and this is certainly true of most laymen—we still understand the *kinds* of things science says and the kinds of things it does not say about the world. Thus, at the very least, we understand the attitude or interpretation which lies behind science and determines what content is permissible.

Restricting the term "life-world," now, to the experienced perceptual horizon, we can say that anyone who lives in the cultural world that includes modern natural science—and this in the sense of understanding, to some minimal degree, the theories of science—not only exists in the life-world, perceives objects within its horizon, etc., but *also* has at his disposal, through the medium of communication, certain theories *about* those objects based on an over-all interpretation of them or attitude toward them. But the essay on "The Origin of Geometry" points to a further aspect of this state of affairs. There Husserl is speaking of geometry as exemplary of a whole range of possible *eidetic* sciences, and does not refer specifically to the geometrized science of *nature*. But what he says applies to it as well. He speaks of a state of culture in which geometry is a living tradition. In such a culture the theories of the geometrician, indeed the whole state of mind which makes them possible (in this case the attitude of idealization per se), are not merely encountered and understood but are accepted, *taken for granted*. While Husserl wishes to make the point that such an acceptance is true to some degree even for the geometricians themselves, it is all the more true, as we have pointed out, for the layman. Not wishing to take upon himself the task of validating the theories, he delegates his authority to the professional geometrician; the latter becomes his functionary in this matter. Now this can apply not only to geometry as an a priori science but also to mathematical natural science, if that science is likewise a living tradition in a culture, as it certainly is in ours. As can easily be seen, accepting and taking for granted the results of science is much more than merely understanding them and having them at our disposal. We may also be aware of other theories and interpretations of the things around us, such as those which endow them with magical powers or correlate daily events to the movements of the stars. We could even be said to genuinely encounter or be acquainted with such theories in the sense that we understand what they are talking about and what they are saying about it. But these are not part of culture as a living tradition, at least not of *our* culture—we who live in the era of science. We not only live in the life-world, perceive and move around among the objects of our spatiotemporal surroundings, but we also have at our disposal and also *accept* a certain interpretation of these objects which is the legacy of science.

Now what exactly does it mean to exist within the life-world, to perceive its objects, *and also* to accept a certain interpretation of them derived from science? Earlier, we spoke of the distinction between what we think about the world and our experience of the world. Husserl, we said, is arguing that we must not allow what we *think* (scientifically) about the world to affect and distort our account of how we *experience* the world. This is the mistake of most modern philosophy. If we can succeed in bracketing our thoughts about the world by setting aside our acceptance of scientific theories, we can reflect on our experience as it really is, correctly understand it, and describe it accurately. But what if our involvement in the scientific tradition were to affect not only our *account* of our experience, our reflective description of it, but also that very *experience itself*? Or better, what if it were to affect our account of our experience *because* it affected the nature of the experience on which we reflect when we set out to give an account of it? This conception takes on plausibility if we remember our distinction between the specific claims of science and the attitude which lies behind it. We can be aware of certain scientific theories, and these can affect our *practice* if we accept them. For example, I do not allow the temperature in my freezer to rise above 32°F because I know that if I do the ice in it will melt. Thus my action is determined by my acceptance of the scientific theory that ice melts at 32°F, which is actually a general statement about the relation between the solidity of H_2O and the length of a column of mercury compared to a fixed scale. My conviction in this matter need not be based on a generalization from my own experience, but is taken over on authority from the scientists who are my functionaries.

Now while such a conviction determines what I do, it cannot be said to determine how I experience things, to affect the manner in which they are given. But from such convictions, as accepted bits of scientific theory, we can distinguish the attitude which determines what kinds of things can be said through specifying the kinds of properties or characteristics of things that can be dealt with scientifically. The underlying attitude of science constitutes a kind of conceptual focus, an attention to some things to the neglect of others. Can such an attitude affect experience in such a way that a conceptual focus becomes a *perceptual* focus, a perceptual attention to some aspects of things and an overlooking of others? Obviously, this is precisely what it does in the case of the scientist, since in order to arrive at his theories he has to pay attention to individual things and events. His theories are, after all, about such things, and both his hypotheses and his confirmations can be said to derive from just this kind of attention to them.

However, we are speaking here not of the scientist qua scientist, but of the layman who lives in a cultural world in which science is a living tradition. Is it possible that his experience is similarly affected, even though he is not actually engaged in the project of science, simply in virtue of his position within the tradition? The life-world has been characterized, among other ways, as the horizon of what is given independently of the scientific interest and of the theoretical interest generally. If participation in scientific culture affects the way things are given, even for those who are not scientists, perhaps this is what Husserl means by saying, in the *Crisis*, that the results of science "flow into" the life-world, that they become validities (or simply valid) *for* it. This is a view which is apparently expressed in the Introduction to *Experience and Judgment*, a work to which we will turn in the next chapter.

9 / *Experience and Judgment* and the Problem of Historicism

BEFORE EXAMINING THE VIEW expressed in *Experience and Judgment,* we must be clear on the peculiar status of this text.[1] Ludwig Landgrebe is listed as the "editor" of this volume, which was first published in 1939, but he informs us in his foreword that his work has been more than just editorial in the usual sense. As far as the main body of the text is concerned, he had to transcribe from shorthand and organize manuscripts written over a period of almost twenty years. He describes himself as responsible for the "literary formulations," while Husserl provided the "raw material" or "conceptual content."[2] But the Introduction, seventy-two pages long, seems to be even more the responsibility of Landgrebe himself. It was written in or after 1935 for the purpose of "relating the sense of the analyses as a whole to the last phase of Husserl's thought" as found in the *Crisis,* and also in order to summarize "those basic ideas of *Formal and Transcendental Logic* which are decisive for understanding the approach of the individual analyses."[3] The Introduction is in part a "free rendering" of ideas from these two

1. Time has not permitted me to use the new translation, *Experience and Judgment: Investigations in a Genealogy of Logic,* trans. James S. Churchill and Karl Ameriks (Evanston, Ill.: Northwestern University Press, 1973), which has just appeared at this writing. The translations in this chapter are my own, and the references are to the original. However, since almost all passages are taken from §§ 6–11 of the Introduction, the reader should not find it hard to find them.
2. *EU,* p. xi.
3. *Ibid.,* p. vi.

works, and "in part based on oral discussions with Husserl and . . . on manuscripts from the years 1919–34. The outline [*Entwurf*] of this Introduction, too, was itself discussed with Husserl and approved by him in its essential content and train of thought." [4] But Husserl never did go over the final text of the work.

One is understandably reluctant, then, to attribute the results of this "quite unique form of collaboration" [5] simply to Husserl, and this is especially true of the Introduction. What we can say is that, to the extent the ideas of the latter do come from Husserl, they come for the most part from the very period in which the *Crisis* was in process. In any case, they speak directly to the problem which faces us now, whoever their "real" author might be. Thus we must examine this text, and in order to be cautious we will attribute its assertions not simply to Husserl but rather to "*EU*" (for *Erfahrung und Urteil*) or to "the text."

The main purpose of the Introduction is to show why an adequate understanding of *Urteil* requires an understanding of *Erfahrung*. To paraphrase briefly, the argument is that judgment is essentially a claim to knowledge. Even when a judgment is merely "entertained," it is entertained *as* such a claim, though the "entertainer" may not be interested in the validity of that claim. This latter is true of the formal logician, who considers the purely formal relations of implication between judgments as such. But in doing so he takes judgment for granted without considering its essential nature. The understanding of what the logician takes for granted requires that it be understood as a knowledge-claim. As such, a judgment is *about* something, an object in the broadest sense. Its claim to knowledge is justified to the extent that its object is *given*. Thus the understanding of judgments as knowledge-claims requires an understanding of how objects can be given to support these claims. The validity or self-evidence of a judgment (*Urteilsevidenz*) must be traced back to the givenness or self-evidence of the object (*gegenständliche Evidenz*). Now anything at all, of course, can be the object of a judgment: essences, numbers, relations, judgments themselves. But the givenness of some types of objects is dependent or is founded upon the givenness

4. *Ibid.*, p. x.
5. *Ibid.*, p. xi.

of others. In order to study the problem of *gegenständliche Evidenz* at its roots, it is necessary to consider those "ultimate substrates" whose givenness is required by all founded types but is not itself so founded. This mode of givenness is what we call experience (*Erfahrung*), in which individual things are directly encountered prior to, and as a condition of, a judgment in which something is predicated of them. Thus "the *theory of prepredicative experience* [*vorprädikative Erfahrung*]—precisely that experience which gives us the most original substrates in objective self-evidence—is the intrinsically first element in a phenomenological theory of judgment." [6]

From here *EU* moves directly to the discussion of the *world*, which is "pregiven as the universal ground of belief for every experience of particular objects." [7] It is not only that every "cognitive activity," every attempt to arrive at the *wahrhaft seiender Gegenstand*, by means of a theoretically grounded judgment, presupposes objects given beforehand; even experience itself, as the prepredicative givenness of particular objects, always presupposes the world as horizon of objects given passively in advance. The discussion here parallels both the Second Section, First Chapter, of *Ideas* I ("The Thesis of the Natural Attitude and Its Suspension") and Appendix VII of the *Crisis*, which we have already discussed: [8] whatever is given is given within the horizon of the world: particular things may turn out to be other than I had supposed, but *the* world remains unaffected, etc. The world is not the object of an "act appearing in its own right" (*eigens auftretender Akt*) in which something is grasped as existing, much less the object of a predicative judgment of existence. Rather, "all this presupposes world-consciousness in the certainty of belief." [9] "And even if it is of the nature of the theoretical interest, when it is consistently carried out to the end, that it is aimed ultimately at knowledge of the totality of what is—and this means the world—this is still something that comes later." [10]

The long § 8 elaborates on the idea of the world as "universal ground of belief" by pointing to the *way* in which the world functions as horizon. The world of experience has a

6. *Ibid.*, p. 21.
7. *Ibid.*, p. 23.
8. Cf. Chap. 7, p. 164–68.
9. *EU*, p. 25.
10. *Ibid.*, p. 26.

structure in virtue of which every object, however unfamiliar, is encountered as falling within a *type* of which we have a prior acquaintance (*Vorbekanntheit*). Thanks to this background of structural familiarity (*Vertrautheit*), every thing directly given has its internal and external horizons which are more or less clearly delineated, but in any case delineated to some degree. It is in this sense that every individual experience presupposes a background of passivity which in its turn prescribes a "fore-ground" of anticipated possibilities to be "filled in" by the actual further course of experience. The world as horizon in this sense is what must be understood if *Erfahrung* is to be understood; and the latter is what provides the substrates for the judgments that the logician deals with in his abstract way. The concrete understanding of logic determines it as *world-logic* (§ 10) in the sense that it presupposes the world as the field in which the activity of judgment finds its application. Thus the understand-ing of logic requires an exploration of experience which extends to its ultimate horizon, a *"return to the world* as it is pregiven—immediately and prior to all logical accomplishments—as the universal ground of all particular experiences, as *world of experi-ence."* This *Rückgang* is further characterized as a *"return to the life-world,* i.e., the world in which we always already live." [11]

But now the text begins to warn us of complications in this project. It turns out that "in the flow of our world-experience, as it is related to the always already pregiven world, [we] will not always find so easily those sought-after, ultimately original self-evidences of experience." [12] It will not suffice simply to take any experiential judgment as an example and ask after the givenness of its substrate-objects. And why not? Because "the world in which we live and in which we act in a cognitive-judging manner, from which everything comes which affects us as substrates of possible judgments, is always already pregiven to us as permeated with the deposit [*Niederschlag*] of logical accomplishments." [13] This means that it is given as something already "worked over," so to speak, by judgmental activity, either my own or that of "others whose experiential acquisitions [I] take over through communication, learning, tradition." [14] And this is true not only of the sense of every object as we encounter

11. *Ibid.*, p. 38.
12. *Ibid.*
13. *Ibid.*, p. 39.
14. *Ibid.*

it as such, "but also of the horizon-predelineation [*Horizont-vorzeichnung*], [i.e.,] of the sense with which it is pregiven to us as an object of *possible* knowledge, as something *determinable*." [15]

In particular, what is taken over from the tradition, and what determines the manner in which the world is pregiven, are the accomplishments of modern natural science. These accomplishments "belong" to the world which is pregiven to us as "adult men of our time." "And even if we are not scientifically interested and know nothing of the results of natural science, *das Seiende* is nevertheless pregiven in advance as determined at least to the extent that we apprehend it [*es auffassen*] as scientifically determinable in principle." [16] Everything that is encountered is taken as belonging to a "universe that is determined in itself" [17] in the manner discoverable by scientific methods in accord with its own concepts. For example, the space and the time of our world, as well as the causal interrelations among events, are taken to be the same space, time, and causality that are dealt with by science. What is overlooked is the "idealization," of which the *Crisis* speaks, which interprets these concepts mathematically. The "mathematization of nature" has become *selbstverständlich* for us; we simply take it for granted.

> Thus right from the start [*von vornherein*] the world of our experience is interpreted [*gedeutet*] with the aid of an "idealization," and it is no longer seen at all that this idealization that leads to the exact space of geometry, to the exact time of physics, to the exact law of causality, and that leads us to see the world as determined in itself in these ways, is precisely already an accomplishment of cognitive methods which are grounded in what is pregiven in our *immediate* experience. [18]

In other words, the world *as interpreted* by the cognitive accomplishment of those who originated modern science becomes the world *as experienced* by us. Those very properties which they ascribe to the real in the manner of a *hypothesis* or *proposal*, as stated in the *Crisis*, have become the properties of the real as it is *pregiven* to us. They began with a pregiven world

15. *Ibid.;* emphasis mine.
16. *Ibid.*
17. *Ibid.*, p. 40.
18. *Ibid.*, p. 41; emphasis mine.

and subjected it to the idealizing interpretation; for us the world is pregiven as *already* so interpreted "right from the start." *Our* cognitive accomplishments, *our* judgmental activity, build upon a pregiven world of experience; but according to *EU*, the latter is no longer a world *immediately* experienced, but a world whose givenness is mediated by the sedimented tradition that we take over in virtue of our membership in the scientific culture, even if we are not scientists.

But the task of *Experience and Judgment* is to trace judgmental activity *as such* back to its roots in experience. It will not be satisfied, then, with an experience which is itself but the deposit of prior judgmental activity, but will seek instead that "immediate" or "original" horizon of experience in which no such activity is presupposed, i.e., the life-world itself. Thus the "return to the original life-world is not one which simply accepts [*hinnimmt*] the world of our experience, just as it is given to us . . . ," [19] for this is a world which is given under the domination of traditionally acquired scientific concepts. A "garb of ideas" (*Ideenkleid*)—the term comes from the *Crisis*—has been thrown over the life-world by the tradition so that it is "hidden" (*verhüllt*) from us.[20] It must be sought out in its hiddenness, must be discovered again. Even before the turn to subjectivity is taken, which will accomplish the full transcendental-phenomenological understanding of the genesis of judgment, it is necessary to return first *"from the pregiven world [vorgegebene Welt]* with all its deposits of sense, with its science and scientific determinations, *to the original life-world."* [21]

There is no doubt that an element of the argument in the *Crisis* is recapitulated in what we have just cited. The transcendental turn requires that we move from our straightforward dealing with the world to a consideration of the world-as-meant, and of the subjective process through which it is meant and given. But this turn must go hand in hand with a proper understanding of the world which is subjected to such a consideration. Husserl's objection to Kant was that he had not had such an understanding, that he had improperly begun with the world as interpreted by science. But the world as interpreted by science cannot be understood except by relation to the world as given

19. *Ibid.*, p. 44.
20. *Ibid.*, p. 48.
21. *Ibid.*, p. 49.

prior to and independently of science, the life-world. Thus Kant's transcendental turn did not begin at the right place, and before that turn can be accomplished now, the idea of the life-world must be worked out. Only if the transcendental turn is applied here can scientific objectivity and every other type of objectivity within the world be genuinely, transcendentally understood.

But equally, there is no doubt that *EU* goes *beyond* the argument of the *Crisis* as just stated. What is suggested in the *Crisis* is that if we can get beyond our tendency to conceive of all consciousness as theoretical—a tendency inculcated by the modern scientific tradition—and concentrate instead on experience which is free of the interest of theory, we will arrive at that "genuine sense of the world" which underlies all theoretical and other interests, the world which all cognitive activity presupposes. According to *EU*, this is not enough. It will not suffice merely to consider consciousness apart from the theoretical interests of science, since—at least in our day—even such consciousness carries with it the sediment of theoretical activity in such a way that the world is given in terms of such activity. It is not enough simply to distinguish between the world as *thought about* in active theoretical thinking and the world as pregiven, or passively taken for granted by such thinking, for even this pregiven world, while still passively accepted, is theoretically determined. Thus *EU* distinguishes further between the pregiven world (*vorgegebene Welt*), with its interpretative covering, and the original world which lies at the basis of that interpretation, the world which, once discovered, will represent the "genuine sense of the world," the genuine point at which the transcendental turn must be effected.

Seen in this way, *EU* clears up a major ambiguity left by the text of the *Crisis* itself. It is hard to tell whether this is Landgrebe's own response to that ambiguity as he himself sees it in the text of the *Crisis*, or whether this is Husserl's own clarification, deriving from those conversations Landgrebe had with him. In any case the text enables us to understand the peculiar way in which the cultural world is introduced into the *Crisis* in connection with the life-world. It is not that the cultural world is seen as part of the life-world, in spite of some of Husserl's remarks which seem to indicate this. Rather, if we understand the life-world as the perceptual horizon, certain elements of the cultural world—especially scientific attitudes toward life-world objects—*flow into* the life-world to the extent that they are accepted or taken for granted. They do this, as we have seen, by affecting the manner in which we experience things.

But *EU* helps further by introducing more precision in terminology. What these elements of the cultural world flow into is the world which is pregiven, the world as it is passively experienced and taken for granted in judgmental activity. Now the point on which the *Crisis* insists, and which is pursued in *EU,* is simply that judgmental activity—scientific activity in particular—*does* presuppose such a pregiven, passively accepted horizon, that it accepts a world prior to and underlying its explicit adoption of a particular scientific or other interest. This is what is called the "life-world" in the *Crisis*. But that text makes no distinction between the pregiven horizon which has already been affected and transformed by the sediment of science— into which its results have already "flowed"—and such a horizon which is not so affected and transformed. It is the *latter,* the genuine and unmediated ground of belief, which *EU* calls the "life-world," while the former is termed simply the pregiven world. The *Crisis,* by contrast, speaks repeatedly simply of the "pregiven life-world." *EU*'s terminological distinction has, of course, one curious result. It is the pregiven world, already permeated by scientific interpretation, in which we—as men of our time—actually live. The original life-world, which is hidden, covered over, and in a sense left behind, seems to be remote from us, at least initially, so that we have to "rediscover" it. It seems odd, terminologically, to characterize as the "life-world" the world in which, in a very important sense, we no longer live. Still, at least this text is an improvement over the *Crisis* in making clear a distinction which the latter does not make.

A Major Problem Raised by *Experience and Judgment*

But if *EU* succeeds in this way in clearing up a major ambiguity in the *Crisis,* it does so only by raising major *methodological* questions which concern the historical reduction, its relation to the phenomenological reduction and the whole phenomenological project, and the possibility of fulfilling that project at all. The implications of *EU*'s conception of the life-world for phenomenological procedure are seen immediately and are pursued as the text continues.

§ 11 begins with the assertion that, because of the manner in which scientific thinking affects the givenness of what is experienced, "the necessary return to the most original self-evidences of experience cannot be accomplished by psychological means." [22] This statement in itself is hardly surprising, and one expects the text to proceed by distinguishing in a standard way between empirical or experimental psychology and phenomenology. But the distinction that actually follows is more sophisticated. For the repudiation extends even to a psychology considered "pure," i.e., one which concentrates strictly on "what is purely experienced and given to consciousness [*das rein Erlebte und bewusstseinsmässig Gegebene*] as such," a "pure internal psychology [*reine Innenpsychologie*]." [23] The reason for this is that, even if such a psychology were to take seriously the problem of self-evidence, pursuing the validity of judgment to its foundation in prepredicative experience, it would necessarily be inquiring into the experiences "of subjects who are already precisely subjects of our world—a world which is already covered over [*überlagert*] with idealizations and is apperceived in terms of this covering." [24] But "striking through" this covering to its "hidden foundation of sense" in "the most original experience" is not a problem that psychology can even pose, "no matter how broadly and purely it is carried out." "For psychological reflection on experiences [*Erlebnisse*] as they are available to inner perception cannot lead back to the origin, in original life-world experience [*Erfahrung*], of this garb of ideas thrown over the world." [25] It leads only to the experience "of a world which, for this subject, stands before him as already ready-made; and this means that it stands before him as a world upon which modern science has already done its work of exact determination." [26] When the psychologist reflects on experiences, the world which is the correlate of such experiences "always belongs" to what he is investigating. But he has no way to get from these experiences to the *"origin of this world itself,"* i.e., the origin of

22. *Ibid.*, p. 45.
23. *Ibid.*
24. *Ibid.*
25. *Ibid.*, p. 46.
26. *Ibid.*

the world as already scientifically determined. To be sure, this world had its origin in "subjective accomplishments"—"activities of cognition, the exercise of scientific methods," etc.[27] But these are accomplishments of "an intentionality *which does not lie open to the gaze of reflection.*"[28] What is required is a return to the subjectivity "through whose intentional accomplishment the world has acquired this form; but it is a *return to a hidden* [*verhüllte*] *subjectivity*—hidden, because its intentional accomplishment cannot be shown [*aufweisbar*] directly [*aktuell*] in reflection."[29]

Thus it is obvious that § 11 of *EU* does not distinguish in the standard way between an empirical psychological and a phenomenological approach to the problem of experience and judgment. Rather, the distinction that we find here is something radically new, brought on as a consequence of new developments found within *EU* itself. What one might expect, when such a distinction is introduced, is a repudiation of an empirical or explanatory psychology which would seek the "origin" of judgment by tracing the conditions, mental or otherwise, under which judgments regularly occur as actual events in the world. But here, such psychology is not even thought worthy of mention. In fact, it is explicitly stated that what is under consideration is a psychology considered "pure," focused strictly on "what is purely experienced as such," and the explanatory or causal approach of most psychology is not referred to. What is repudiated is psychology's *way of access* to experiences, whatever it may do with them—e.g., in the way of explanation or mere description—once it has them. And what is that way of access? "*Reflection.*"

But why does this repudiation of reflection as a way of access amount to a repudiation of *psychology*? Is *reflection* not also the key to *phenomenological* method itself? To be sure, in order to be phenomenological in the full sense, reflection must, as we saw in Chapter 1, be *radical*. This means that it takes in the *object* of the experience on which it reflects and at the same time "brackets" it, i.e., considers it purely *as* meant in that experience; and ultimately, this "object" that is bracketed must be the whole world. This movement constitutes the

27. *Ibid.*
28. *Ibid.*, p. 47; emphasis mine.
29. *Ibid.*

phenomenological reduction. Furthermore, the results of reflection must, according to Husserl, be subjected to an eidetic reduction whereby they are taken merely as examples of essences that are sought. But whatever the peculiar features of reflection which determine it as phenomenological, it is still *reflection*, i.e., a turn from the straightforward consideration of objects to the consideration of the experiences in which they are given.

Although it does not say so explicitly, perhaps *EU* should be taken as repudiating only that *form* of reflection which is operative in psychology, and not reflection per se. Leaving aside the problem of explanatory psychology, what would differentiate psychological from phenomenological reflection? We have spoken little of Husserl's views on psychology since Chapter 1, where we dealt with his earlier repudiation of explanatory psychology. Now we must take into account his later views on psychology. As distinguishing characteristics of phenomenological method, we have mentioned the eidetic reduction and the phenomenological reduction; let us consider these in turn. First, is psychological reflection different from phenomenology because it is not susceptible to eidetic reduction? Not according to Husserl. What is grasped in psychological reflection can be subjected to "ideation" through imaginative variation in such a way that the *eidos* of the psychic and of various psychic structures is attained. There not only *can* be, but indeed there *should* be, behind empirical psychology, an *eidetic psychology* which clarifies its basic concepts, as we have seen in Chapter 1.[30] Thus psychology is by no means restricted to being a science of fact, as opposed to a science of essence. In order to carry out meaningful experimental investigation of regularities among factual occurrences, psychology must be clear on the basic kinds of occurrences it is investigating. But this is true of the scientific investigation of *any* domain, e.g., physical nature. It must be remembered that the term "science of essence," as opposed to "science of fact," is *not* one that applies to phenomenology alone. There are many sciences of essence, and phenomenology is but one of them.

But what of the phenomenological reduction? Phenomenological reflection, as we said, focuses not only upon experiences but also upon the objects of these experiences, the latter being bracketed, i.e., considered exclusively *as* they are meant in the

30. Husserliana IX, pp. 72 ff.

experiences focused upon. But the approach is not excluded from psychology, either. In fact, Husserl insists that because all experience is intentional, any consideration of it which does not take into account its object-as-meant is missing the point. Thus he calls for a psychology that is not only eidetic but also *intentional*. This is what Husserl means by the "phenomenological psychology" to which he devoted so much exposition, especially in his lectures. And he explicitly mentions, as part of such psychology, a "reduction" termed the "phenomenological-psychological reduction." [31] But what of the further provision that the phenomenological consideration of the object-as-meant be expanded to include the ultimate horizon of all objects, the *world*? Surely, this is what finally distinguishes even phenomenological psychology from phenomenology in its full sense as *transcendental* phenomenology.

Yet even this is not what constitutes the difference. It is not *whether* the world as such is considered, but rather *how* it is considered, which provides the distinction between phenomenological psychology and transcendental phenomenology. Psychology, too, can consider not only experiences and objects-as-meant, but also the *world-as-meant*. Indeed, again it *should* do this if it is properly to understand its subject matter, experience (consciousness, the psyche); for it is of the nature of experience to be directed ultimately toward the world as horizon. But psychology does not make the full *transcendental* turn because it considers its subject matter—experience, object, world-as-meant —"on the ground of the world," i.e., it takes this whole complex as something which exists *in* the world as a whole, i.e., as a part of the world. It takes for granted the existence of the world, of which minds and their experiences constitute one *region* alongside other regions and which is interrelated with those other regions. Thus while such a psychology would indeed consider the world-as-meant, it would not, like transcendental phenomenology, consider the world *exclusively* in this way; for it would also involve a straightforward, unexamined acceptance of the world. Transcendental phenomenology, by contrast, renounces this acceptance altogether, and has the world before it in only *one* mode: *as meant*. And this difference also affects its acceptance of consciousness, as we have seen: the relation of consciousness to the world is not that of existing *in* the world,

31. *Crisis*, p. 236.

but strictly that of *intending* the world. True, an intentional psychology would also *consider* consciousness exclusively in terms of its intentions; but, because of its underlying, non-transcendental approach, the consciousness that it considers in this way would still be taken as existing *in* the world. This whole discussion turns, of course, on the fundamental distinction between the natural and the transcendental *attitudes*. In spite of all that it takes from phenomenology, an intentional psychology would still be based on the natural attitude.

This difference in attitude is, of course, of paramount importance for Husserl. At the same time, it can be seen that if psychology is pursued to its limits by following the demands of its own subject matter—that is, if it not only recognizes the intentional character of consciousness but also sees that this requires a consideration of the *world*-as-intended—then this difference in attitude is the *only* thing that separates a "genuine" psychology from transcendental philosophy. This is why, from the mid-1920s on, Husserl saw the pursuit of psychological subject matter as a way of access to phenomenology: once psychology had been pushed to its limits within the natural attitude, the shift to the transcendental attitude would, he thought, suggest itself. This is the approach followed in the *Encyclopedia Britannica* article,[32] and indeed, as we have seen, it was to have been the basic approach of the *Crisis* itself prior to the inclusion of the life-world section. It is, in fact, the approach of the present Part III B. Furthermore, Husserl repeatedly insisted that psychology, if properly understood, is "parallel" to phenomenology in the sense that everything it says about consciousness can be transformed into a phenomenological assertion by shifting to the transcendental attitude.[33] In other words, it is not *what* is said, but rather the "sign" under which it is said, that makes the difference: phenomenological reduction amounts to a "change of sign."

What we have just said reflects the most advanced state of Husserl's researches on the nature of psychology and its relation to phenomenology. And what is peculiar about *EU* is that when it refers to psychology, it clearly has this fully developed Husserlian concept in mind. Not only does it speak of a psychology which is "pure"—one of Husserl's usual terms for an

32. Husserliana IX, pp. 237 ff.
33. *CM*, p. 38.

intentional, phenomenological psychology—in the sense that it is focused "on what is purely experienced and given in consciousness as such." [34] It even says explicitly that "to the experiences [*Erlebnisse*], as the psychologist . . . finds them, belongs the *world as the correlate of the experiences* he is investigating. . . ." [35] And yet such a psychology is rejected as a way of access to the life-world, and what is given as the reason for this rejection is psychology's method of *reflection*. But what distinguishes psychological from phenomenological reflection is neither its subject matter—as reflection it is focused on experience—nor its reference to the world, nor the actual content of the descriptions that result, but only the attitude under which it is performed. The difference lies in the interpretation, we might say—i.e., transcendental or natural interpretation—to which its results are subjected. Now this rejection hardly squares with Husserl's notion that the results of psychology are valid for phenomenology if only this interpretation is changed. Phenomenological and psychological inquiry differ not because one is reflective and the other is not but only with regard to whether or not their reflection is transcendental.

THE REJECTION OF REFLECTION

THUS IT IS HARD to uphold the interpretation that *EU* rejects only psychological reflection, especially if psychology is understood as phenomenological psychology. In any case, *EU* says not that it rejects psychological reflection, but that it rejects psychology *because* it is based on reflection. It is reflection that is inadequate as a means of access to the life-world. And indeed, on the basis of what precedes it in the text, this rejection of reflection as such is easily understandable. Being "men of our time," our world is permeated by the sediment of the scientific tradition. We are so much a part of that tradition that our world, in the very way it is given, prior to all judgmental activity, is shot through with determinations derived from scientific thinking. Now if we reflect on *our* experience, we who are "men of our time," and if our reflection takes into account the world that is given in such experience, what is the character of

34. *EU*, p. 45.
35. *Ibid.*, p. 46.

the world that thus confronts us reflectively? Clearly, it is the world that is thus pregiven, "ready-made," permeated by idealizations taken over from the tradition. This is the only world to which we have *access* in reflection. And as *EU* says, to reflect upon this world is not to discern *its* origin in the "original life-world."

But the serious problem raised by this consideration is whether, in its rejection of reflection per se, *EU* is also rejecting that form of reflection that figures in phenomenology itself. If phenomenology is indeed characterized by its reflective method, albeit radical, and if reflection is judged inadequate as a means of access to the life-world, we arrive at the peculiar result that phenomenology as it has been understood up to now is wholly incapable of getting at the life-world. Indeed, a method which is confined to reflection would seem to condemn us to a hopeless relativism. Reflection involves turning from objects given to the description of the manner in which they are given. In reflecting, we could attend to the forms of such givenness and the forms of consciousness in which it is effected. We could "radicalize" our reflection by expanding it to include the whole world as the horizon of the given, and by bracketing our straightforward acceptance of the world, and our reflective turn could then legitimately be called "transcendental." Our procedure could even be made eidetic by concerning itself with the essential structures of the givenness of objects as we encounter them. But what would be the result? Our description could never extend beyond what is available to us as "men of our time." The sense of the world, of objectivity, and of our experience that would result from such reflection would be limited to a particular historical phenomenon: we would be describing *only* the world of those of us who happen to exist at this particular time in a culture which bears the stamp of the scientific tradition. Clearly, this would fall short of the "genuine sense the world has for us all," where the "all" refers precisely to the universality which transcends historical differences. Of course, the claim that philosophy is incapable of transcending its historical situation is none other than the "historicism" that Husserl had attacked, along with psychologism, in "Philosophy as Rigorous Science" and the *Logical Investigations*. Is this the fate of phenomenology once historicity is taken seriously?

This is, needless to say, hardly the conclusion drawn by *EU* itself. In fact, its whole point in discussing the pregiven, historically determined world is that philosophy must transcend it, get at its roots. But if reflection is incapable of accomplishing this, how is it to be accomplished? What *does EU* propose as the method for arriving at the original life-world, for "striking through" the cloak of ideas to its "hidden foundation of sense"? The pregiven world, with its covering of idealizations, according to the text, is the sediment of "a historical development [*eine Geschichtlichkeit*] through which the world first acquired the sense of an objectively determinable world existing 'in itself'." [36] The return to the original life-world must "pursue [this] historical development, which is already deposited in [the pregiven world], back to its origin." [37] All the "deposits of sense" (*Sinnesniederschläge*) that are "at hand [*vorliegt*] in our present experience" must be "dismantled." [38] This activity of dismantling (*Abbau*) involves "an inquiry back . . . into the subjective sources from which [these deposits of sense] have arisen, and thus into an accomplishing subjectivity which does not belong to the subject who, reflecting psychologically [*psychologisch sich besinnend*], sees himself already confronting the ready-made [*fertig gewordene*] world. Rather, it is that subjectivity through whose accomplishments of sense the world as it is pregiven to us—*our* world—has become what it is for us." [39]

Thus the text seems to be telling the philosopher of our time that he must address himself to a subjectivity *other than his own* in order to arrive at the "original life-world." Presumably, this "other" subjectivity is, specifically, one which exists not in our world, or our time, but rather at the beginning point of that tradition of which we are the heirs, one whose activity is responsible for the idealizations which now "cover" our world as a matter of course and determine the manner in which its objects are given to us. We must turn from the consideration of *our* world, and *our* experience of it, to the world and the experience of the person or persons who made our world as it is. For them there was no difference, as there is for us, between the pregiven world and the life-world. An interrogation of their experience will presumably put us in contact with that life-world which has been lost to us by virtue of the force of tradition.

Thus *EU* has brought us to a seemingly paradoxical

36. *Ibid.*, p. 44.
37. *Ibid.*
38. *Ibid.*, p. 47.
39. *Ibid.*

position: everything turns on an understanding of the "original life-world"; yet, as we have seen, in a sense the life-world is not even the world in which we live. Now we are apparently being told that the subjectivity to which we must turn, if we are to understand anything else, is not our own but that of some remote ancestors. It is no wonder that reflection will not do, if we define reflection as the subject's consideration of his own conscious life. Presumably, the result of this interrogation *will* eventually be an understanding of our own experience and, in particular, of the nature of judgment. But this understanding is not to be gained by the sort of direct examination that we associate with reflection. Such an examination would only be misleading.

But the difficulty inherent in *EU*'s proposal is obvious: how do we, in our time, make the kind of contact with the historical originators of our tradition that would enable us to understand how they experienced the world? We can read their works. Will this suffice as a means of access to the world in which they lived?

According to *EU* there is more that we can do. We need to understand the accomplishments of these predecessors, but it is not as "particular historical personages" that we turn to them.

> We could not understand [their accomplishments] if we could not reproduce [*nachvollziehen*] these accomplishments in ourselves, if we could not experience [*nacherleben*] this arising of the accomplishment of idealization out of original life-experience [*Lebenserfahrung*], that is, [if we] could not complete in ourselves this return [*Rückgang*] from the covered-over life-world, with its garb of ideas, to the original world-experience and life-world.[40]

In this reproduction (*Nachvollzug*), then, the accomplishments that were previously hidden become accessible to us.

At first sight, these passages seem to be nothing more than *EU*'s "free rendering" of the argument in the *Crisis* for what we have called the "historical reduction." Like the *Crisis*, *EU* is operating with a notion of the *historicity* of consciousness— indeed, here the notion is worked out even more explicitly than it is in the former work. The subject is seen as standing within a tradition whose concepts he takes for granted, i.e., whose concepts play the role of *Selbstverständlichkeiten* in his con-

40. *Ibid.*, p. 48.

scious life. Given the aim of coming to terms with these *Selbstverständlichkeiten* and transforming them into *Verständlichkeiten,* the philosopher must turn to their origins in his own intellectual background: it is not enough simply to declare himself free of these prejudices; he must root them out by reliving them. Furthermore, the language recalls what Husserl says about his approach to the historical figures at several points throughout the *Crisis:* it is necessary to "strike through the crust" of objective history,[41] to "reconstruct the train of thought" that motivated Galileo,[42] etc.

But the fact of the matter is that *EU* has lead us to an even greater paradox: on the one hand, the reasons for the necessity of historical reduction are even stronger than those offered in the *Crisis;* on the other hand, *EU* robs us of the very means of carrying out that reduction.

It is easy to see why *EU* presents "stronger reasons" for the historical reduction than the *Crisis.* This is because it pictures the human subject as being more deeply embedded in the tradition. Not only does he inherit certain concepts from it, i.e., concepts of reality, of the world, of subjectivity, etc., which determine for him the *Sachen und Probleme* of philosophy, but, what is more, his inheritance determines the very way the world is given to him. It is not only his thought about the world but his very experience of the world that is affected. The more thoroughgoing the effects of history on the subject, then, the greater the need to come to terms with it, to bring it to light in the manner of a reduction.

But the possibility of such a reduction becomes problematic if we ask ourselves just how the *Nachvollzug* of the accomplishments of our predecessors is to be achieved, given the presuppositions of *EU.* Presumably, what is meant are analyses like that of the Galileo section of the *Crisis.* Recalling that analysis, we remember that its "reconstruction" of Galileo's "train of thought" involved, first of all, an understanding of his goal—the achievement in respect to physical nature of the kind of clarity and intersubjective agreement found in mathematics. Then it traced the fulfillment of this goal in the application of ideal geometrical concepts to the experienced world—or, more precisely, the application of the experienced world to those

41. *Crisis,* p. 18.
42. *Ibid.,* p. 23.

concepts, through the procedure of idealization. Galileo "proposes," as Husserl puts it, to deal with the real world scientifically only to the extent that its experienceable features can be treated as instances of ideal geometrical properties and relationships. His greatness lies not only in this proposal, but also in the degree to which he was able to carry it out by finding more and more aspects of the real which could be treated in this way—including the so-called "secondary qualities," as they were called by later philosophers.

But how are we able to *understand* Galileo's accomplishment —we who live in an age so thoroughly dominated by his thought? Clearly, the analysis of Galileo in the *Crisis*, and the understanding we are supposed to achieve through it, can only succeed if we have access not only to Galileo's intellectual accomplishment of mathematization but also to the world which he confronted and sought to deal with in this way. In other words, we must place ourselves in a world which *preceded* Galileo's accomplishment in order to be able to "reproduce" it in ourselves and thus to understand it in the way it must be understood.

Yet this is the very thing that *EU* says we cannot do. As the heirs of Galileo and the whole tradition of modern science, we have supposedly lost contact with the world that preceded that tradition. That contact, however, is what is needed if we are to carry out the investigation prescribed. *EU* seems to leaves us at an impasse. It exhorts us to recapture the original life-world which has been "covered over" by the sediment of tradition; it directs us to relive the intellectual accomplishments of those who originated that tradition in order to effect the recapture; but the possibility of this recapture seems to presuppose the very contact with the original life-world that we seek. Otherwise, living as we do in the already mathematized world of science, it seems we can only speculate as to the nature of an experience and a world in which this mathematization had not yet occurred.

The only helpful hint offered by *EU* is the term "dismantling" (*Abbau*), a term also found in one of the *Beilagen* to the *Crisis*.[43] The idea seems to be that we can somehow subtract the idealization from our present experience, remove or take apart what has been superadded to the world by the function of tradition,

43. Husserliana VI, p. 498.

and thereby arrive at what was present before this process began. But we are given no further clue as to the nature of this procedure. Without an idea of what was there before, how are we to know what has been superadded? Again, a circle begins to appear. What is more, such a dismantling procedure seems to suggest a kind of negative construction, rather than a recon-struction or reproduction in us, of the original life-world in its relation to the idealizing accomplishment. This is a far cry from the phenomenological insistence on grasping in original intuition the thing itself.

But this is what the rejection of reflection has left us with. Since we no longer *live* in the original life-world, since the world no longer *presents* itself to us in this way, we cannot simply turn, in the manner of reflection, to the *way* in which it is given. Reflection is the form of intuition in which we make the kind of contact with the world-as-given that is required by a phenomenological description. Yet now, for reasons we have seen, reflection will no longer do. If the procedure of "dis-mantling," and the resultant construction of the original life-world, is still to be described as a *phenomenological* procedure, then the term has surely changed its meaning.

SUMMARY

AT THIS POINT perhaps we should pause to summarize the results of our examination of the Introduction to *Experience and Judgment*. We turned to it because, whatever the status of its authorship, it provides a possible solution to a problem that develops in the exposition in the *Crisis* of the concept of the life-world. The problem was that of the relation between this concept, as it emerges in the *Crisis* as a result of what we have called the "historical reduction," and certain statements of Husserl's concerning what is properly called the "cultural world." Simply expanding the concept of the life-world from its original status as perceptual horizon to include cultural phenomena, which is suggested by some of Husserl's remarks, seems not only to conflict with other things Husserl says but also to deprive the original concept of its genuine phenomenologi-cal significance. Hence, we explored the idea of the cultural world's "flowing into" the life-world as preceptual horizon by

determining the manner in which things are perceptually encountered. Though it is only hinted at in the *Crisis*, this idea is
developed, as we have seen, in the Introduction to *EU*.

At first this idea seems attractive. Not only does it clear up
the above-mentioned ambiguity in the *Crisis;* it also has a certain intrinsic plausibility. After all, is it not the case that we
actually *see* and *experience* things in terms of our inherited
ideas? Some parts of the *Crisis*, like Husserl's earlier philosophy,
might have led us to believe that the structures of perception
are absolute and universal, unaffected by our engagement in
history. But what is significant about the *Crisis*, as we have
tried to argue, is that, for the first time in Husserl's career,
history, or rather the historicity of human subjectivity, is really
taken seriously. Is it not the case that the conception outlined
in *EU* is simply the ultimate "seriousness" with which history
can be taken? Viewed in this way, it seems to round out and
support many other aspects of the *Crisis* as well. As we have
seen, such a strong concept of the historicity of consciousness
renders even more urgent the need for historical reduction.
Furthermore, it seems to make more understandable what we
have claimed is Husserl's critique of his own earlier views:
Husserl, like other philosophers before him, had approached the
problem of the world in terms of the scientifically interpreted
world, not because he had simply overlooked the life-world but
because this is the way the world appeared in his actual experience of it. His mistake, we might say, was the mistake of
phenomenology itself as he then understood it: he simply reflected on the world as it presented itself to him as a "man of
his time."

However, if this conception seems intrinsically plausible and
for other reasons attractive, in the end it brings us, as we have
now seen, to a hopeless impasse. For the only thing consistent
with the aims of *Experience and Judgment,* and indeed with
the project of transcendental phenomenology itself, is to trace
this historically determined world back to an "original" world,
the life-world, on which it is built. But the means prescribed for
carrying this out seem impossible to fulfill. Such a method presupposes the very thing it hopes to achieve: acquaintance with
the "original life-world." In the end *EU* seems to leave us
stranded in the very position it exhorts us to escape from:
engagement in a world determined by our historical situation.
Unless we can make some sense of the apparently unphe-

nomenological method of *Abbau,* we are condemned to history, and historicism seems vindicated after all.

There is yet another difficulty presented by this train of thought. We have said that *EU* operates with a concept of historicity even stronger than that of the *Crisis.* But in the text this concept is elaborated by only one example. It is only men of *our* time who are said to be affected by the historical-intellectual tradition in which they exist. In a sense this is perfectly understandable: it is to us, after all, that this book, with its program for philosophical investigations, is addressed. We are to turn from *Urteil* to *Erfahrung,* and we need to be warned as to how our experience is affected by our particular historical situation. We are told of our own tendency to experience the world in terms of the mathematical model of modern science, whether we are scientists or not. Then we are instructed to turn to that subjectivity in which this model was not yet taken for granted, but from which it originated. Only when we arrive at and understand such a subjectivity and its experience will we understand the true origin of judgment in the life-world.

Thus we are directed to envisage a subjectivity, such as that of Galileo, whose world was not yet "covered over" with the "garb of ideas" that characterizes our world. But, we might ask, is it not the case that Galileo *also* lived in a cultural world, and that *his* experience was as much affected by the concepts of his own historical situation as our experience is by ours? To be sure, he was free of the particular forms of experience that we, as his heirs, owe to his very activity. But he was not free of all historicity. Indeed, the concept of historicity from which the analysis of *EU* is derived seems to be a *general* concept applying to all conscious subjects alike, whatever their particular place in history. It is a characteristic of subjectivity generally that it is engaged in history, that it inherits certain *Selbstverständlichkeiten,* and that these involve a certain interpretation of the world or of being. The particular content or character of this interpretation varies, of course, from one historical period or tradition to another. But some interpretation, some set of traditional *Selbstverständlichkeiten,* is always present. Indeed, we usually think of a pivotal historical figure like Galileo not as one who initiates a way of looking at the world *ex nihilo,* in a cultural vacuum, as it were, but as one who introduces a *new* way of looking at things and effects a break with the old—in his case, the Aristotelian-medieval—way.

Thus, in seeming to direct us to the origin of the modern, mathematical way of viewing the world in order to find the "original life-world," *EU* seems to be projecting the idea of a kind of "age of innocence," an experience free of *all* conceptualization. Even if such an age were conceivable, we would hardly be justified in placing it in the Renaissance. The *Crisis* itself, it must be said, does not seem to conceive of Galileo and his age in this way. While Galileo is obviously chosen for examination because of his key role in *our* cultural world, Husserl presents him precisely as a revolutionary figure who overthrew the dominant conceptions of his time. Furthermore, Husserl is at pains to show the degree to which Galileo's new conception owed much to the past, namely, in its indebtedness to the mathematics of the ancients. Indeed, the *Crisis* makes much of that feature of the Renaissance which is customarily associated with it and even gives it its name, i.e., its conception of itself as a rebirth, a return to and revival of the Greek view of man's relation to the world, at least in respect to his cognitive goals.[44]

This picture of the relation between Galileo and his time should lead us to question not only *EU*'s suggestion of a kind of "age of innocence" prior to the beginnings of modern science, but also the very conception of historicity on which it seems to rest. For, after all, the significance of Galileo was that he was *not* totally a child of his time, that he and his contemporaries were able to break away from their own tradition and initiate a new one.

The relation between the Renaissance and Greece, mentioned but not dwelt upon in the *Crisis*, is what had led Husserl in the Vienna Lecture to focus precisely on the Greek ideal of knowledge as the true origin of our preconceptions concerning the world and man's relation to it. Galileo's mathematization provided the means for fulfilling the idea of a unified, all-encompassing knowledge of the world on which every rational being must agree, but that ideal itself was Greek; in fact, the origin of this ideal is, according to Husserl, the origin of philosophy itself in its broadest sense. In the Vienna Lecture itself, Husserl "reconstructs" the Greeks' "train of thought" in much the same way he does Galileo's in the *Crisis:* a growing awareness of the discrepancies between our different conceptions of the world

44. *Crisis,* p. 21.

goes hand in hand with the idea of a world "in itself," independent of our subjective views of it, or of the views of our societies, the idea of being that persists through change—and the problem of our access to that being.[45] Whatever the differences over the centuries in the conception of this being "in itself," and in the view of how one comes to know it, man's relation to his world is conceived in terms of the idea of a pure cognitive relation to this "in itself"—*theōria*.[46] In this sense, philosophy is a Greek invention, and Husserl conceives of "Europe," in the spiritual rather than the geographical sense, as the community of heirs to the Greek philosophical ideal. As in the *Crisis,* Husserl stresses the necessity of understanding how this theoretical stance arose out of a pretheoretical attitude toward the world.

Following the line of *EU,* does this mean that we now have to project the supposed "age of innocence" back to the time prior to the origin of philosophy itself? But even here Husserl puts great stress on the *cultural* world of prephilosophical civilization. Even the creation of philosophical culture was not the creation of culture itself, but again a shift from one world-view to another. Husserl claims that the prephilosophical world view can be understood as a *practical* relationship between man and his world, as opposed to one which seeks knowledge of "true being" apart from its practical consequences.[47] And such a practical relationship in culture goes far beyond the social store of techniques developed for dealing with the immediate environment in order to procure the daily needs of life. Even the "mythical-religious" concerns of man, which extend to encompass the world as a whole, are not "theories" about the nature of the universe but expressions of a practical relationship between man and the powers that govern the world.[48]

Clearly, *EU*'s quasi-historical search for some primitive consciousness in direct, culturally unmediated relation to the world will not do. It is the very function of culture to "mediate," in the sense of providing its members with an interpretation of the world, a set of concepts that are taken for granted. To find a form of experience that bears no trace of such mediation, we should have to envisage man in a state in which he is *totally*

45. *Ibid.,* p. 278.
46. *Ibid.,* p. 280.
47. *Ibid.,* p. 282.
48. *Ibid.,* p. 283.

unknown to us: man without culture, not only prehistoric man but precultural man. Is man without culture still man? Even if he were, the search for him would be justified only if the history of culture were regarded as a steady accumulation, a form of growth in which layer was simply added to layer without any radical breaks. And this is certainly incompatible with Husserl's own picture of the radical transformation which took place with the birth of philosophy, and again with the revolution of the Renaissance.

Thus we should revise our critique of *EU*'s notion of the "original life-world." Earlier, we said that the text had left us without any access to such a world, and that we seem on that account to be condemned to a form of relativism. Now we must ask whether the concept of the "original life-world" itself makes any kind of sense at all. Do we have any reasons or evidence for supposing a basic structure of experience upon which all particular cultural forms are built? Perhaps there are as many "life-worlds" as there are cultural forms, which have neither common structures nor a common ancestor. This would make Husserl's earlier (i.e., pre-*Crisis*) use of the term the only correct one. If this represents the final consequence of the train of thought opened up in *Experience and Judgment*, it also represents the ultimate vindication of historicism.

10 / Historical Relativity
and Transcendental Philosophy

OUR EXAMINATION of the Introduction to *Experience and Judgment* seemed to lead to a vindication of historicism. If this consequence is valid, the claim of phenomenology to the status of transcendental philosophy—in fact, the possibility of any transcendental philosophy at all—is seriously threatened. Indeed, if Husserl had followed the train of thought we have developed in the last chapter, he might well have uttered the statement often attributed to him: "Philosophy . . . as rigorous science—*the dream is over.*" [1] Of course *EU* itself nowhere asserts such a vindication of historicism, and even seems to be pointing in the opposite direction; thus, one could question the validity of our interpretation of that text in the last chapter. Furthermore, even if our interpretation of *EU* is accepted, one can question the status of *EU* itself as a statement of *Husserl's* views, for reasons we outlined at the beginning of Chapter 9. Yet, as we have seen, this text provides a possible answer to certain ambiguities that arise in the course of the *Crisis* and, as such, constitutes a valuable aid in the interpretation of Husserl's last work. Taken in this way, *EU* deepens and intensifies the notion of historicity already present in the *Crisis*, and seems more aware than the latter text of the implications of that notion. As we have presented it, *EU* simply follows through to a paradoxical end the development set in motion by the idea of "historical reduction."

1. *Crisis*, p. 389. Often quoted as if it were Husserl's own view, this is a sentiment Husserl is attributing to the present age, as is clear from the context.

This is the paradox with which Husserl leaves us at the end of his life. As we stated at the outset, the nature of Husserl's late manuscripts leaves us without any clear answers. It is not even clear whether he is explicitly aware of the conflict between transcendental philosophy and historicism as we have described it; in any case, he presents us with no clear-cut resolution to it. On the one hand, Husserl seems not to despair of the possibility of transcendental philosophy; this is clear throughout most of the *Crisis*. On the other hand, the ambiguities of that text, taken together with a plausible interpretation of *Experience and Judgment*, raise serious doubts about that possibility. We must emphasize again that this is an interpretation we have made, not one that is offered by Husserl or even Landgrebe. Still, on the basis of reflections similar to those found in our interpretation of these texts, many others in our time have reached the same conclusion concerning the historicity of conscious life.

The question before us, and the question we shall examine in this chapter, is whether this conclusion is to be accepted and what obvious consequences might be drawn for the fate of philosophy as rigorous science, i.e., as transcendental philosophy. Our purpose here will be to examine the historicist conclusion on its own merits, to see whether it represents a coherent alternative to the idea of transcendental philosophy. Before proceeding to the task, let us summarize briefly the manner in which this conclusion has been derived from Husserl's idea of "historical reduction."

FROM HISTORICAL REDUCTION TO HISTORICISM

"HISTORICAL REDUCTION" is the name we gave to the procedure that Husserl, in his last attempt to present and ground phenomenological philosophy, evidently considered a necessary part of his method. The necessity of this new procedure had impressed itself on Husserl, as we saw, because of his growing recognition, in the years prior to the *Crisis*, of the historical character of transcendental consciousness. What this recognition amounts to is a theory of the role of certain prejudices or *Selbstverständlichkeiten* in conscious life which are comparable in function to the prejudices of the natural attitude itself, but which are historical in character. These prejudices, then, derive not so much from the nature of consciousness itself as from the engagement of consciousness in a particular historical situation. They constitute the conceptual sediment of tradition which is inherited by individual consciousness in its dealings with the world and with others; and which is unacknowledged and unexamined as such.

A philosophy that is dedicated to freedom from prejudice must come to terms with this unacknowledged heritage. It is not enough that a philosopher declare his emancipation from all prejudices if his cultural inheritance still operates surreptitiously as he constructs his theories. Like the natural attitude itself, the cultural heritage of the philosopher can be deprived of its taken-for-granted status only if the philosopher raises it to the level of conscious awareness by reliving it and making explicit what was previously hidden. This we saw as the motivating force behind Husserl's "historical and critical reflection" on Galilean science and the manner in which it was integrated into the philosophy of the modern period. The criticism of "physicalistic objectivism"—including rationalism and empiricism—was developed along lines familiar to readers of Husserl, but as the exploration proceeded to include "transcendental subjectivism"—primarily Kant—Husserl's criticism developed into an important revision of transcendental philosophy which applied even to his own earlier phenomenological version of it. It was found that transcendental philosophy, while ostensibly directed against its objectivist predecessors, actually took over uncritically from them its concept of the *world*. Husserl's concept of the life-world, which developed out of his study of Galileo and which in the *Crisis* was directed against Kant, was seen to overcome an objectivist tendency in his own concept of the world prior to the period of the *Crisis*. We showed the dominance of this objectivist concept in Husserl's earlier thought in order to make clear the degree to which Husserl's historical reflections brought about the recognition of certain unacknowledged prejudices in his own thinking.

As we developed Husserl's theory of the life-world, we saw it initially as representing the fulfillment of the phenomenological project of describing the world and overcoming the historically acquired hindrance to that fulfillment. The philosophical-scientific tradition was seen as inculcating in us certain ways of thinking about and interpreting the world we live in, and leading us to take the world, so interpreted, to be the world *as* we live in it, *as* it is directly given in our experience. Historical reduction has the function of revealing the philosophical-scientific interpretation precisely *as* an interpretation, a certain way of thinking about the world, and of allowing us to distinguish it from the world as we actually live it, the world of which science is a conceptual interpretation. In arriving at the life-world, we arrive at that "general structure" which underlies all historical relativities, that structure which "is not itself relative."[2]

But certain ambiguities in Husserl's presentation of the life-world concept in the *Crisis* gave rise to the suspicion that the picture was not so simple. While the foregoing interpretation seemed to presuppose a sharp distinction between life-world and cultural world, certain of Husserl's expositions seemed to suggest a peculiar confluence of the two. In trying to unravel the difficulty of the relation between life-world and cultural world, we came upon the notion, suggested by some of Husserl's remarks, that the cultural world actually flows into and affects the nature of the world as it is directly given. Rather than consisting simply in inherited ways of thinking about or interpreting the world, historical prejudice actually shapes our way of *experiencing* the world. It was this idea, which seems to be developed in *Experience and Judgment,* that led us to the present impasse.

It is important to recognize the fact that *Experience and Judgment*—if our interpretation is correct, and if it reflects Husserl's own thinking—demonstrates that history is being taken "seriously" by the philosopher to a heightened degree, in contrast to the train of thought that gave rise to the "historical reduction." In fact, we should distinguish two levels of Husserl's newly acquired "historical consciousness": the first underlying the historical investigation of the *Crisis* and finding its resolution in the dominant concept of the life-world that is presented there; and the second arising in a different conception of the life-world, which emerges in the *Crisis* and gives rise, according to our interpretation, to the impasse of *Experience and Judgment.*

In the first case, historical prejudice is recognized—and this is what is new to the *Crisis* period, by contrast to Husserl's earlier writings—as operating under the surface, as an initially

2. *Ibid.,* p. 139.

unacknowledged heritage which cannot simply be disowned by fiat but must be revived. But what does it operate on, what does it affect? Merely the *philosopher's* ability to correctly discern the structure of his world and of world-consciousness at its deepest and most basic level. He is heir to an intellectual tradition, and it is his intellect that is shaped by his historical situation. He inherits certain ways of *thinking* about the world, and these keep him from attending to and simply *seeing* the world as it really is. The objectivist tradition, according to this view, never was a way of *seeing* the world; it was only a conceptual framework for interpreting the world that *is* seen for purposes of scientific inquiry. The historical reduction, by making us aware of the interpretative and conceptual character of objectivism, has the same function the phenomenological reduction was always meant to have: it returns us to a position of pure *seeing*. The emphasis on *seeing* in phenomenology was never as simple as some critics have made out: it never amounted to the claim that we only need to look in order to see. The rigors and dangers of the phenomenological reduction, as described with great emphasis by Husserl, attest to this: it takes great effort to get ourselves into the position where we *can* see at all. Now the historical reduction, as we have seen, adds to that effort: In order to arrive at this position, it is not only the prejudices of the natural attitude that have to be overcome, but those of the historical situation as well. But the implication is that this position can, at least in principle, be attained. Having overcome the prejudices of modern objectivism, including its hitherto unrecognized effect on transcendental philosophy, Husserl had at last arrived at the life-world, and life-world–consciousness, as the realm to be described.

As we have seen, the second level of Husserl's "historical consciousness" attributes a much greater role to history. Not only do historical prejudices operate under the surface, hidden from the historically naïve philosopher, as was true also at the first level. What they constitute is not merely a conceptual framework which dominates the philosopher's approach to the world and hinders his direct access to it. Rather, the structures of the historical culture world filter down, as it were, and affect —indeed *become*—the structures of the immediately experienced world. It is true that they begin, in the case of the modern world, as an intellectual accomplishment, a theoretical approach to the pregiven world; but once this approach has done its work and become established through the power of sedimentation, the pregiven world it began with no longer remains intact. In fact, in the terminology of *EU*, what is *pregiven* to the heir of such a tradition is precisely the world as interpreted by that tradition. And the philosopher who is such an heir is affected not merely in his capacity as philosopher—i.e., as one whose task is to effect a theoretical grasp of his world—but in his very capacity as perceiver, in his very manner of experiencing and living in the world. We have seen how this has affected the role of *reflection* as the key to phenomenological procedure. Given the function of history just outlined, the philosopher who turns his reflective gaze upon his conscious encounter with the world and on the world as he directly encounters it therein will come upon nothing more than a reflection (in the sense of a mirroring) of the historical tradition in which he lives. It is no longer a matter, then, of overcoming, through the process of historical reduction, the intellectual frameworks inherited from the past and present and of reestablishing oneself in a position to *see* the world-structure as it is apart from such frameworks. The assumption at the first level is that the structures of the experienced world remain ever the same "for us all," and we can grasp those structures if only we can free ourselves from inherited theoretical frameworks. It is this assumption that is undercut by the second level, for these structures do not then remain the same. The individual philosopher, subject as he is to his tradition, cannot hope to *return* reflectively to the transhistorical structure of world-consciousness in himself, because there is no such structure in himself to return to. There is only the historically determined structure deriving from his place in history.

Thus the very purpose of historical reduction, as it was introduced into phenomenological method, cannot be fulfilled. The "position of seeing" that was to be attained through such a reduction is in principle unattainable. One might say, then, in a paraphrase of Merleau-Ponty's famous remark about the *phenomenological* reduction,[3] that "the most important lesson which the *historical* reduction teaches us is the impossibility of a complete reduction." More than this, one must ask whether

3. *Phenomenology of Perception,* trans. Colin Smith (New York: Humanities Press, 1962), p. xiv.

the aim of such a reduction can even be partially fulfilled or whether the notion of the task itself makes any sense. Any putative accomplishment of a historical reduction, such as that carried out by Husserl in the *Crisis*, would have to be seen as something else entirely. In spite of its claim to overcome the prejudices of the philosopher's historical position, it could be shown, perhaps, to abide in those prejudices after all. It might be shown that Husserl's "return," via the historical reduction, to the life-world as the constant underlying meaning-fundament of science, and his phenomenological description of it, is, after all, simply the historically determined reflection of one who, in spite of himself, experiences the world in terms of the categories of modern science.

It might be argued that something like this has been shown by another well-known philosophical account of the world, that of Heidegger. In the *Crisis* we find Husserl speaking of the "formal and most general structures of the life-world: thing and world on the one side, thing-consciousness on the other." [4] Here he speaks of the "world-form of space-time" and outlines his concept of the world as horizon.[5] On the side of world-consciousness, as we have seen, it is perception that constitutes the fundamental form of such consciousness. But Heidegger, in *Being and Time*, speaks of the "worldhood of the world" without reference to perception or even consciousness,[6] and also attacks the notion of the "thing" as the fundamental mode in which entities are encountered within the world.[7] "Proximally and for the most part" (*zunächst und zumeist*), it is as *equipment* (*Zeug*) that entities are encountered,[8] and the passive sort of observation that philosophers talk about under the heading of "perception" is actually a secondary and derived mode of encounter. It is only in this secondary mode that entities with the status of "things" or "objects" appear, torn from their place in a complex of equipment and endowed with a neutral and objective status. Heidegger's analysis can be seen as undercutting some of Husserl's descriptions in the same way that

4. *Crisis*, p. 142.
5. *Ibid.*
6. Except in order to criticize these notions. See *Being and Time*, trans. John Macquarrie and Edward Robinson (New York: Harper & Row, 1962), pp. 88–89.
7. *Ibid.*, p. 96.
8. *Ibid.*, p. 97.

the latter were meant to correct the scientific interpretation of the experienced world. Space, too, for Heidegger, is not so much the spatial horizon of perception as it is the practical space of work, in which things "have their place" not primarily in relation to the perceiving subject, but rather in relation to the work to be done.[9] Though Heidegger's analysis does not criticize by name Husserl's account of the life-world (indeed, it predates it by several years), it can be seen to apply to it insofar as Husserl carries out his description at a level (that of perception and the perceived) that Heidegger regards as secondary. And, in criticizing philosophers who conduct their analysis at this level, Heidegger makes it clear that they are simply reflecting the prejudices of the modern age with its science-oriented notion of experience.[10]

In this way, then, we could perhaps discern the power of the *historically-taken-for-granted* in the account of a philosopher who, at least originally, thought he could overcome that power. But this is not all. The "ultimate seriousness" with which history is now taken by the philosopher could penetrate even deeper into Husserl's project. Let us think back once again to the motivation of the "historical reduction" as we presented it in Chapter 5. Husserl became aware, we said, of the manner in which philosophers take over from the tradition not so much the finished doctrines and theories of their predecessors, but their very manner of posing questions and setting problems, i.e., their notion of the task of philosophy as such. In this sense, we said, Husserl's critical account of the development of modern philosophy was not a rehearsal of various "theories" or "views," in the manner of a history of ideas, but an attempt to get at "the primal establishment of the goals" of modern philosophy[11] in order to show how we are "heirs of the past in respect to the goals which the word 'philosophy' indicates, in terms of concepts, problems, and methods."[12] The main thrust of Husserl's presentation is to show how succeeding generations of philosophers, beginning with the rationalists, took over from Galileo and other scientists the physicalistic approach to the world, and then set up all philosophical problems relating to the world

9. *Ibid.*, p. 136.
10. *Ibid.*, pp. 122 ff.
11. *Crisis*, p. 71.
12. *Ibid.*, p. 17.

without subjecting that world-concept to an appropriate philosophical scrutiny. Husserl's presentation, conceived as a "historical reduction," aims to help *us* to avoid falling prey to the same unexamined presuppositions. And these presuppositions are not so much theories as ways of posing philosophical problems.

But it is clear that, just by formulating the project of historical reduction in the way that he does, Husserl brings his own notion of philosophical goals and problems to bear on the matter at hand. As we have presented it, Husserl's discovery of the general notion of the unacknowledged heritage leads him to the idea of historical reduction *because* of his dedication to the idea of philosophy as the emancipation from prejudice. He puts the reduction into effect in order to root out the particular prejudices of the modern period, which are found, according to our interpretation, to have infected even his own philosophizing. But it does not seem to occur to him that the very idea of rooting out prejudices is a goal that he *takes for granted* without question. As we know, it is an idea that is constant throughout Husserl's career, and, if much of Husserl's philosophy has now changed with respect to his concept of the world and even his idea of phenomenological procedure (i.e., through the introduction of historical reduction), it has changed precisely out of allegiance to the same overarching goal of freedom from prejudice. At the very deepest level, this motivation seems to remain unchanged and unchallenged. It apparently does not occur to Husserl to ask whether this aspect of "the goals which the word 'philosophy' indicates" might itself constitute, like other notions he examines, a prejudice taken over from the tradition, a legacy of Husserl's formation as a philosopher in the tradition of modern thought.

In *Wahrheit und Methode*, Hans-Georg Gadamer speaks of the "prejudice against prejudices" (*das Vorurteil gegen die Vorurteile*) as a peculiarly modern phenomenon. "An analysis of the history of concepts shows," he says, "that it is first through the Enlightenment that *the concept of prejudice* receives the negative accentuation that is familiar to us." He goes on to point out that prejudice means literally: decision before the fact, before the facts are in and a final decision can be reached. " 'Prejudice' thus in no sense means: false judgment; rather, in its concept lies the idea that it can be valued both positively and negatively." [13] But the modern period has focused on prejudice as unfounded or ungrounded judgment and, Gadamer suggests, has confused this with false judgment, which is to be eliminated. Gadamer mentions Descartes, whose "hyperbolic doubt," of course, consisted precisely in treating merely ungrounded judgments as if they were false judgments. And we need hardly mention the degree to which Husserl admired Descartes as a philosopher, despite the thoroughness with which he criticized him.

Such considerations lead us to see Husserl, then, as a philosopher caught, so to speak, in his own net. In the very process of "coming to terms with history" in his philosophy, in the process of trying to root out and overcome the indebtedness to the past that is his by virtue of the nature of conscious life, Husserl exhibits himself as an example of the sort of historicity whose recognition has prompted the new approach of the latest phase in his thought. Attempting and claiming to have set aside historically acquired prejudices which stood in the way of a phenomenological grasp of the structure of world and world-consciousness, Husserl seems, at a deeper level, to exhibit such prejudices in his description of the life-world. And, as we have seen, the very motivation to overcome prejudice, historically or otherwise acquired, is itself the expression of a historical prejudice, i.e., what Gadamer calls the "prejudice against prejudices." Husserl's philosophy seems to end up in the same position as any other philosophy, according to the view of those who describe philosophy as *Weltanschauung,* or the culminating expression of a historical period's view of the world.

HISTORICISM AND SKEPTICISM

IT IS TIME NOW to pause and reconsider the ideas we have been developing since the beginning of this chapter. Are they valid? As stated they seem to describe an inexorable progression in which the originally claimed status of Husserl's philosophy is steadily undermined and replaced by the most radical sort of historicist relativism and skepticism. And all of this follows, it seems, from a plausible interpretation of *Experi-*

13. *Wahrheit und Methode,* 2d ed. (Tübingen: Mohr, 1965), p. 255.

ence and Judgment which itself is taken as an interpretation of Husserl's last work, *The Crisis of European Sciences*. Are there any considerations that would lead us to question this progression or the conclusions which seem inevitably to derive from it? Husserl himself, of course, provides arguments in "Philosophy as Rigorous Science" against historicist relativism and its skeptical consequences, so we might turn to them for guidance. But as we have seen, at that early date Husserl had little appreciation for the historicity of conscious life, whereas, later in his career, and culminating in the *Crisis* itself, the notion of historicity was developed which has led to the present position. It might seem that we could return to the arguments of "Philosophy as Rigorous Science" only if we abandon what we have described as the major methodological development in Husserl's later thought.

Still, we may find that some of those arguments, subjected to significant reinterpretation in keeping with later developments, may be of some help.

Let us recall first that, just as the need for historical reduction impressed itself on Husserl because of the growth of the idea of historicity, so this idea in turn grew out of the practice of phenomenological method as articulated in the *Ideas*. That is, it was the practice of phenomenology *as* transcendental philosophy which originally revealed the idea of historicity, and, as we repeatedly stressed, historicity was conceived as an essential feature of *transcendental* subjectivity itself. As we saw, two areas of phenomenologial investigation—genetic phenomenology and the theory of intersubjectivity—converged to produce this concept; both of these areas were ignored in the *Ideas,* but were not unknown to Husserl, at least as problems, even during that period. Once the temporal character of conscious life, already explored in the early lectures on internal time-consciousness, was developed into the full-fledged genetic theory of the *Cartesian Meditations* and *Formal and Transcendental Logic,* Husserl was already using the terms "history" and "historicity" to characterize the essence of transcendental consciousness. This meant not only that consciousness, initially conceived as act or intentional experience, consisted of a flowing multiplicity of such acts in a "stream of consciousness," but also that because of the structure of retention, the past constitutes a stock of abiding possessions or a "background" for each experience. Put more simply, the past has meaning or significance for present consciousness; it plays a role in the givenness of what is given.

With the full-fledged development of the theory of inter-subjectivity, finally, in the *Cartesian Mediations*, the term "history" began to take on something more like its usual sense. Just as subjectivity is essentially *temporal*, so it is essentially *communal* in its constitution of the world. And just as it *exists*—regarded from the static point of view—not merely in its own world but in the world of the community of which it happens to be a part, so it inherits, in its temporal aspect, not only its own abiding possessions but those of its community as well. It is in this sense, in inheriting and appropriating from the community the "background" that it brings to present experience, that subjectivity exhibits its essential historicity.

Now it is this concept, when applied to the *particular* philosopher—Husserl himself, or anyone else who is engaged in the business of philosophy—that motivated the procedure of historical reduction we outlined in Chapter 5. And what that procedure requires, as we saw there, is attention to the *particular* circumstances of the philosopher's philosophical-historical situation. But the concept of historicity is not itself *particular* in this way; it is a notion which claims to state the essence of subjectivity purely as subjectivity, i.e., whether it is that of a philosopher or not, and whatever its particular historical situation may be; and it applies to the particular philosopher *because* he is an instance of this essence. Thus the need for historical reduction develops out of the recognition of a concept that claims essential status; the very motivation for performing the historical reduction depends on a concept whose validity is assumed to be universal. This is simply to say that the concept of historicity is not itself historical, where by "historical" we mean: valid only for a particular historical time and circumstance. Or at least, insofar as it serves as the motivation for historical reduction, it is not *taken* as being historical in this sense. Thus the whole idea of historical reduction makes no sense except on the assumption of this ahistorical truth.

But if such an ahistorical truth serves as the assumption of the need for historical reduction, it serves just as surely as the assumption for the view that such a reduction is incapable of being carried out, i.e., the view that seems to result in the triumph of historicism. Indeed, as we saw, the development toward this conclusion begins when the concept of historicity just outlined is taken even more seriously than it had been before, i.e., when the force of historical prejudice is seen as involving not only the manner in which we think about and interpret the world but also the way in which the world is given in immediate experience. What gets "relativized" according to this view is the structure of world-givenness as such, so that the idea of a universal or ahistorical essence of world-structure becomes at best totally inaccessible to the philosopher and at worst a completely senseless idea. But this relativization itself has sense only on the basis of a presupposed structure of world-consciousness which ensures the relativity of world-structure by virtue of its essential historicity. What this view *asserts* is the dependence of the structure of world-givenness on a conceptual framework of prejudices that subjectivity inherits from its historical-cultural milieu and is unable to escape from to any sort of ahistorical grasp of the structure of world-givenness "as such." What this view *assumes*, in order to be asserted at all, is that subjectivity is "in itself" of such a nature that its world is structured, that its mode of existence is to be in such a historical-cultural milieu, and that the particular structure its world has is a function of whatever historical-cultural milieu it happens to exist in.

Looked at in this way, historical relativism seems to fall prey to the difficulties Husserl pointed to in "Philosophy as Rigorous Science." It is one thing, as he notes there, to take cognizance of the fact that the history of philosophy represents a chaos of conflicting theories which gives no evidence of agreement or even progress toward agreement, and to conclude by induction that the prospect is not favorable that any such agreement will ever be reached. It is quite another to argue that such agreement—which would indicate philosophy's achievement of a scientific status—is in principle incapable of being achieved because of the essential historical limitations of human knowledge.[14] When the case for relativism is stated in this way, it matters little whether the reasons adduced are those of historicism, psychologism, anthropologism, or whatever. The point is that the case for relativism is being made on the basis of a general theory of human cognitive capacities, and the theory itself claims objective status, whether about the human psyche, the human species, or the nature of history. Either this theory is valid, in which case the thesis it supports is undermined, since there is at least one theory which escapes the supposed

14. *PRS*, pp. 122 ff.

limitations of human knowledge; or the theory is subject to the same limitations, in which case it cannot serve as the basis for the unrestricted claim that those limitations exist. As Husserl often pointed out, skepticism as a universal claim always contradicts itself, since it renders invalid its own status as a claim.

In the case of historicism, what happens when its claim is applied to itself in this way? To say that the claim "all human knowledge is historically limited" is itself historically limited is, for one thing, to say that this claim expresses the prejudices of a particular historical period. This means that other historical circumstances may lead men to the contradictory claim: i.e., that *not* all human knowledge is historically limited. This would be a harmless—and obviously true—conclusion, and would leave open the possibility that one of the contradictories is true. But the claim of historicism goes farther than this. "Historically limited" in this case does not mean merely "a product of the times" or the like; it means that the claim cannot have objective validity, i.e., it cannot be true. But then its contradictory is true, by standard canons of logical inference, and some knowledge is not historically limited and thus can be objectively valid. The skeptic may object to invoking canons of inference at this point, appealing to the historical relativity of logic itself; and if we point out that he appeals to it at some times and not at others, he may simply claim for himself the right to be inconsistent. But here the discussion must end.

Of course, a skepticism which is mitigated or limited in a certain way does not suffer these difficulties. It may claim that no objectively valid knowledge is possible *except* the knowledge that no other objectively valid knowledge is possible. Any attempt at rebuttal would have to leave formal considerations for substantive ones and ask for the basis on which the partial skeptic's claims are based. This might force him to admit other exceptions to skepticism besides the one already admitted, and the scope of his claim might be gradually undermined. But there is no formal reason why such a skepticism, circumscribed to some extent, cannot be maintained.

Perhaps such a partial skepticism, rather than a total one, is actually the outcome of the train of thought described at the beginning of this chapter. After all, what was really declared "historically relative" was not everything, but rather something quite specific, namely, our experience of the world; what was called into question was not all philosophical claims, but only the attempt at a universal and non- or transhistorical description of the structure of world-givenness such as that which seems to be the aim of Husserl's original theory of the life-world. This need not be all there is to philosophy, as evidenced by the fact that there is also a theory of the historicity of consciousness, whose validity is not called into question. If this is the final outcome of the train of thought that grows out of *Experience and Judgment,* we can perhaps say that, although Husserl has accepted the consequences of taking history seriously by giving up (or tacitly admitting that he must give up) much of the scope of his phenomenology (i.e., its theory of the world), his philosophy does not degenerate into complete historicism because it holds onto the universal validity of its theory of consciousness.

There is something unsettling and somewhat contrived about this solution. The partial skeptic, like any other philosopher, is called upon to substantiate his views. He must substantiate not only his claim that certain kinds of knowledge are not possible— the ideas of *EU* seem to constitute a substantiation of the view that access to the life-world is not possible—but also his claims *to* knowledge on which his negative claims are based. In the case of the "partial historicism" we are now considering, the advocate of this position must account for the fact that he can arrive at a theory of consciousness (including its historicity) that is itself nonhistorical, i.e., not limited by the blinders of history. It is hard to see how such an advocate could establish that historical prejudice, which admittedly stands in the way of a transhistorical theory of the world, does not likewise stand in the way of a theory of consciousness. The historicist argument concerning the theory of world-structure asserted that, since our way of perceiving the world is a function of our historical situation, our *reflection* upon the world-as-perceived will itself be a function of that historical situation. But if our reflection upon the world-as-perceived is thus affected by history, why not our reflection upon consciousness itself? After all, the historical-critical investigations of the *Crisis,* while primarily aimed at modern theories of the world, also criticized modern theories of consciousness as being infected by historical prejudice. If some theories of consciousness are thus infected, why not the theory of the proponent of (partial) historicism?

Perhaps such a proponent could argue that, in the case of the theory of consciousness, it is possible to overcome historical prejudice and get at the truth. But if it is possible here, why not elsewhere as well? Again he must explain why the theory of consciousness is exempt—at least potentially—from the force of historical prejudice, while the theory of the world is not.

It seems that perhaps the best case to be made out at this point for the view we have been describing—what we have called a "partial historicism"—is that it does take for granted, as the basis of its skeptical claims, its theory of the historicity of consciousness, and that it assumes this theory to be saying something essentially (ahistorically) true of consciousness. To say that it takes this theory for granted is not to say, of course, that it simply adduces this theory ready-made and unexamined. Indeed, as we have seen, the theory is carefully worked out along phenomenological lines and presented in great detail. What we mean is that this theory serves as a basis for certain historicist claims about the possibility of a theory of world-structure, and that, in serving that function, it has the status of an essential claim about consciousness. That is, the phenomenological procedure followed in arriving at this theory is assumed to be capable of arriving at essential descriptions of consciousness. But no support is produced for its claim to that capacity; the best that can be said is that such a "partial historicism" is not inconsistent, in that it allows for the possibility of some form of escape from complete subjugation to history.

THE PROBLEMS OF "PARTIAL HISTORICISM"

BUT IF HISTORICISM, now partial rather than absolute in its scope, is not inconsistent with itself, it is still open to question upon other grounds.

It has been pointed out that this historicism is based on a conception of consciousness, developed phenomenologically, which states the essential historicity of human exeprience. We traced the development of this conception in Husserl's career in Chapters 3 and 4. Now it is to be noted that this conception amounts to a theory or description of consciousness, and that it is *phenomenological* in nature. What we mean by this is simply that, as we saw in the course of tracing this theory, it is a development and elaboration of Husserl's earlier views, a deepening and broadening of the investigations carried out in the *Ideas* and elsewhere. Far from abandoning or reversing the basic notions of the first formulation of Husserl's theory, this development draws upon it and expands it. In particular, of course, it draws upon and elaborates Husserl's most basic notion, that of the *intentionality* of consciousness. As we saw in Chapter 1, Husserl's whole procedure amounts to an assumption of, rather than an argument for, the intentionality of consciousness: to effect the phenomenological reduction is to treat consciousness exclusively *as* intentional and in no other way. While the early central notion of "intentional experience" or "act" is subsequently placed in larger contexts—attitude, temporal or dynamic background, community—it remains central, and these larger contexts are ultimately meant to elucidate it and add to our understanding. Furthermore, the notions of attitude, temporal background, and community are themselves treated in thoroughly intentional fashion.

Now the essence of intentionality, of course, is the "of-ness" of consciousness, its relation to what is other. We traced the development whereby it became clear that the intentional relation of consciousness to an object is ultimately to be considered in terms of its relation to the world as a whole. And while the thoroughgoing intentional consideration of consciousness makes it improper to speak of consciousness as being *in* the world (in the sense of a part of it), it is also true, as we noted in Chapter 1, that consciousness is nothing without its relation to the world. This brings with it a corollary concerning the nature of phenomenological investigation: there can be no intentional consideration of consciousness which is not at the same time a consideration of that *of* which it is conscious. Any phenomenological account of consciousness must then be at the same time an account of the world—understood, to be sure, as the world-as-meant or the world-as-experienced.

This raises an obvious question for the partial historicism which is now under consideration. This view proposes a theory of consciousness which is yet a further outgrowth of the phenomenological theory. In particular, it proposes the theory of the historicity of consciousness. But, as we have seen, partial historicism assumes the ahistorical validity of this theory. That is to say, it outlines a theory which will be true of consciousness regardless of its particular historical circumstances. Consciousness is such as to be historical; the particular character of the prejudices that it inherits from its situation will vary from one situation to another, but what is not variable is the fact that it has this structure. But if there is a structure of consciousness that is invariable in this manner, does it not follow that there is also a structure of the world that is likewise invariable? This seems to follow if the theory of historicity is still a theory of the intentional structures of consciousness. For however consciousness may be newly described by this theory—as prejudice-laden due to its social and temporal dimensions, etc.—it is still consciousness *of* . . . that is being described in this way. In order to describe the manner in which its historicity affects its manner of experiencing the world, one must still assume that experience takes place, that it is *of* something, that this something is ultimately something of the world.

To this it could perhaps be replied that, to be sure, the theory of partial historicism considers consciousness to be intentional and thus to stand in relation to the world. What it denies is that this world has an *invariant structure* throughout all historical periods and that such a structure can be grasped by a reflective transcendental philosophy. To be conscious is indeed to be in the world, or in a world. But while our world is that structured by modern science, the ancient Greek's world is structured in an entirely different way, and still different from this is the world of the Chinese peasant or the primitive tribesman. We cannot hope to penetrate these worlds or to find something common between them and our own.

But is it possible to maintain a phenomenological theory of consciousness and say no more than that "consciousness is intentional and that it stands in relation to a world"? Does the theory of consciousness not already indicate to some degree the form this relationship takes? To speak of the world in the phenomenological manner is already to give that relationship a certain structure. For the phenomenologist the world is treated not as the "universe" of science or traditional metaphysics but as the ultimate *horizon* of whatever is experienced. At the very least, the focus-horizon, figure-background, or foreground-background analogy is invoked in the use of this term. And it is to be noted that these notions involve the characterization not so much of the form of experience as of *what* is experienced, i.e., they involve a structural characterization of the world as experienced. The concept of *space* is clearly involved in these notions, and, as we have seen, not merely by analogy. It is hard to see what the phenomenological concept of world would be if it did not involve, at least in part, consciousness standing in relation to a space spread out before it; thus the figure-background concept is not merely the analogical expression of a functional relationship but also refers literally to the structure of the world as experienced.

And what of the concept of *time*? The theory of the historicity of consciousness draws heavily, as we have seen, on the phenomenological notion of the temporality of consciousness. But can there be a temporal structure of consciousness which is not at the same time the consciousness of a temporal world, i.e., a world in which things *happen*, a world of events? And both the idea of temporal event and that of spatial figures imply a certain articulation of the world, i.e., they imply a world that consists for the subject of identifiable *objects*—in the broadest sense of the word—that are distinguishable from each other and from the subject himself.

Horizon, space, time, object, event—these seem to be indispensable correlates of a phenomenological theory of consciousness, and they amount to a minimal but still articulate account of the structure of the world-as-experienced. Is it not necessary to say that, just as we cannot make sense of the "historical relativity" of experience without an ahistorical theory of consciousness, so we cannot make sense of it without this minimal —and likewise ahistorical—theory of the world? And does this not assure us that in spite of all relativity there is a bedrock of unchanging world-structure which remains invariant and upon which the play of historical change runs its course? These considerations take us back, then, to the initial theory of the life-world in the *Crisis* which we outlined prior to Chapter 8.

We recall that that theory began to be questioned when it was suggested, first by random and puzzling remarks in the *Crisis,* then by implication in *Experience and Judgment,* that historical prejudice effects the most basic structure of world-givenness, in particular perception itself. We developed this by noting that theoretical structures—for example, those of the physical sciences in the modern period—not only exist as ideal formations but also have a content, i.e., they speak about the world we live in. When they are inherited by the conscious subject from his historical-cultural milieu, it is as such content that they are appropriated. It is not so easy, then, to separate possession of such theoretical structures from the actual experience of the world, since these structures bear directly upon the world around us. When Husserl speaks of the results of theory "flowing into" the life-world, it is plausible to interpret this as meaning that the one set of structures actually transforms the other or usurps its function. Turning to *EU*, we saw this view actually asserted. We noted in both cases, too, that this theory not only makes sense but has a kind of intrinsic plausibility to it. Is it not the case that our experience of the world is a function of what we—implicitly or explicitly—believe about the world, and that what we believe is in turn a function of the historical prejudices of our time and culture?

But how plausible is such a notion, really? One certainly hears it expressed often enough today. Indeed, it is almost regarded as a truism. But can it actually be cashed in by showing exactly how we experience the world in terms of the scientific theories we inherit? Or does its "plausibility" really reflect a prejudice we inherit from an overwhelmingly historicist age? Surely we do not directly experience the world we are told about in accounts of atomic theory. To move to a much simpler level, do we in fact experience or live in a world deprived of secondary qualities, one in which such qualities are actually experienced— rather than merely interpreted, after the fact—as merely psychological, as existing in us rather than in the objects?

Turning the historicist's notion of historical prejudice back upon himself, it is easy enough to devise an account which would show that his claim about the structures of experience is just an exaggeration of prevailing historicist views. The growth of historical knowledge, especially in the nineteenth century, brought with it the famous "historical consciousness," which can be looked upon as a revival of the *physis-nomos* controversy of ancient Greece. Increased knowledge of ancient and also non-Western societies drove home a recognition of how much the values, morals, and metaphysics of such societies contrasted with those of modern Europe. One can picture a growing fascination and amazement over the fact that what we take for granted, as deriving from the very nature of things—norms governing one's relations with others, ideas of the proper order of society or of the structure of the universe—can be viewed so differently by others. These alien conceptions came to be looked upon not so much as wrong conceptions but as merely *different* conceptions, so that modern Europe was eventually seen as being itself merely one historical formation among others. The term *"Weltanschauung"* was an apt expression for the manner in which various features come together, in a given cultural-historical period, to make up a coherent and unified picture, so comprehensive as to leave nothing untouched. If we invoke the notion of *Gestalt*, it is easy to suppose that even the simplest and most seemingly direct form of experience is a function of such an over-all picture. From this point of view, any philosophical attempt to arrive at a fundamental structure of experience which is not subject to the influence of such an over-all picture seems naïve and oblivious to the insights of "historical consciousness."

But this view is a generalization or extension of the notion of *Weltanschauung* beyond the domain in which it was originally developed, and it remains to be seen whether this extension is legitimate. Great differences in such matters as values, society, the structure of the universe are actually discovered in historical investigation; but do we actually discover the differences that are alleged in the case of the fundamental structure of world-givenness? How could we go about discovering them at all? Indeed, it could be argued that in order to discover those cultural differences that we can actually point to, we must assume a common structure of world-givenness. For how could we understand buildings, monuments, and artifacts that serve as evidence without assuming that these were experienced by those who made them? And in doing so, must we not assume something, however minimal, about the manner in which they were experienced? And how can we understand the documents that we decipher and interpret as further evidence, unless we take them first to refer to a world whose structure is that of our own? Is it possible, then, to show, to demonstrate in any way, that differences in world-view penetrate to the level we are discussing, or is it only a surmise? If such differences existed, would we have any access to them?

By the same token, how could we ever show that our own structure of world-givenness is merely a function of our over-all world-view? But here it might be argued that one example of such showing has already been adduced. We referred to Heidegger's account of the "worldhood of the world" and noted that it might serve as a critique of Husserl's theory of the life-world. As we saw, some of Heidegger's key notions differ markedly from those of Husserl; and Heidegger's treatment suggests that Husserl's theory might, in spite of his efforts to the contrary, still be an expression, in his account of the structure of world-givenness, of the form of experience shared by all those who live under the influence of modern science and philosophy. Thus the fact that his account centers on perception and the perceived object can be seen as derived from the essentially contemplative function of experience involved in science, as opposed to the active *Besorgen* made central by Heidegger. The concept of "object" is explicitly rejected by Heidegger as constituting the fundamental mode in which entities-within-the-world are encountered; and while both "horizon" and "space" are involved, they are used in very different ways.

But here it must be noted that Heidegger's implicit critique— if we are right in reading it as such—makes its point only by contrasting one account of world-structure or worldhood, which it considers wrong or historically limited, with another such account, which is presumably the true account. It invites us to recognize and appreciate the degree to which philosophical accounts of experience and the "worldhood of the world" are affected by historical prejudice, but it does this by presenting us with an alternative account which is presumably not itself encumbered by such prejudices and which is an adequate description of the world as we actually live it. So if Heidegger's account actually does stand in a critical relation to Husserl's theory of the life-world, which is similar, as we have suggested, to the manner in which Husserl's own theory criticizes his earlier views, it cannot be taken as an argument for the impossibility of any theory of world-structure which escapes the limitations of historical prejudice. Quite the contrary. It merely suggests that Husserl's theory has to be rejected or revised in an effort to get at the true account.

To put it in another way, should the historicist view be correct, Heidegger would be in exactly the same position as Husserl or any other philosopher with regard to the structure of world-givenness: he would be able to do no more than give expression to the prejudices of his own historical world-view. But this is certainly not the spirit in which Heidegger's account is put forward. It is clear that his intent is to cut through and overcome such prejudices in a way that his predecessors have not been able to do.[15] Whether or not Heidegger succeeds in this is a question we do not intend to take up. Whether his theory con-

15. Many commentators agree that the Heidegger of *Being and Time* is still operating within the "transcendental" tradition in this sense. See, for example, Gadamer, *Wahrheit und Methode*, p. 241.

stitutes a valid criticism of Husserl's, or whether it is ultimately more reconcilable with it than it would first seem, are separate questions. Our only point is that the project of such an account, and the very idea of a valid critique of the previous theories of Husserl and others, presupposes a possibility which is denied by even the partial historicism we have been discussing: the possibility, namely, of penetrating to and adequately describing the actual structure of world-givenness that underlies all historical change.

OUR TASK IN THIS CHAPTER was to evaluate on its own merits the historicist position that seemed to flow from the development of the concept of historicity in certain passages of the *Crisis* and in the Introduction to *Experience and Judgment*. We have examined some of the difficulties that beset the philosopher who attempts to put forward a full-fledged historical skepticism, and we have noted that a retreat to a partial or mitigated skepticism similarly presents great problems.

With the historicist conclusion thus called into question, we are inclined to reexamine the train of thought that led up to it. We asserted at the beginning of this chapter that the historicist conclusion derives from the development set in motion by the idea of "historical reduction," which was in turn the methodological outcome of Husserl's insight into the essential historicity of consciousness. If this development leads to paradoxical conclusions, must we reject that insight and its methodological implications altogether? In our concluding chapter we shall see whether the notion of historicity and that of historical reduction can be maintained without leading into the impasse of historicism and without totally compromising the idea of transcendental philosophy.

11 / The Project of
Transcendental Philosophy

THE CONSIDERATIONS of the last chapter have led us to question the idea of historical skepticism. It should be made clear that we questioned it *as* a coherent philosophical position; that is, we were able to subject it to criticism only by supposing that its proponents were willing to put forward the reasons for maintaining it. Naturally, this is the only way that this or any other form of skepticism, or indeed any philosophical position at all, can be subjected to criticism. If the doctrine is held merely as a matter of unsubstantiated belief, there is nothing that can be said against it. This puts the skeptic in the position of a dogmatist, of course, a position he may find uncomfortable.

In any case, our criticism took this form: that the historicist position could only be supported by appeals to a theory of consciousness which is not itself subject to the major stricture of historicism. Only by asserting that consciousness is essentially —and thus ahistorically—characterized by historicity can the historicist give any substance to his view. We went on to point out that if the historicist is willing to concede this much, but wishes to argue for skepticism with respect to everything else— notably a transcendental theory of world structure—he must face the fact that his theory of consciousness itself has certain implications for the structure of the world and that even this argument for skepticism seems to take that notion of structure for granted.

We suggested at the end of the last chapter that these difficulties in the historicist position might lead us to go back and question the train of thought that led up to it. That train of thought was presented primarily in our interpretation of the Introduction to *Experience and Judgment* and focused on the manner in which historical prejudices were said to effect the way we experience things. That interpretation culminated in what we called the *rejection of reflection* as the basis of transcendental-philosophical assertions. Are we now, because of the considerations of the last chapter, in a position to declare that interpretation invalid and to reaffirm the status of reflection which is at the heart of transcendental philosophy? After all, if the skeptic, daunted by our critique and in full retreat, claims the validity of his historical view of consciousness, does he not do so precisely on the basis of reflection, at least in part? Does not any theory of consciousness resort ultimately to the reflections of the theorist upon his own conscious life? Are we not in a position, now, simply to blot from the record the exaggerations of *Experience and Judgment* and return to the practice of the phenomenological version of transcendental philosophy?

REFLECTION AND HISTORICAL REDUCTION

WE WOULD BE MISTAKEN if we thought that the considerations of the last chapter established this much. The fact is that these considerations contribute nothing themselves to the support of any putative transcendental philosophy. Nor, strictly speaking, do they establish even the possibility, in principle, of such a philosophy. All they really show is how difficult it is to *deny* such a possibility in any definitive way. Or, more precisely, they show that even any attempt to deny it presupposes to some extent the very possibility that is being denied.

Clearly, much more is needed if the validity of the transcendental project—at least in Husserl's terms—is to be reestablished. In particular, the topic of *reflection* must be reexamined, and it must be shown that reflection is capable of more than a mirroring of the historical-cultural prejudices of the philosopher who happens to be reflecting. And this in turn depends on a final refutation of the thesis that historical-cultural prejudices not only affect the way we think about and interpret the world of our experience, but also transform that very world by shaping the way in which it is given in direct experience.

We touched upon this topic in the last chapter, but again

our attacks on this thesis are not sufficient to establish in any definitive way the possibility of a reflective transcendental philosophy. All we were able to do was to cast doubt on the soundness of this thesis by showing that it, in turn, is not substantiated. We pointed out that, while it seems to be a plausible extension of the notion of historical prejudice, in order to be established firmly it would have to show exactly *how* our perceptual experience is a function of the historical period in which we live. We noted further that any attempt to show this would either be itself subject to the same historical prejudice; or, if it succeeded, it would be at the expense of what it had declared impossible—namely, it would have made contact with the "true" structure in order to contrast it with the one supposedly limited by historicity. Pointing out these difficulties in the historicist position does not succeed in establishing the opposite view: that a definitive emancipation from historical prejudice has been achieved by any particular description, or even that such an emancipation can in principle be achieved. This much could be established ultimately only if a phenomenological description of the structure of world-givenness could be put forward in such a way that it guaranteed its own freedom from historical-cultural prejudices of any sort. And certainly we cannot claim to have accomplished this.

Thus we should not claim too much success for our attacks on historicism. As we said, all they really show is that the possibility of transcendental philosophy, on the Husserlian model, cannot be denied in the skeptical manner of the historicist. But while this does not in itself establish the actual success of any transcendental philosophy or even the possibility in principle of such a philosophy, it can be said to leave the possibility *open.* The possibility that is left open is that reflection can succeed in arriving at a characterization of the world and of consciousness that is more than the expression of a set of historical prejudices. In other words, the possibility that is left open is that Husserl or some other philosopher has succeeded, or might someday succeed, at the transcendental project. The reason we do not say that the possibility of such success is *established* is that we are unable to *deny* unequivocally that historical prejudices *do* affect our way of experiencing the world and thus the reflections we make upon that experience. But we are also unable to *assert* this. What this amounts to is that there are no clear-cut canons or criteria according to which a particular case of reflective investigation could be adjudged to have succeeded where another has failed.

But here it is important to recall the procedure of historical reduction, the train of thought that led up to it, and the purpose for which, according to our interpretation, it was devised. If the historicity of consciousness is taken with the ultimate "seriousness" proposed by the historicists, of course, the historical reduction becomes a useless procedure. But if we put aside the excesses of historicism, historical reduction at least offers some aid in the transcendental project. Based as it is upon the recognition of the historicity of consciousness, of the role of historical-cultural prejudices in conscious life, this reduction consists in the attempt to make those prejudices explicit, hold them up to view, retrieve them from their habitual role as unexamined *Selbstverständlichkeiten*. Again, there is no guarantee that this procedure can succeed completely, but the point is this: it allows us considerably more than the mere pious hope that, in our philosophizing, we are not merely mirroring the prejudices of our age. As we have argued, it was because of Husserl's recognition of the inadequacy of such a pious hope (as expressed in the "philosophical epochē" of the *Ideas*), that the procedure of historical reduction was developed and put into practice in the *Crisis*.

In this way, historical reduction has a dual function in the undertaking of transcendental philosophy. First, it acts as a counter to the pretensions of any straightforward reflections that are carried out in historical naïveté, warning that such reflections may be mere expressions of historical prejudice. Thus it serves a critical function, as it did when it caused Husserl, as we saw, to reject his earlier conception of the world as one which expressed the prejudices of a science-oriented philosophy. Second, in exercising this critical function, it at the same time holds open the possibility that reflection can succeed in arriving at a philosophical description which is not encumbered by such prejudices. Here reflection operates in concert with historical reduction, keeping one eye, so to speak, on the historical perspective that the latter reveals. The philosopher's aim, as always, is to establish ahistorical truth. But instead of being historically naïve, he proceeds, through historical reduction, with the explicit consciousness of the historical context within which he operates.

We are making a distinction here between reflective procedure and historical reduction as philosophical methods, and it should perhaps be pointed out that historical reduction as we described it is itself, in its own way, a reflective procedure. As we pointed out before,[1] far from being an attempt at a history of ideas or a history of philosophy in any objective sense, historical reduction is the philosopher's recounting of the tradition as it exists *in him* through his participation in the historical-cultural milieu. In this sense it is the philospher's reflection upon his own conscious life. But, as we also saw, in one important sense it differs from that form of reflection which serves as the basis for phenomenological method, as described in Chapter 1. The latter is specifically aimed at descriptions which go beyond the particularity of both the philosopher who is reflecting and his historical situation. In Husserl's language, such reflection is subjected to an eidetic reduction, according to which what is sought are patterns or essences descriptive of all possible conscious life and world-givenness. Historical reduction, by contrast, aims precisely at the particular, in this case the particular configuration of historical-cultural prejudices peculiar to the philosopher and his own age.

This gives us a better idea of how these two procedures, with different aims and different subject matters, work together. The philosopher who performs both, as Husserl tries to do in the *Crisis,* is in a position to contrast the results of his phenomenological-eidetic reflection with the results of his historical reduction. If the latter is successful in bringing to the fore the relevant prejudices of the philosopher's historical position, he has something against which to test the putative essences of his phenomenological reflections. Such a test can never establish *positively* that such phenomenological results are indeed the transhistorical essences sought. But as long as the results of historical reduction—in the form of a characterization of the dominant prejudices of the philosopher's age—are clearly before his mind, he can at least guard against naïvely giving expression to *them.* To be sure, this "test" is only as successful as the historical reduction itself can be in bringing to light those prejudices. There is always the danger that such a reduction has succeeded only partially.

But can the historical reduction ever succeed fully? Can the philosopher ever become conscious of and display completely the prejudices of his age? This is but the reverse side of the question of whether transcendental philosophy itself can ever

1. Cf. Chap. 7, pp. 179–80.

be accomplished. As we have said, we have no positive answer to the question. But as long as the *possibility* remains open, the procedure of historical reduction has a *raison d'être*. It may have to be carried out repeatedly, with each accomplished reduction subject to further criticism; but as long as its purpose is not declared a priori incapable of being fulfilled, as in historicism, it has at least the prospect of being more than mere treading in a circle.

Just as reflection needs historical reduction to curb its pretensions, so historical reduction needs the project of reflection in order to give it a purpose. Only when the two procedures are seen as operating together can we make any sense of the puzzling notion of *Abbau* or "dismantling" which was mentioned in *Experience and Judgment*.[2] What is puzzling about that notion, we recall, was that it was presented in a context where reflection was apparently rejected as a valid method for transcendental philosophy. But if the possibility of valid reflection remains open, then the process of dismantling the successive levels of historical superstructure can have some end-point, some prospect of reaching a level that no longer needs dismantling.

After exploring and rejecting—or at least calling into question—the historicist interpretation of *Experience and Judgment*, we are able to draw some tentative conclusions on the major problem posed by this book: that of the extent to which Husserl's version of transcendental philosophy is able to "take history seriously" or "come to terms with history" and still survive. What our account shows is that the "ultimate seriousness" with which history is taken by the historicist position means not at all "coming to terms" with history but rather *succumbing* to history. If our criticisms in the last chapter are correct, a total commitment to historicism makes impossible even the theory of the historicity of conscious life. It is precisely Husserl's position in the *Crisis*—minus the ambiguities that led us to historicism—that comes to terms with history by both acknowledging the force of historicity and trying to deal with it in philosophical terms. Since it leaves open the possibility of a valid reflective theory of consciousness, it at least allows for the validity of the very theory of historicity on which its reductive procedure is based. And since it leaves open the possibility of a

2. Cf. Chap. 9, pp. 227, 230–31.

valid reflective description of the structure of world-givenness, it can proceed on the assumption that historical prejudice can be overcome in arriving at such a description.

While this allows us to say that in a certain sense Husserl's version of transcendental philosophy survives, it is also obvious that it does not simply survive intact, at least as outlined in our first chapter. This is true first of all because, once history is taken seriously, phenomenology can no longer be *exclusively* a philosophy based on reflection. The reflective procedure embodied in the phenomenological reduction is now subject to the constant surveillance provided by the historical reduction. Because of the acknowledged pervasiveness of historical prejudice, there is always the danger that reflection will be something less than it claims for itself under the rubric of phenomenological reduction, i.e., that it will be merely the mirroring of such prejudices. This is the danger that historical reduction is designed to guard against.

Because of the difficulty of obtaining the completeness of any historical reduction, the reflective procedure and the whole phenomenological enterprise are endowed with a certain *tentativeness*. It is not as if the historical reduction could be carried out once and for all and left behind. It must be constantly renewed. It must be remembered, too, that since the focus of a historical reduction is the prejudices of a given historical period, each new period and each philosopher attempting to philosophize reflectively in that period will have to carry out a new reduction pertinent to his own age. Husserl's remarks about "constructing the 'novel' of history for purposes of self-reflection [*Selbstbesinnung*]" [3] suggest that each new age must write its own novel. Far from accomplishing this goal once and for all, as if history had ended and the forces of historicity were overcome, Husserl suggests a process of constant return to reflection on the philosopher's historical situation, a process that should go on as long as there is history.

Thus the tentativeness of the reflective philosophical enterprise is of a quite specific sort. To a certain extent, of course, the results of phenomenology should always have been considered tentative in the sense that they should remain open to criticism. This much is true of any philosophical theory, and it is true also of phenomenology, despite some of the early claims to definitive-

3. Husserliana VI, p. 556.

ness on Husserl's part. But the theory of historicity, developed by Husserl himself, provides a particular point of view from which to criticize the deliverances of reflective philosophy. While it leaves open the possibility of the success of such a philosophy, it demands that its claims be constantly measured against the results of historical reduction. If the historical reduction has to be constantly renewed, this does not mean that each philosophical age is condemned to a never-ending treadmill and is incapable of escaping from its own situation. There *is* the prospect that philosophy can come to results which would satisfy the perennial demand for rigorous science in the form of transhistorical truth. But the message of the theory of historicity and the historical reduction is that the philosopher can aspire to such transhistorical truth only if he is at the same time constantly making present to himself the particularity of his own historical situation.

PHILOSOPHY AND THE TRADITION

ONE INTERNAL INCONSISTENCY may seem to have plagued the notion of historical reduction from the start. This notion developed because of the theory of historicity, as we saw in Chapters 3 and 4; and what that theory states is that it is *essential* to conscious life that it be engaged in a historical situation such that it embodies the prejudices of that situation. Such prejudices may vary from one situation to another, but what is essential is that there be some stock of prejudices which form the "background" of ongoing experience. Now what may appear problematic is that, if such prejudices are really *essential* to the life of consciousness, then according to the ordinary understanding of the term "essential," we cannot conceive of consciousness without them, and any attempt to overcome them would be futile. Consciousness without historical prejudice would not be consciousness. Yet we have repeatedly described historical reduction as a process of overcoming such prejudices. Does the possibility of historical reduction negate the claim of the theory of historicity insofar as the latter makes an essential claim about consciousness?

Perhaps the best way to approach this problem is to compare the historical reduction with the *phenomenological* reduction as described in Chapter 1. The phenomenological reduction can be characterized in a very general way as the project of overcoming the natural attitude. But, as we saw, the whole point of this exercise is to get oneself into a position where one can adequately describe the natural attitude itself. The natural attitude is the over-all stance (*Einstellung*) of consciousness in relation to the world, and it is within this framework that phenomenology pursues and tries to grasp all the rich detail of conscious life. In this, of course, its aim is to outline what is essential to consciousness as such and to the world as given to consciousness. Thus its characterization of the natural attitude is intended as a description of the very essence of consciousness. As the term "natural" implies, this attitude is of the nature of consciousness—consciousness, so to speak, in its natural state. Yet in order to recognize this, phenomenology must overcome that state; it must renounce its own participation in the natural attitude, the better to see it for what it is. Thus the same paradox appears: if the natural attitude is really essential to consciousness, how can phenomenology succeed in overcoming that attitude?

It must be admitted that this *is* a paradox and that it exists at the very heart of the phenomenological enterprise. We already discussed it in Chapter 1 when we characterized the reduction as going "against the grain" of consciousness, as being "unnatural," even "artificial." [4] If the historical reduction is paradoxical, then, it is no more so than the phenomenological reduction itself.

But perhaps more can be said in defense of the phenomenological reduction, in spite of this paradox. There is a very special sense in which the phenomenologist "overcomes" the natural attitude. As we saw in Chapter 1, it is not as if he gives it up entirely and goes on to something else. Because it is precisely the natural attitude that he is describing, he must keep one foot constantly in that attitude—he must continue to live the natural life of consciousness—in order to have something to consult in his descriptions. This is what Husserl refers to as the "zigzag" procedure. Strictly speaking, then, it is not so much that the phenomenologist gives up the natural attitude: he remains in it while at the same time striking an attitude of detachment. The purpose of his detachment is not that the

4. Cf. Chap. 1, p. 36.

Selbstverständlichkeiten of the natural attitude be done away with, but rather that they become visible and open to description. Simply to live in the natural attitude is to live under these taken-for-granted prejudices and not be aware of them as such. To perform the reduction and carry out phenomenological description is to free oneself from these prejudices only to the extent of becoming aware of them for what they are.

Understanding the reduction in this way, perhaps the best way to put the matter is to say that while the natural attitude is indeed in some sense "essential" or "natural" to consciousness, the essence of consciousness includes the possibility of the kind of detachment that makes the reduction possible. That is to say, if phenomenology is itself possible, then consciousness must be seen as being capable of grasping itself and its own operating principles.[5] We are not saying that this capacity has been realized to the fullest extent by Husserl, or even that it can in principle be realized. Indeed, the subject matter of this book has been to a large extent the question of the very possibility of phenomenology, a question we do not claim to have answered in any definitive way. But at least, in this regard, we can say that an affirmative answer can be self-consistent and is not as paradoxical as it first appeared.

As for the *historical* reduction, perhaps a similar account suggests itself. Here, too, we could say that the real purpose of such a reduction is simply to make visible and open to description prejudices that previously operated as taken-for-granted *Selbstverständlichkeiten*. In this case, the prejudices in question are historical rather than "natural" in character, but their function in the life of consciousness is similar, as we saw, and this function is what dictates to the philosopher a procedure similar to phenomenological reduction. Here, too, the philosopher must remain *in* his historical situation rather than simply leaving it behind, in the sense that he must relive and bring to consciousness those prejudices peculiar to his historical situation. Perhaps we could say, then, that what the historical reduction accomplishes is an "overthrow" of such prejudices only

5. Two studies which elaborate richly on the paradoxes of this principle are: Klaus Held, *Lebendige Gegenwart* (The Hague: Martinus Nijhoff, 1966); and Jacques Derrida, *La Voix et le phé-. nomène* (Paris: Presses Universitaires de France, 1967), English translation by David B. Allison, *Speech and Phenomena* (Evanston, Ill.: Northwestern University Press, 1973).

to the extent that the philosopher can achieve an attitude of detachment and hold them up to view.

But here it will perhaps be objected that we are carrying the analogy between the two reductions too far. After all, the two procedures are not merely parallel but have a certain relationship to one another. It is true that they both consist of bringing to consciousness certain prejudices that act in similar ways in the life of consciousness. But first there is the difference we have already pointed to in this chapter, namely, that the historical reduction aims at the particular (i.e., the particular features of the philosopher's historical situation), while the phenomenological reduction seeks out what is essential to consciousness as such, under all historical circumstances. But second, and more importantly: as we saw in Chapter 5 where we introduced the historical reduction, *its* purpose is precisely to free the philosopher from his historical prejudices, to remove them, so that he can succeed in the business of phenomenological reduction and thus transcendental philosophy. The prime example of historical reduction, the treatment of modern philosophy in the *Crisis*, confirms this interpretation. The point is to overcome the prejudices of a philosophy oriented toward scientific inquiry in order to get at an adequate transcendental description of the world. Far from simply remaining under the sway of his historical situation while at the same time achieving the detachment that allows him to describe it, the philosopher's purpose here is to escape his situation in order to assure himself the possibility of an adequate phenomenological description. It would seem, then, that the historical reduction, if successful, *overcomes* historical prejudices in a much stronger sense than that in which the phenomenological reduction overcomes the prejudices of the natural attitude.

But this interpretation of the historical reduction is only partially correct. It is true that in the process of historical reduction actually carried out in the *Crisis* (which is what we have focused upon here), Husserl's attitude toward the modern tradition has been primarily negative and critical. As we have seen, he is critical of the manner in which the scientific abstraction of Galileo was integrated into the philosophical program in both objectivism and traditional transcendental philosophy; and, if our interpretation is correct, he is also critical of himself insofar as his own earlier philosophy embodied the mistaken emphasis of that tradition. But it should be clear that the reduction has a positive side as well. In attempting to render present to himself the tradition under which he operates, Husserl not only wishes to uproot and discard those "shifts of meaning" which have misled the philosophical quest; he also wants to make clear and hold fast to what is right about the tradition. We have seen this in his treatment, for example, of Descartes, Hume, and Kant. These philosophers are not simply taken to task for their wrongheadedness; they are criticized primarily for failing to recognize the significance of their own most profound insights, and for failing to follow them through. Thus their positive contribution to the tradition is acknowledged while their mistakes are being criticized. And in doing this, Husserl is saying that part of the tradition under which we stand, as philosophers of the present, is not to be rejected but precisely maintained. Historical reduction serves the purpose of finding out what that part is as well as discovering wrong paths and dead ends. This may involve understanding certain philosophers "better than they understood themselves," but it is by no means equivalent to simply rejecting them.

But this positive side of the historical reduction involves much more than giving credit to individual philosophers for their still-valuable insights, just as its negative side is more than merely a critique of this or that philosopher. On both sides Husserl is after a hidden unity of motivation that gets established and is handed down, precisely in the manner of a tradition, often only obscurely understood by those who participate in it. Thus, he says, "We must inquire back into what was originally and always sought in philosophy, what was continually sought by all the philosophers and philosophies that have communicated with one another historically." [6] We must learn "what, through all these philosophers, 'the point of it' ultimately was, in the hidden unity of intentional inwardness which alone constitutes the unity of history." [7] The historical inquiry not only tells us what we must avoid, but is also "the deepest kind of self-reflection aimed at a self understanding in terms of what we are truly seeking as the historical beings we are." [8]

In answer to the objection made to our interpretation of historical reduction, then, it can be said that the purpose of

6. *Crisis*, pp. 17–18.
7. *Ibid.*, p. 73.
8. *Ibid.*, p. 72.

this procedure is not simply to divest consciousness of its historicity. The positive side of the reduction reveals that the outcome is not a consciousness unrelated to its history, but rather one which is clear on the nature of that relationship. Consciousness after the reduction—assuming the latter succeeds—is still a consciousness which takes over its project from the past. But it has a clarified conception of the project and thus is unlikely to be diverted into the sort of byways Husserl sees in most of modern philosophy.

The negative side of the historical reduction is most evident in the *Crisis* text itself, because Husserl focuses there on the modern tradition beginning with Galileo and Descartes; and he is anxious to make his point that the very project of modern philosophy was misguided from the start. As he says, "The European crisis has its roots in a misguided rationalism," and he understands this rationalism very broadly as "the European development from the seventeenth to the nineteenth centuries." [9] But the *Crisis* also makes the point that both the Renaissance in science and its philosophical legacy considered themselves to be a rebirth of the original philosophical project initiated by the Greeks. As we noted at the end of Chapter 9, it is in the Vienna Lecture that the reduction is extended back to what Husserl considers the very origins of philosophy in the Greek notion of *theōria.* The great figures of early modern philosophy sought to recapture the ancient ideal and bring it to realization, but they failed. As is so often the case in a developing tradition, the original ideal has been lost sight of. The purpose of Husserl's "historical and critical reflections" is likewise to recapture the ideal as it was found in ancient Greece, and also to discern it in and in spite of the various flawed attempts at its realization in the modern period.

Perhaps the best idea of the complementary positive and negative sides of the historical reduction can be gleaned from the following passage from the *Crisis:*

> If he is to be one who thinks for himself [*Selbstdenker*], an autonomous philosopher with the will to liberate himself from all prejudices, he must have the insight that all the things he takes for granted *are* prejudices, that all prejudices are obscurities arising out of a sedimentation of tradition . . . and that this is true even of the great task and idea which is called "philosophy." All

9. *Ibid.,* p. 290.

judgments which are to count as philosophical are related back to this task, this idea.[10]

What is peculiar, and even paradoxical, in this passage is that it contains the theme of the philosopher as one who liberates himself from *all* prejudices, and the notion of prejudices as obscurities arising from the tradition, and then goes on to say that even the idea of philosophy itself—presumably including the task of liberating oneself from all prejudices—is such a prejudice.

Now if everything that comes to us from the tradition is prejudice, and all prejudice is *simply* to be overthrown and rejected, then the "great task and idea which is called 'philosophy' " must also be overthrown. This is hardly what Husserl is telling us. To be sure, certain conceptions of the task must be rejected. But the point is to clarify the proper sense of the task, a sense which exists in the very tradition of doing philosophy—even when it is done badly—and must be sought out. What must be eliminated is not its "traditional" character as such—the fact that it is handed down and that it serves as the ultimate presupposition of philosophical work—but rather its obscurity, an obscurity which results from a lack of historical awareness and which allows the task to be misconstrued and misapplied. The process of achieving historical awareness—historical reduction—unearths and rejects obscurity for the purpose of clarifying and holding fast to the task and idea of philosophy clearly understood.

This brings to mind the passage from Gadamer, quoted in the last chapter, about the "prejudice against prejudices." [11] There is no doubt that, for Husserl, freedom from prejudice is one of the fundamental ideas of philosophy itself. He expresses this view in various ways at different times in his career. In his rather ahistorical reflection on the nature of science in the *Cartesian Meditations*, it is expressed as the demand for self-evidence as the basis for judgment.[12] In a more historical mood, in *Formal and Transcendental Logic,* he sees the Platonic dialectic as the beginning of science in the sense of giving an account in response to the skeptical criticism of any assertion.[13]

10. *Ibid.,* p. 72.
11. Chap. 10, pp. 245–46.
12. *CM,* p. 10.
13. *FTL,* p. 2.

In the Vienna Lecture, it is the notion of *theōria* as the tested and grounded assertion that starts the history of philosophy on its way.[14] The contest is always between mere opinion and knowledge based on insight, between the naïve or straightforward and the reflectively criticized, between *Selbstverständlichkeit* and *Verständlichkeit*, the taken-for-granted and the understood. If this idea constitutes the *Urstiftung* of philosophy in Greece, phenomenology represents the *Endstiftung*, reflective self-criticism carried to its limits and based on a method that will assure its success.[15] Far from being peculiar to the Enlightenment, as Gadamer claims, this idea is seen by Husserl as characterizing philosophy from its beginnings.

Whatever its origins, what is interesting is that Gadamer himself seems to be subject to the prejudice *against* prejudices; what is suggested by his remark is that, because this notion is a prejudice, it ought to be given up. But in keeping with his own gloss on the term, indicating merely a judgment that still has to be tested, the "prejudice against prejudices" need not be rejected simply because it is a prejudice. It may be that the project of liberation from prejudices, once understood and clarified, is to be embraced, especially if provided with a method which will make feasible its realization.

In Husserl's philosophical career, the development of a method for the liberation from prejudice (initially the prejudices of the natural attitude) came first. This was the phenomenological reduction. In developing this method, he was simply attempting to realize a received and unexamined notion of what philosophy should do. Then, through his insights into the historicity of consciousness, he was led to reflect on the *Sachen und Probleme* of philosophy as a historical legacy. As we have seen, this was the occasion not only for criticism of the philosophers of the modern period, but also for self-criticism on Husserl's part. Considerable revision, especially in the case of his concept of the world, resulted from this reflection. But above all, this reflection was aimed at recapturing the true *Sachen und Probleme* of philosophy, the original impulse which started philosophy on its way. This led him to inquire beyond the modern period and back to the ancient Greek ideal—though not in any scholarly way, and not with the detail he devotes to modern

14. *Crisis*, p. 280.
15. *Ibid.*, p. 71.

philosophy. At the origin of the philosophical tradition Husserl discerns the will to emancipation from prejudice, freedom from subjugation to authority, autonomy of judgment. The understanding of this goal is the key to understanding the history of philosophy as the succession of (failed) attempts at its realization. But it is also the key to the understanding of phenomenology itself as a method. In the *Crisis* Husserl goes behind the practice of the method to discover what "the point of it" is, and he finds this point in the unity of the philosophical tradition.

At the same time, as we have seen, Husserl's historical reflections serve to curb the pretensions of a straightforward reflective philosophy in its claim to liberation from prejudice. Far from being merely a metaphilosophical reflection upon phenomenological method, historical reduction must henceforth go hand in hand with that method if it is to have any possibility of success. As we have expressed it, the philosopher who aims at transhistorical truth cannot proceed in historical naïveté, but must at the same time make present to himself his own historical situation, including his inheritance of the over-all philosophical project.

As for this project itself, if it is a "prejudice" in the sense of being taken over from tradition, it is no longer a "prejudice" in the sense of being hidden or unexamined. But, even as such, it might be objected, is the project of philosophy not something inescapably "particular"? We made the point that while the phenomenological reduction, supplemented by the eidetic method, aims at essences, the historical reduction is aimed at the particular—i.e., the particular features of the philosopher's historical situation. Now we have seen that, at the limit, the historical reduction encompasses, in its positive aspect, the underlying project of philosophy from its earliest beginnings. Broad as this scope may be, extending from the ancient Greek world to the present, it is still a particular episode in the long history of the world, one of which we still happen to be a part.

Husserl himself seems to recognize this in repeatedly referring to philosophy as something somehow peculiarly "European." Europe, for him, of course, indicates a historical and cultural, not a geographical concept. But the fact remains that he sees philosophy as something that arose at a particular time and place and lives on as a direct descendant of its particular origins, whether it realizes it or not. Indian and Chinese thought, he says, do not belong within this tradition, and it is a mistake to call them science or even philosophy. Philosophy is peculiar to the spiritual descendants of the Greeks.[16] Yet at the same time the project of philosophy has universal significance, its fulfillment, in the form of phenomenological transcendental philosophy, is the solution to the crisis not only of Europe but even of mankind.

Husserl is often accused of a sort of cultural chauvinsm in his last writings when he expresses sentiments such as these. His seeming dismissal of Oriental thought and his elevated conceptions of the destiny of the European spirit are not easily accepted in a relativist and somewhat xenophiliac age in which the European spirit seems to have failed. But if we look closely at his characterization of the origin of the philosophical task in Greece, we see that it begins with the recognition of the difference between a cultural world and the world as such. The paradoxical essence of the European spirit, for Husserl, lies in its attempt precisely to transcend the limits of any cultural world, including that of Europe in the empirical historical sense. What was born with the European spirit was the ideal of a nonrelative truth, that is, a truth that is neither European truth, Chinese truth, etc.

Husserl's response to the particularity of the philosophical project is thus very different from that of the later Heidegger, for example. Heidegger, who has obviously given up the transcendental quest of his earlier work, seems to regard philosophy as an episode in the history of mankind that has run its course, spent itself, said everything that it can say.[17] Husserl cannot agree, primarily because he regards the project of philosophy as largely unfulfilled. The emergence of phenomenology as transcendental philosophy is not the end but the possible beginning of its fulfillment. If Husserl's lately developed historical consciousness makes him more aware of his own—and philosophy's—dependence on the tradition, and of the inherent limitations of the transcendental project, it still leaves open its possibility as a working philosophy with some *raison d'etre*. This conception also places Husserl in a very different position from that of a Hegel, who could be seen as Heidegger's opposite pole. For Hegel, philosophy has said all that could be said, but also all that needs to be said. What begins in a particular time and place develops

16. *Ibid.*, pp. 284–85.
17. See "Das Ende der Philosophie und die Aufgabe des Denkens," in *Zur Sache des Denkens* (Tübingen: Max Niemeyer, 1969), pp. 61–80.

into the attainment of an absolute standpoint. The philosopher who occupies that standpoint can comprehend history without remainder because history has essentially come to an end in his thought.

It is true that the attainment of such an "absolute standpoint" —the idea of nonrelative, transhistorical truth—is essential to Husserl's philosophy. But it plays the role of an unfulfilled *telos*, a project which gives philosophy its sense. In the end, far from seeing himself at the end of history, Husserl sees himself—and any other philosopher—immersed in it and having to come to terms with it. If there is a philosophical way beyond history, it must consist in a continuing process of confrontation with history.

Husserl draws together some of these thoughts in the following passage:

I know, of course, what I am striving for under the title of philosophy, as the goal and field of my work. And yet I do not know. What autonomous thinker has ever been satisfied with this, his "knowledge"? For what autonomous thinker, in his philosophizing life, has "philosophy" ever ceased to be an enigma? . . . In that obscure "knowledge" . . . the historical is concealed; it is, according to its own proper sense, the spiritual inheritance of him who philosophizes; and in the same way, obviously, he understands the others in whose company, in critical friendship and enmity, he philosophizes. And in philosophizing he is also in company with himself as he earlier understood and did philosophy; and he knows that, in the process, historical tradition, as he understood it and used it, entered into him in a motivating way and as a spiritual sediment. His historical picture, in part made by himself and in part taken over, his "poetic invention of the history of philosophy," has not and does not remain fixed—that he knows; and yet every "invention" serves him and can serve him in understanding himself and his aim, and his own aim in relation to that of others and their "inventions," their aims, and finally what is common to all, which makes up philosophy "as such" as a unitary *telos* and makes the systems attempts at its fulfillment for us all, for us [who are] at the same time in company with the philosophers of the past (in the various ways we have been able to invent them for ourselves.)[18]

18. *Crisis*, pp. 394–95.

Index